FAITH IN
HISTORY

For Levon

FAITH IN HISTORY

Armenians
Rebuilding
Community

Susan Paul Pattie

SMITHSONIAN INSTITUTION PRESS

Washington and London

© 1997 by the Smithsonian Institution
All rights reserved

Permission has been generously given to reproduce the following copyrighted works. The poem "The Lamp" and sections of the poems "We Will Refuse and Say" and "Prayer on the Threshold of Tomorrow" from *Sojourn at Ararat: Poems of Armenia*, compiled and edited by G. Papasian. Copyright © 1987 by G. Papasian. Published by Publishers Choice, Mars, Pennsylvania. The poem "Melkon" from *I Remember Root River*, by David Kherdian. Copyright © 1981 by David Kherdian. Published by The Overlook Press, Woodstock, New York 12498.

Copy Editor: Susan A. Warga
Designer: Kathleen Sims

Library of Congress Cataloging-in-Publication Data
Pattie, Susan Paul
　　Faith in history : Armenians rebuilding community / by Susan Paul Pattie.
　　　　p.　cm.
　　Includes bibliographical references (p.) and index.
　　ISBN 1-56098-629-8 (alk. paper)
　　1. Armenians.　I. Title.
　　DS165.P28 1996
　　909'.0491992—dc20　　　　　　　　　　　　　　　　96-7579

British Library Cataloguing-in-Publication Data is available

Manufactured in the United States of America on recycled paper
03　02　01　00　99　98　97　　　　　5　4　3　2　1

∞ The paper used in this publication meets the minimum requirements of the American National Standard for Information Sciences—Permanence of Paper for Printed Library Materials, ANSI Z39.48-1984.

For permission to reproduce illustrations appearing in this book, please correspond directly with the author. The Smithsonian Institution Press does not retain reproduction rights for these illustrations individually, or maintain a file of addresses for photo sources.

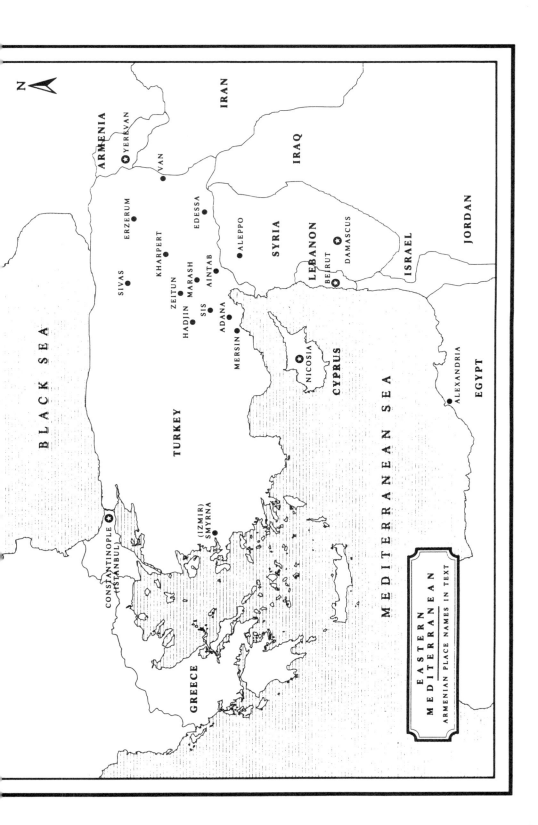

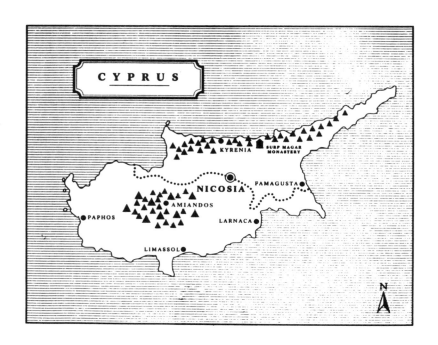

CYPRUS

SURP MAGAR
MONASTERY

KYRENIA

NICOSIA

FAMAGUSTA

AMIANDOS

PAPHOS

LARNACA

LIMASSOL

N

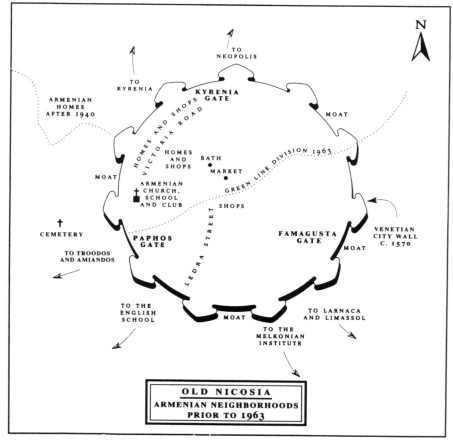

TO
NEOPOLIS

N

TO
KYRENIA

ARMENIAN
HOMES
AFTER 1940

KYRENIA
GATE

MOAT

HOMES AND SHOPS

VICTORIA ROAD

HOMES
AND
SHOPS

BATH

MARKET

MOAT

ARMENIAN
CHURCH,
SCHOOL
AND CLUB

GREEN LINE DIVISION 1963

SHOPS

CEMETERY

PAPHOS
GATE

LEDRA STREET

FAMAGUSTA
GATE

VENETIAN
CITY WALL
C. 1570

TO TROODOS
AND AMIANDOS

MOAT

TO THE
ENGLISH
SCHOOL

MOAT

TO LARNACA
AND LIMASSOL

TO THE
MELKONIAN
INSTITUTE

OLD NICOSIA
ARMENIAN NEIGHBORHOODS
PRIOR TO 1963

Contents

Preface

I am half Armenian, am married to an Armenian, and spent two years in Cyprus as a child. When choosing a fieldwork site, I was drawn to Cyprus, where I felt something could be learned about the ways different ethnic groups interact and how this changes over time. After an initial attempt to avoid working with Armenians, out of a false concern that I was too close to the subject, I realized how few ethnographic accounts have been written about Armenian life in the Near East or the Mediterranean.[1] And when I began, I soon discovered that I was close to the subject only in a very abstract sense, one that little impressed some people.

Because I was born and raised in America, the product of a "mixed marriage," a Protestant, and only just learning Armenian, many people were not too shy to tell me that I was the personification of the sad future in store for the Armenian nation—assimilation, Westernization. But as the work continued and it appeared I might be serious, this attitude mellowed considerably, and people often praised my mother to me for having raised her children to be aware of being Armenian. It was difficult to explain that she had not consciously tried to do this. At the same time, my personal "ideal Armenians," my mother's brother and mother, were certainly very different in attitude, interests, and habit from many of the people I met in Cyprus and London. Until then it had never occurred to me that there might be a way of being Armenian different from that of my uncle and grandmother, and it took some time to realize how many different ways of feeling Armenian there are.

My marriage to an Armenian from Cyprus just as my fieldwork was beginning clearly had an important influence on the work. In a small community most families know each other, and as a musician, Levon was well known himself. The goodwill and trust that went along with that had the advantage of opening doors more easily and quickly than I could have done alone, even given the great importance of hospitality. But it also meant arriving with part of my identity already accounted for, since I was now attached to a certain family with its own history.

In any fieldwork situation, being a man or a woman must make some difference to relationships, but gender is only one aspect of a person among others, including age, marital status, family, interests, personality, and probably appearance. These easily discernable features are important as one makes first impressions (and forms them oneself) but begin to fade as more solid connections are formed on other bases. While in Cyprus I gradually changed my own self-presentation, starting with clothes, as I realized that I was constantly and seriously underdressed. Women of my age (at that time I was in my mid-thirties) and older dressed much more formally and fashionably. At one point I remember feeling quite proud of myself for having guessed correctly and worn a "nice" dress to a coffee morning—until my gaze fell to floor level, where I noticed pairs and pairs of shiny high-heeled shoes and one pair of dusty, dirty flats, which were my own. I never did give up walking between homes and appointments, something that was accepted as only slightly less eccentric than my early efforts on a bicycle.

How are we judged in the field? What are the different expectations associated with a fieldworker of a particular gender and age? Does it make a difference in terms of information gathered? Women were very friendly, warm, and receptive in both London and Cyprus. Many made every effort to think of new ideas to help me. Often my day would be programmed by a friend or relative who had thought things over and decided that my study would not be complete if I did not meet a certain person or see a special event or place. All of these arranged events were greatly appreciated, but equally valuable were the informal times spent around kitchen tables together. Men were also willing to talk, inviting me to their shops, clubs, and offices and making suggestions for further investigations. Whether it was because of my friendship with their wives, relationships with my husband and family, or common interest in the subject, I always felt welcomed by men as well as women.

Armenian Cypriots are multilingual, speaking Armenian, English, Greek, Turkish, and often some French and Arabic in varying degrees, depending on their generation and particular education. I began to learn Armenian as my fieldwork started and by the midpoint of the research found that I could follow the changes in language used during a single conversation. There was always a drift toward English, however, as all in London and most in Cyprus speak it very well. Why worry about speaking Armenian at all, then? For one thing, a few people do not speak English, and others are uncomfortable with it. Just as important, however, I found that learning Armenian enabled me to be part of casual group conversations and also helped me get an idea of current language use. In this way, French and Turkish were also useful, and Greek certainly would have been, had I had the time to learn. Because of the particular development of the Armenian community in Cyprus, few members of the oldest generation spoke Greek well, while young people now speak Greek as fluently as their elders spoke Turkish. Unless otherwise noted, in this text *Greek* is used to mean vernacular modern Greek as it is spoken in the cities of Cyprus. This is not the Cypriot dialect (which is still spoken in some villages) but has a recognizable accent and a number of particular expressions. *Demotiki,* modern spoken Greek, learned at school, is often called "proper Greek" by older Armenians concerned about grammatical mistakes in their vernacular.

Most conversations, whether primarily in English or primarily in Armenian, included phrases, words, and even whole sentences in other languages. Armenian, Turkish, or Greek words that are regularly used when speaking another language or that are hard to translate succinctly are shown in italics, with a translation supplied either immediately or in the glossary. I have not indicated the crossovers in language in the translations of conversations.

Fieldwork consisted of a series of extended visits to Cyprus between 1983 and 1988 while I was based in London. This method brought along its own advantages and disadvantages. The continuation of contact over five years gave the study a longitudinal dimension. Working in London in between trips to Cyprus also meant keeping in contact with Cyprus, even at such a distance, as events and people there figure extensively in the lives of Armenians in London as well. The disadvantages are equally obvious. The shorter periods I spent in Cyprus created a rush to get certain things done in a limited amount of time, whereas the traditional longer stay allows a gradual progression of friendships, meetings, and events to occur and gives a more day-to-day view over the course of the year. This aspect emerged in London.

Information, impressions, and ideas were gathered by arranging interviews (that is, by making an appointment to ask certain people specific questions); through more informal conversations with individuals and groups of people; by reading articles, letters, and memoirs written by and about Armenian Cypriots; through attending parties, social activities, and other events; by visiting institutions (schools, churches, clubs); and by generally hanging around as much as possible, at workplaces and in homes. I used a tape recorder when it appeared that it would not intrude. Several people asked me to record their comments because they had something particular they wanted others to know about. Most frequently I took copious notes while we spoke. This is clearly impossible at parties or on the street, so in those cases I wrote as much as I could remember immediately afterward.

Names have been changed except in a few instances in which the person or incident is very well known (Bishop Saradjian, for example). The titles *Mr., Mrs.,* and *Miss* are used as Armenians and other peoples of the eastern Mediterranean do, with the first name most of the time. Today such titles are frequently not used with people of the same age or younger, and I have followed this pattern.

Since the conclusion of my fieldwork there have been many important events and developments in the lives of these communities, such as the opening of new Melkonian Institute buildings, more Londoners returning to Cyprus to work or to retire, and new internal political divisions. Within the wider Armenian world, change has been more dramatic, including the 1988 earthquake in Soviet Armenia, conflict in the Caucasus, the disintegration of the Soviet Union and the independence of the Republic of Armenia, and further troubles and then a tentative peace in Lebanon. This study necessarily covers a limited period but should provide some basis for understanding the ways in which people react to these and other changes and incorporate them in their lives.

Acknowledgments

Many people have been instrumental in the creation of this book, and without the help and cooperation of Armenians in Cyprus and London, it would have been impossible. Why do people trust a stranger with their stories and precious memories? It seems that in talking and remembering we make some sense of our own lives—and this must be what the anthropologist is doing also. Ethnography is always a form of collaboration, resting on the contributions of many, and I hope that in this book people will recognize their ideas and experiences. I wish to express my deepest gratitude to all the many people in Cyprus and London who spent hours and days of their time patiently explaining in animated conversation, always accompanied by very generous hospitality. I have been extremely fortunate to have become part of a larger family and formed very close friendships through this work.

From the beginning I felt very much at home in Cyprus. This may be due to some childhood memories, but I am sure it is in much larger part the result of the very warm reception I was given there. The names of those who went out of their way to help would fill several pages here, and I can mention only a few. These include my "Cyprus parents," Nouvart and Hercules Panayotides-Djaferis, who made both Levon and me a part of their family and household. Their support goes far beyond their calm and comfortable home and has been a major factor in enabling productive and enjoyable stays in Cyprus. Thank you also to Salpy Eskidjian and Arlene Nahikian, who both helped to gather information in Cyprus. I am grateful to Marie Boghossian and Hagop Palamoudian, who contributed copies of their informative memoirs. Shakeh Horomian was one of the first people to take me in hand and chauffeur me from place to place. Ano Eskidjian, Elsie Utidjian, their families, and many cousins from the Aynedjian, Kazandjian, and Bedelian clans all helped in so many ways, not least of which was in providing wonderful company.

I am also very grateful for the financial support of the Benlian and Essefian Trusts of London, the Detroit Armenian Women's Club, the University of Michigan Department of Anthropology, Rackham Graduate School, and the National Endowment for the Humanities. Many thanks to Vigen Boyadjian, then of Viglen Computers, who enabled me to join the computer age, and to Dan O'Brien, who helped me through the final technical hurdles.

People who took on the task of reading and commenting on certain chapters along the way are especially appreciated, including Taqui Altounyan, Bedo Eghiayian, Aram Kerovpyan, Akabi Nasibian, Genie Nazarian, and Hratch Tchilingirian. I remain very grateful to Lindsay French, Nicholas James, Ruth Mandel, and Fran Markowitz, each of whom has helped in many ways, as friends and critics in this project and others. Dr. Ara Paul and Shirley Paul, the Ann Arbor extension of our family, have generously shared their home and encouragement at every step.

At the University of Michigan I was fortunate to find a variety of influential teachers, each of whom contributed to the eclectic blend on the following pages. Aram Yengoyan, Conrad Kottak, Susan Harding, and Ronald Suny each provided stimulating ideas. Peter Loizos, in London, has read many drafts of this manuscript, and I remain deeply grateful for his encouragement and sane guidance. Detailed and invigorating critiques given by Michael Herzfeld were a tremendous boost at a time when the manuscript had become far too familiar to tackle. I am especially thankful for these. Thanks also to Bill Merrill and to Sue Warga for helpful suggestions during the editing process on ways to corral the still scattered ideas and create a book.

I would most like to thank my family. My parents, Mark and Helen Pattie, have always been encouraging no matter what, or even in spite of, the project at hand. My mother-in-law, Sirvart Chilingirian, shared many memories and wise perceptions that were especially helpful. And my husband, Levon Chilingirian, has been an integral part of this work, teaching me Armenian, taking notes at lectures, discussing ideas, and reading the manuscript at every stage. His own work has been equally important, filling our home with beautiful music.

Chapter 1

Dzur Nstink, Shidag Khosink
Let's Sit Crooked and Talk Straight

This is an ethnography of Armenians in Cyprus, a people undergoing great changes. It is also a study of continuity and regeneration that spans generations and international borders. In public, church and secular leaders speak and write of an ideal Armenian; in their own homes, however, people talk of changes and flexibility. Memories of the past, contingencies of the present, and hopes for the future intertwine in the creation of identities. People ask themselves and each other what it is important to keep, to remember, to change. What does it mean to be Armenian? an Armenian Cypriot? an Armenian Cypriot living in London?

In Nicosia, Wednesdays are half days for the shops, and men gather at the cultural clubs in the afternoons to socialize. One week, after lunch and siesta time, I was invited to join one of the groups. Several men came to greet me and offer a seat in the middle of the room, where a number of chairs were gathered. "Ah! *Pari yegar!* Welcome!" Others were already in the back room playing backgammon or cards; across the patio, in the opposite building, a few other men and women had gathered to plan future club events.

Speaking in a mixture of English and Armenian, we chatted as others joined us. The men first discussed how many Armenians were still in Cyprus. The estimates varied widely, but in the end a consensus was reached: between 1,700 and 1,800. "The main thing, though, is the political uncertainty," said one, and the others agreed. "The trend of the youth is to find their fortunes elsewhere—not just the Armenians, I mean, but the Greeks

1

too, and probably the Turks, but we don't know about them. There are plenty of scholarships, and many go to England or other places, and they get used to the life there." Looking around, I realized that all the men present were around fifty or older.

Someone else added that the Cypriot Armenian community is like a witches' brew. "Everything is in it. The people are from everywhere, and they are trying to extend their roots here. Look at me. Half of my family is in Hayastan [now the Republic of Armenia] and half is in America."

"Yes," added his neighbor. "I'm from Kharpert, but my wife is from Adana, you see."

Mr. Shant, a tall, older man, leaned forward, finger raised. "Now, *Kharpert* is a mispronunciation from our Turkish-speaking days.[1] It should really be *Karpert*, 'stone castle.' But we have forgotten that." He looked around and continued, "My family was also from Kharpert. When the troubles came to us in 1915, I became separated from my family— except for my small sister, my aunt, and my grandmother. We stayed to- gether and began walking, wandering toward Hayastan. The others went south to Der Zor. . . . We were from Kharpert, and we walked north, through mountains and snow, to the Russian frontier. My auntie—she was a young girl herself—she had taken an Armenian alphabet book with her, and so wherever we sat, she opened that book, and we learned Armenian."

He paused and looked at us. "Doesn't a race of this character have a right to live in this world? She was thinking of the future. The book would last longer than a loaf of bread. I remember the pictures in the book, and learning to make the letter *r*."

While Mr. Shant was speaking, Vrej, a young teacher from the Mel- konian Institute, the Armenian secondary school in Nicosia, was pacing back and forth agitatedly behind us. When the older man had finished, Vrej sat beside me and told me that Mr. Shant used to be his teacher at the Melkonian. The young man had come from Turkey and knew no Arme- nian when he arrived.

"Mr. Shant taught me my Armenian. Not just the language! But he taught me what it is to really be Armenian." Looking at the dignified Mr. Shant, I wondered what Vrej meant, but the young teacher was a step ahead. "You must tell her the story that you told us when we were stu- dents. I can *never* forget it, it affected me so much! About Hayastan."

Mr. Shant knew what he meant. "But it's not about Cyprus," he said. "I don't know if she wants to hear."

"She must! Yes, tell it!"

Mr. Shant began slowly, quietly, and the other men leaned forward to listen.

"When we arrived in Hayastan, it was . . . unbelievable. The hunger, the poverty—you can't imagine it. And yet we were so happy to be there. But it was a terrible time for the people, so much starvation. We were taken to an orphanage, and we were the fortunate ones. Even though there was no food. For dinner, say, two walnuts.

"Why walnuts? Because Hayastan is famous for its walnuts. They're easier to find than anything else. Of course, sometimes you break the nut and there is nothing inside—it's rotten or old. The rule was this: If you break two walnuts and there's nothing in either, you take the empty shells to the teacher and get one more. If you're lucky, that's a good one. If not, bad luck. . . .

"We were ten, eleven years old, and my little sister was seven. Before the organization of schools, we found time to forage. We'd look for anything to eat. If you've noticed the almond trees after the rain, there's resin on the bark, for example. We would eat it with the bark. Anything to survive. We used to go to the fields. And there somebody found some sort of root, like a carrot but flesh-colored. He ate it . . . and he was satisfied for the moment, but after a while it all came out. It didn't make any difference. He ate it anyway, and he told his friends to do the same. Under these circumstances, a child who has always been hungry, he never remembers a full stomach. . . .

"A child wanders under the trees and looks for a walnut that the crows have dropped. Imagine, a child of seven or eight finding a walnut and breaking it up and seeing that it is excellent and keeping it clenched in her fist and taking it to her brother to share. . . . "

Mr. Shant's voice trailed off, and his own clenched fist was trembling. Looking up from my notes, I saw that his face was suddenly wet with tears, silent ones, and they continued to flow. We looked at each other as everyone quietly shifted in their chairs. I wished I knew what to say. "Your sister . . . she was full of love . . . even though she was so hungry," I ventured. He nodded graciously. The others shifted again and murmured that those had indeed been difficult times.

Mr. Shant collected himself and looked back down from the ceiling at Vrej. "Don't ever ask me to tell that story again in front of people." Then to me he added, "I can never tell that story without crying. . . . It says something about not just one person but about the Armenians as a race."

"Everything is embedded in that story," said Vrej.

For Armenians, one particular event has bound and preoccupied the personal and collective imagination in this century: the devastating deportations and massacres in the Ottoman Empire in the late nineteenth and early twentieth centuries. The upheaval and displacement Armenians went through later in Cyprus will be familiar to their Greek and Turkish neighbors, who have also been affected by the troubles in Cyprus,[2] but the experiences of Armenians in Cyprus are also echoed in Hirschon's (1989) portrayal of Greek refugees from Asia Minor settling in Piraeus. There the past is a reminder of tragedy and loss but also an emblem of pride, continuity, and strength.

Who are the Armenians? In their words, Armenians are people who not only have survived terrible pogroms but also can look beyond that to a glorious and ancient past: the first Christian "nation"; an early, distinct alphabet; continuous tilling of the Anatolian soil for 2,500 years. Like the Asia Minor refugees, Armenians in Cyprus also found reasons for particular pride in their personal pasts or the pasts of their old villages or towns. These histories embody behavior or values that they deemed worthier than those of their non-Armenian neighbors or even those of fellow Armenians from other areas.

The young teacher said that "everything" was embedded in Mr. Shant's story of the walnuts. Like others I heard, this tale combined depths of misery and deprivation with optimism and innocence, here expressed by the sister's love. Often someone would turn a story of total abjection into one that demonstrated the heroism of a family member or, sometimes, one that made the point that certain Turks or Kurds did help Armenians to escape or survive. Hope was rarely far behind the despair that was still so deep. Sacrifice for family or nation was another frequent theme, as was the importance of learning.

During my fieldwork, people often brought up the subject of identity, both personal and communal. They discussed how life had been, how it should be, and, again, what was important to remember. One way in which my own work was understood was that of putting such memories on paper to preserve them for posterity, to keep them for the day when the next generation(s) might be ready to listen—as surely they would, eventually. While waiting for that day, older Armenians often voiced a wistfulness and concern similar to that witnessed by Boyarin among Polish Jews in Paris, who noted a "shortage of cultural heirs" in the community. Like their Jewish counterparts, Armenian children do have some information about their parents' and grandparents' lives—especially those parts that form the political memory—but these younger people are selective, and they are busy. Their interests and ambitions are aimed toward the future. In a comment that is as applicable to Armenians as it is to the Paris Jews he worked with, Boyarin adds, "Loss of homeland and family is a recurrent theme in Jewish popular memory; but the 'loss' of one's children to a different cultural world, common as it may be, remains in large measure an unalleviated source of pain" (Boyarin 1991, 11).

Succeeding generations occupying the same territory have been known to accuse each other of not understanding the other's world. In cases where people have been displaced or have emigrated, there are often real gaps in the collective memory, ones that can be only partially bridged through the telling of stories about the past. The fewer the common experiences and collective memories that are shared between people, the more difficult it is to share the present. But the present is always there in the remembering, forming the "social framework for memory" (Halbwachs 1992, 38). Details may remain the same but take on a different aspect, even different meanings, as the social environment changes. It is true that in retrospect we almost always understand events differently—sometimes better—than we do when we are living through them. This is due not simply to removal from the scene or to growth in individual wisdom, but also to the claims and ideas of current life.

Halbwachs notes that social memory nearly always places the golden age of any particular group at the "beginning," in the distant past, and portrays the present as a process of dissolution, assimilation, and procession toward anarchy. It is the role of the old to remember, to provide an anchor of continuity with the past (Halbwachs 1992, 48). Among Armenians in the last decades of the twentieth century, the older people uprooted from eastern Anatolia—the survivors of the pogroms—have a special, revered status. Their memories are considered precious, both as a link to the old world that predated the event and as concrete ways to contest contemporary Turkish disclaimers of responsibility.[3]

The respect shown for Mr. Shant is in part because of his own personality, for he is a dignified, generous, intelligent, and witty man who has spent his life in service to his community. But he is also respected because of this role as a survivor. Even if he were unable to speak so eloquently of the experience, the role remains fundamentally important, a living link with the central event. Halbwachs describes older people generally as "guardians of the common treasure" (1992, 48), and this is particularly apparent here.

Political groups emphasize and commemorate certain features of common stories. In between commemoration of the past, on the one hand,

and its collective construction and reconstruction, on the other, is remembering: passing on memories within families, between teachers and students, among friends meeting together over a drink. Older people may choose to tell their stories in different ways—or in some cases not at all. But frequently older people find that political groups and even their own families are not so very interested in the many other aspects of their past daily lives that are not related to the pogroms, and they sit contemplating and cultivating their memories alone or with other older people with whom they can check and revive images of events, places, and people.

There are many occasions, though, in family homes, clubs, and shops, when a mixed group will begin chatting about general subjects and the discussion will gradually give way to one of the older people present, a survivor who is ready to tell her or his story. The others may have heard a version of it many times before and listen to be polite, out of respect. Or they may have been thinking about the story in some other context and invite the speaker to relate it so that they can go over the details again. In some cases the speaker is asked to go over the familiar ground for young people or a newcomer like myself.

Social memory, most often through personal narratives, forms an integral part of this book. This is also a study of the present, however, and a variety of voices will be heard discussing people's contemporary lives in the Armenian communities of Cyprus and London. As earlier studies have shown, Armenian diaspora communities place a formal emphasis on church, language, and history as the cornerstones of their culture.[4] The general recognition of links among these different aspects does not prevent disagreement over the appropriate emphasis on each, nor a lack of consensus over their proper manifestations.

The Armenian diaspora has been said to most resemble the "archetypal" or "ideal" diaspora of the Jews,[5] but the concept of diaspora has undergone many changes, in terms of both the definition of the word and the ways diaspora is experienced. Whether an "ideal" diaspora exists is an open question, the complexities of which will become clear through the narratives on the following pages. For many centuries the Armenian world has been based on interconnected communities without an umbrella government of their own. The stories of individuals, like those of the collective, reflect continually changing relations between majority and minority cultures, the change from being subjects of empires to citizens of nation-states, and ongoing mutations of ethnic and nationalist self-definitions.

Though some would posit the necessity of a homeland for the existence of a diaspora,[6] in this case homeland clearly has been a contested and evolving notion. It is shaped by the personal experiences and ambitions of people at particular times and by the desires and plans (and varying degrees of success of these plans) of intellectuals, teachers, priests, and political leaders. It can be the utopian vision of the future that is expressed in popular poetry and argued over in kitchens and coffee shops. It might be the nostalgic remembrance of home, the "old country," by a displaced refugee who is waiting to return. Homeland can mean all this at once, even to the same person, and takes specific shape only in the discourse of nationalist ideology. For centuries there has been no single, clearly defined center and periphery acknowledged by all Armenians. This is changing as the new Republic of Armenia consolidates power, but it does not negate the experience of centuries of diffuse connections among communities around the Near East and Caucasus, later spreading around the world. The question of return is equally ambiguous, as people have been haunted by the memories of the smells and sights of their old village or town while gradually becoming more at home in their new space, in diaspora. The confusion increases as political parties emphasize ideological notions of homeland, detached from personal experience but rooted in past and contemporary history. Again, this has taken new shape since the independence of Armenia, in 1991, but the question of whether emigration to that state is a true "return" for those whose ancestors never lived there remains the focus of debate.

As in the past, the cement of diaspora communities, within and between them, is family. Networks of people related through descent or marriage remain of great importance, though the specific ways in which this is true have changed. The national church, from early times, and the political parties and cultural organizations that have grown up over the last hundred years provide an infrastructure that links communities on a more formal level. Though the Armenian diaspora is far more widely spread at this end of the century, modern innovations have made connections quicker, easier, and fundamentally different than in earlier times. Telephones, jet airplanes, fax machines, international banking and finance, and the various media all serve to pass information immediately but also reinforce the role of kin as a resource, wherever and however far away they may reside.

Françoise Zonabend observes that a group derives its identity in part from the collective memory of a history that is not shared with others (Zonabend 1984, 203). While this is demonstrated in the chapters that follow, it is also clear that collective memories are contested from within and that history *is* shared with others, in its living and in its retelling. As

Eric Wolf argues, we often incorrectly depict the world as a "global pool hall" (1982, 6) in which bounded entities bounce off one another, spinning in different directions. Looking toward both the Near East and Europe, living in the interstices of a variety of societies, maintaining links both with these societies and among their own communities, Armenians demonstrate the dynamic connections and mutual influences of peoples and cultures. As a transnational people, Armenians frequently compare themselves to their neighbors and to Armenians living in other countries. They note the "witches' brew" mentioned earlier, ways in which different Armenian diaspora communities borrow from their host cultures. This widens the question of culture and how it is shared and transmitted not only between generations but across borders. This study explores the relations within two local communities, the links between them, and their place in an international diaspora, noting, as Michael Herzfeld (1985, xii) does for Crete, that these concentric circles of identity are subject to much and constant debate by the people themselves.

In this study I consciously shift the emphasis away from politics and toward the less organized, more private experiences of people—though public, organized life is never far away. Most of the "stuff" that community is made of is not the "different approaches of its subsections, their rivalries and disagreements" that Tala'I (1986, 252) suggests, but those different approaches *in addition* to individuals and their families (who may or may not be active in community organizations, and who may even be repelled by them) and the informal as well as formal life that they make together. One must study the public, formal teaching and debate over community symbols, ways of expressing Armenianness, and so on, but to ignore the underlying layers of private and less-formal public life among family and friends is to lose sight of the process of cultural change.

There are many ways of being or "feeling" Armenian (Bakalian 1993) and a variety of ways of reacting to and living in diaspora. The following chapters will explore the complex of symbols articulated by the people of the Armenian communities in Cyprus and in London and their transmission over several generations. Underlying themes and ideas are presented in chapter 2 in anecdotal and narrative form. Chapters 3 through 7 are ethnohistorical, following dispersion from the homelands, the building of community in Cyprus in the early part of the century, later disruptions and losses, the decrease in population, and the rebuilding. Chapter 8, which begins with the 1950s, looks at those who chose to rebuild in London rather than Cyprus. Views of language, religion, and history are examined in chapters 11 through 14 and are set against a context of family interactions and relationships, which are analyzed in chapters 9 and 10.

The interplay of cultural change and religious belief (especially where religion and nationalism overlap), the dual spiritual and functional roles of the national church, and the nature of faith in both will be explored in the conclusion. The purpose of this book is to give expression to the complexity of the lives of people who call themselves Armenian, exploring the processes of culture in diaspora, the mutual influence of values and ideas, and the tensions between public and private identity.

Chapter 2

Batmeh Nayenk
Conversations in the Field[1]

"How is your project coming along?"
We were standing in a crowded room at a party in Nicosia— a middle-aged man who had already been a great help, a young woman, an older couple, and me.

"Well, it's okay. . . . "

"It's very interesting, what she's doing, you know," Haig explained to the older couple. "Writing a book about Armenians in Cyprus—about our culture, important things to remember."

"And how things are changing," I started to add.

"What culture?" Someone else joined us. "We have nothing, we are so anglicized already. Look at the Beirutsi, the Barskahays, Armenians from Beirut and Iran, and compare us."

"Nonsense!" the older man, Mr. Garabed, protested. "We speak Armenian, we have very good schools, a beautiful church! Of course we can help you learn about Armenians."

At this point I said, "You see, I am really interested in the everyday life of Armenians in Cyprus, what's important to you, not an ideal culture." I stopped as I saw Mrs. Maro's eyes open wide and her smile falter.

"Yes, you know what is important?" Mrs. Maro told me. "Families are being split up. We have one daughter. We let her go to study in England and she lives there now. We never see her. It's terrible."

"Maro, enough. She doesn't want to hear this. You know, Shushan, it is language that is—"

"Our daughter was studying at college and she met an Englishman. He's very nice, and they are happy together." Mrs. Maro hesitated. "But they got married and now they live there. That's not the way it should be."

"You must miss her," I began, but the young woman joined in at the same time.

"It's the insecurity. You must write about that. It is difficult to live here and not know what is going to happen."

"That's why *Hay tad* is so important," added another who had come into our circle, using a phrase that means "the Armenian cause" and implies working toward the politicization of Armenians, the rebuttal of Turkey's denial of the Armenian massacres, and, for some, the return to an independent homeland.

"*Hay tad* is nothing, nothing will come of it."

"We go to visit her maybe once a year now—or they come here in the summer for a vacation. It's not enough, it's not the same. You can't imagine how I miss her."

"*Aman,* Maro—that's enough! Of course we miss her! Everyone here has the same problem, you know."

"We phone sometimes. . . . " Mrs. Maro's words were drowned out by a heated discussion of the problem of young people not going to church. She murmured a good-bye and wandered across the room, through the sea of bright silks, jewelry, and tailored suits.

This conversation, early in my fieldwork, immediately brought out many of the often conflicting dreams and concerns of people in Cyprus. It was difficult to talk about everyday matters. How and why should one do it? After all, it is so *ordinary*. But identity was brought up everywhere at every opportunity, though initially I avoided asking questions about it, feeling that this was an overrated and possibly artificial issue. Conversations, however, often involved explicit debate over what Armenian culture might be or might have been, whether it was possible for it to continue in diaspora, and whether the collective, the nation, should be given priority over the individual and the family. After one young woman had analyzed her personal identity and then that of the community, I asked if she had been reading articles about theories of ethnicity or national identity. She had not, she said. Nor had the many others whom I later heard discuss similar issues. Some of these ideas are absorbed through their analysis in the Armenian press as well as from related topics treated in other media, but many people suggested that it is living in diaspora that makes them conscious of different levels of identity and of the flux that surrounds them.

This chapter includes conversations and anecdotes that give some context to the shaping and articulation of ideas and images of identity and community. Recurrent themes are then drawn out. These themes are not, of course, the only ones possible. They struck me, however—most of them many times over, from different directions and in various ways—as the framework of an invisible shared background for the group, one that is both conscious and unconscious and which incorporates information, "truths," and attitudes shared in varying degrees.

"How do you decide whom to talk to?" many people asked. In fact, relatively few meetings involved a prior decision on my part. My single rule was to keep as much variety of age, sex, politics, and occupation as possible in scheduled meetings and otherwise allow one acquaintance to lead to another. At first these introductions were especially important, as I was learning Armenian and needed to know in advance whether and how well the person spoke English or if I should bring someone to translate. Most people spoke at least some English, a large number spoke it extremely well, and many were fluent. As I gradually learned Armenian my confidence grew to the point where I thought I was ready to contact an unknown person alone.

Someone had suggested I meet Mr. Boghos, an older man who made *basterma,* a very spicy, garlicky dried filet of beef, and *erishkik,* a spicy beef sausage that is also called *soujouk.* Feeling very confident indeed, I decided to look up his address and phone number instead of asking for help. Then I had a twinge of doubt at the thought of speaking Armenian on the phone. Why not just stop by his shop and ask for an appointment? The address was right in the middle of town, so it would be much easier than telephoning. And Nouvart said it was a great idea. I could buy some *erishkik* at the same time. She did not ask exactly where I was going.

So I set off on a favorite walk, through the municipal park, past the rows of tall date palms and colorful flowering trees, through the remnants of the Paphos Gate, and along the narrow streets inside the wall of the old city. Walking slower and slower, I passed the right street number, but no one was inside—and the shop seemed to be full of textiles. I glanced back; the men from a grocery store I had just passed were at their door, watching. I looked the other way and saw that another merchant was watching, too. What else was there to do? I went to the merchant and asked, in English, if he knew Mr. Boghos. "Yes," he replied very slowly, looking over my shoulder. "There he is now," he added with a smile.

One of the other three onlookers, a lean, wiry older man, was walking toward us. He looked at me with head cocked and asked something in Greek.

"Are you Mr. Boghos?" I ventured in Armenian.

"Yes!"

"I'd like to buy some *erıshkik,* please," I said, happy to have a concrete reason to be there. But he looked bewildered. I went over it again in my mind and decided that it must be my Armenian. "Is this your shop?" I gestured toward the fabrics.

"Yes."

"Uh, do you make *basterma?*" It still seemed possible somehow.

"No."

I was running out of ideas by this point. But then I saw another head pop out of a shop farther along, and soon a familiar figure was running to the rescue.

Ared arrived and started talking in Armenian as fast as he was running, first to me: "Look, you are better off if you don't go into people's shops while they are working! We'll arrange for you to come to the club one Wednesday afternoon and you can talk to the men there and we'll talk about all of this and so on"—all of this at ninety miles per hour, but I got the gist of it and agreed that it was a good idea.

"I'll come on Wednesday, yes, thank you. But just now I was trying to buy some *basterma*—" I mumbled that I had also been trying to make an appointment but that now I wasn't so sure. "—er, actually, *erishkik* from Mr. Boghos," I said, stumbling to a close.

The two men looked at each other, and Ared caught his breath. "*Erishkik?*" Suddenly broad smiles appeared on both faces. "Okay, okay! I'll get it for you! How much do you want?" laughed Ared.

I didn't understand at all. "Where? Where will you get it?"

"Don't worry! I'll get it. How much?"

"No, no, please, don't trouble yourself! Don't worry about it! I'll get it. Just tell me—"

"No, it's too far. I'll go in my car!"

I was utterly lost. Finally they explained that there was another man of the same name who did make *basterma* but who lived a couple of miles away. I sighed, surrendered Nouvart's money, and agreed to wait with the other Mr. Boghos while Ared drove off. The day was not turning out exactly as I'd planned, and as I followed Mr. Boghos into his shop I wondered what I should have done differently. Thinking of Ared's words, I apologized for taking up his time. "Maybe I should wait outside?"

"No, no!" He pulled up a chair and ordered tea to be delivered from a nearby shop. He sat in the door and we tried to talk. He spoke no English and was very discouraged by my Armenian at first, but that changed a little as we struggled along. Fortunately, he already understood something about my work from what Ared had said outside, and he thought it was a good idea.

"So, you will write a book about what life was like so that the young people do not forget?"

"Well, yes, but I'm also interested in what the young people are doing."

He carried on with his own train of thought. "Yes, what they're doing. It's terrible! They don't know Armenian!" He gave me a meaningful glance. "They're marrying foreigners, not listening to the older people! It's not the same anymore!"

I tried to continue the conversation in the same direction. "What do you think is most important for me to write down for the young people to remember?"

He thought a bit and looked out the door toward the sunny street, then turned back to me and began again, full of passion. "You must tell the young people that they *must* marry Armenians. Otherwise Armenians will disappear. Write that down!"

I listened, watching him, waiting for the next part.

"Write *that* down!" he repeated. I was being slow—he'd meant it literally. "Write it down so you don't forget! Why are you holding a notebook?" So I did. He leaned over and looked at it. "What language are you writing in?"

I was embarrassed. "English."

"Eh, you see?" He stared back out the door as if willing Ared to return and save him. Eventually he sighed and looked back at me. "It's easier for you."

"But what about here in Cyprus now?" I asked. "Why did you say the young people don't speak Armenian? They do."

"They do now. But they will forget their Armenian eventually. This place is becoming more and more Greek, especially since 1974. It's completely Greek. There's no life for us here. Look at me. I speak more Greek than Armenian. There's only Ared on this street. Otherwise all the shop owners are Greek. My helper is a Greek. It's become easier for me to speak Greek."

Just then Ared flew to the door with the *erishkik*. "Don't forget Wednesday!"

And Mr. Boghos by this time almost seemed sorry that I was leaving and very kindly invited me back: "Monday afternoons aren't busy, you see." I wandered back home feeling properly chastised but at the same time happy to have stumbled upon a new and interesting acquaintance, impressed once again by the spontaneous hospitality and the patience of the people I encountered.

In this chance meeting themes were expounded that already sounded very familiar to me. Mr. Boghos expressed concern over language, assimilation, and intermarriage (often I found that unmarried people were most strident on this latter subject). He expressed a general fear that the Armenian people would drift off into obscurity. At the same time, his and Ared's behavior demonstrated that certain values and habits continue—hospitality, interest in each other's (and my) affairs, willingness to drop the work at hand and do a favor, entertain, talk.

Though young people were sometimes criticized by their elders, as Mr. Boghos did, for becoming absorbed in life outside the community and with the *odar* (non-Armenians) through school, work, and leisure, this was more often given as a resigned observation. As one of the men at the party I mentioned earlier noted, it is something sad but perhaps inevitable. It happens to all of them, and in fact parents often set up the process through their early choices in education for their children. Young people, on the other hand, responded to this by saying that they were doing things that made sense at their age and at this end of the twentieth century. They still considered themselves Armenian, they said, and perhaps as they grew older they too would spend more time with only Armenians, speak Armenian, insist that their children speak Armenian—and pass on their history. Meanwhile, the history most familiar and meaningful to them was a general knowledge of the Ottoman massacres and deportations of Armenians. Great respect was shown to the grandparental generation—as seen in the story of Mr. Shant in chapter 1—in recognition of the difficulties they had overcome and the role they played as symbols of survival and in rebuilding community life.

In this context, a number of young people felt it was very important that I hear as many stories of the massacres and deportations as possible. It was evident that for both survivors and their families, memories and perceptions of the massacres greatly colored attitudes to daily life in both subtle and more-conscious ways.[2] At times members of the oldest generation would encourage and push each other to tell me the stories of their own deportations. In other instances, a spouse or friend would try to derail someone from "carrying on about it again." "It's over, finished," they would say.

It seemed that the majority of young people had gained their most detailed information about the massacres from school, written accounts, history books, published memoirs, recited poetry, and more generally from posters, photographs, songs, and lectures at school, clubs, or church. Whether the stories were heard in more intimate surroundings varied between households and personalities. Some parents felt their children and grandchildren had not really wanted to hear about it or said they couldn't bring themselves to tell them of such horrific experiences. I found that in our private conversations and interviews, men usually dwelt more on the adventurous aspects of this childhood experience, while women held back neither tears nor gruesome details. This changed in more public places, where men tended to deliver a less personalized, more rhetorical account.

Mrs. Haiganoush had been a young child when her family was deported. Though she said, and it was clear, that the experiences of those years had made a powerful emotional impact on her and continued to bother her greatly, she had never told her own children the story. She wondered aloud whether anyone who had not been through such an ordeal could possibly appreciate not only the terror felt at the time but also the scars it left on one's psyche. Even so, she said, she had really wanted to tell her children and her husband, but the time had never seemed quite right. There was dinner to make, clothes to wash, the children to get ready for school, their adventures to listen to, her husband's concerns, family plans—everything and anything. And why disturb them?

But she herself remained disturbed, carrying these terrible memories alone. We spoke in London, where she lived with her family, and when she began, the words poured out, their rush unimpeded by the tears that flowed alongside. Mrs. Haiganoush described part of her family's journey from Kharpert. Having walked three days, they were at the river's edge, a branch of the Euphrates. A priest's wife, lying beside her, had been shot the night before and thrown in the river.

"It became morning. Everyone is sad, there are no men." Earlier the men in the caravan had been separated from the women and killed in Malatya. "Women and little children. What's going to happen? Are they going to throw us all in the water? What will happen? And you would see things in the water . . . someone would say it's a man, someone would say something else. Horrible things. They said they were going to make us pass over to the other side of the river.

"They killed a few other boys. We had already stayed there quite a bit. They killed people not because they had to, but for the enjoyment of it. That's the worst part. In the morning, at that river's edge, there was a boy of ten to twelve years old. This I will never, never be able to forget. He got up early in the morning to fetch water. You know there are those gourds that have a big belly and you can hollow it out, dry it, and it serves as a jug. It's light. How could you carry something heavy around? He took it to get water. To wash, to drink, for his mother—who knows? There was the sound of a gun. A gun was fired from above. Very simply, they had taken aim just to see if they could shoot somebody down or not. So that they could be sure.

"Another woman had gone to get water. That boy dropped the gourd from his hand and the water took it and it went away. And he stayed there like that, as if dazed, a small boy of just eleven or twelve. The woman who had gone for water shouted, 'Whose boy is this? He's been shot!'

"They had taken aim from above and had already shot him in the foot. Of course all the people got up together and ran. The mother came, the poor woman. The brother. They came at once. The gendarmes came, too, and saw that he had been shot in the foot. They threw him in the water. *Aman Astvadzim!* [Oh, my God!] You should see those people, frozen in place. Nobody says anything, nobody can speak. What will you say? They [the gendarmes] are pushing the little one into the water. The little one knows how to swim. He swims and he comes back, swimming. They push him back with a stick. They find a stick and beat him into the water so that the water will take him away. He swims back. This is such a horrible picture that they should make it into a film so that people could see what the Turks are like, that it isn't just murder, it's—in the act of killing they are getting pleasure, to see how they can kill.

"Then, finally, they pushed him and he was gone. The people gave a big sigh together. He's free, they thought. The boy's gone. Because they had pushed him into the depths with that big stick. The sound of the people is still in my ears. Still . . . he must have been freed. How much could he be tortured? They thought he was gone. But—he came back again! Swimming, he came back! He came and they all went back. They had also thought that he must have been finished, that is, that he was gone. All of a sudden he took his head out of the water and he started swimming back! Maybe he was a villager. It seems he was a villager and he knew how to swim. They must have lived near a river. He came and we could see that he had no strength left. Just like this, like an animal, his hands on the ground, he was looking at the people. 'Help!'"

"Did anyone . . . ?" I asked hesitantly.

"Who is going to help? The mother ran. The brother ran. They [the gendarmes] came, they came, and one of them hit the brother, too. Then he immediately began bleeding. The mother forgot the first one and immediately wrapped her headscarf around the second son so that the soldiers wouldn't see that he was wounded too and throw him in the river too. At that place, in front of so many people, in front of the women, he [one of the gendarmes] took out a gun and emptied it into the ear of the child and threw him back in the water.

"This is . . . I mean, it's not a story. I saw it with my own eyes. And though many years have passed—I was six years old—it's impossible to forget it. Impossible. Those who died, who were beaten, who were wounded."

We shuddered and sat quietly together until the vivid images started to fade. Mrs. Haiganoush began to apologize for "burdening" me with her troubles.

Not only her own generation but those that have followed have had to come to terms with the incredibility and horror of what was done. There is a popular notion that the generations can be characterized by different reactions: the survivors, stunned, trying to rebuild their lives; their children, ignoring their parents' worries, assimilating and building a life in a new country; their grandchildren, showing not just interest but anger at the injustice and the desire to do something about it. However, I found much more variety within generations than between them, and considerable overlapping of these categories of reaction.

While Mrs. Haiganoush had not told her own children her story, other survivors felt a need to talk about their experiences. In London a woman in her late fifties who had been raised in Cyprus spoke of how she had heard of the massacres.

"One day, when I was six or seven, my mother said, 'Armineh, sit down by me. I'm going to tell you a story.' I was very excited and sat down, crossed my arms, and waited with wide-open eyes and open mouth. 'I'm going to tell you a story about a little girl—how she became a refugee, how she came to an orphanage, and so on,' she said. I said, 'It's you, the little girl, isn't it?' And it affected me very much—to this day.

"Father was a teacher and had collected Armenian orphans after the massacres and taken them to an orphanage in Alexandretta. Then to Port Said and then to Beirut, where he married one of the orphans. At night we were so interested in the stories about their lives—the older people. There was nothing else to do, of course, but we loved them. We especially listened to my mother, who was very forceful and vivacious and talked about her days at the orphanage and during the massacres.

"When we came to Cyprus, people were semiliterate. Mother was educated compared to them and could read and write. And she would sing Gomidas.[3] We thought, as little kids, that we were really something special. The refugees spoke Turkish, but *we* spoke Armenian."

Mrs. Armineh felt very proud of her mother's courage, but she also indicated the pride felt by families who spoke Armenian and were knowledgeable in Armenian matters when most around them spoke Turkish and were relatively uneducated. This is a division that was not based entirely on wealth. Certainly teachers' families were neither well-off nor secure.

Mrs. Armineh became a teacher at the Melikian-Ouzunian primary school, where most in the next generation first heard about the pogroms. Hratch, now in his late twenties, recounted how it had impressed him.

"This is one of the few things I *really* remember from primary school. Mrs. Heghineh was our teacher. She was *very* nice. We loved her. But one day she was telling us about the massacres and the deportations. All of these people killed, carried away, kidnapped. And she was telling us very sadly, very depressed, and I couldn't understand why she wasn't angry and shouting! I put up my hand and I asked her, 'Didn't they fight back?' 'No,' she said. I couldn't believe this either. 'Why not?' She told us they couldn't. They didn't have any guns. And I think she really believed that then. That's what people were told, and they believed it. But I was a little boy. It didn't make sense. I thought, why didn't they have hunting guns or knives or anything? They could even have used sticks and stones! *Why* did they let the Turks do that to them?

"It made a big impression on me, and those days, for a long time afterward, I used to imagine myself back during that time and I would hide behind a door with a *big* stick and wait for the first Turk to come along. Even after I stopped doing that, I wondered about it for a long time.

"Now it's different. Now they are telling us that people *did* resist. Some people did fight back, and I am very happy to hear that. It makes a big difference to me."

Hratch came out from behind the door and dropped his imaginary stick as his mother called from the other room for him to calm down, not get so worked up. He remembered an appointment at one of the clubs and took off at high speed, calling, "Don't worry, Mum!"

"I *do* worry, and I don't understand," she said as his car pulled away. "His father and I care about what happened—it's terrible, of course—but we never pushed it on any of our children. What's the point? What can anyone do about it? The big countries will do whatever they want. And Turkey is their friend. They will never even admit they did it. Why should anyone get so excited about it? Let him concentrate on his own life. It's almost time to start a family."

When I passed by another house that week, Mrs. Araxi was sitting on a sofa with her two teenage granddaughters, surrounded by pieces of paper. Astghig was looking through poems her grandmother had saved for one she could recite at the April 24 commemoration of the 1915 massacres the following week.

"It's really difficult. Look at this, it's so self-pitying! 'Why us, God? Even the flowers are better off!' I can't say something like that. That's what so many of them are like. And there are two other choices, I figure, out of what we've been looking at. It happened to us and now we must fight. I mean, we must work harder and try to build up our lives again. Or the other type—it happened and now look at us! Aren't we great? I think I believe that we must work, I don't know. But we can't find just the right poem, anyway." She returned to the pile to see what her grandmother had found.

Hratch and others were busy organizing the commemoration at one of the youth clubs that year, and he invited me to attend. The walls of the staircase leading up to the club were lined with large plasticized photographs of atrocities committed during the deportations—piles of skulls, miserable and bony children, men hanging from scaffolding. This was exactly the same set of photos I had seen a year earlier on the walls of the museum of the Armenian convent in Jerusalem. Upstairs young people were beginning to gather, some arranging chairs and the podium, others sweeping the floor.

A few parents were in the crowd, but many more older men were gathered in the smaller adjoining rooms playing backgammon or cards. This disappointed some of the young people, but by the time the program began there was no space in the room for the card players, as nearly a hundred people, mostly young, crowded onto the closely packed small chairs. We arranged our knees and listened to an hour of songs, a short lecture, and recitations of poetry, including the one that had been selected by Astghig and her grandmother.

Briefly outlined, the poem, which was written by Siamanto, describes a small group of Armenians who, having escaped the deportations, are hiding in a dark cave. Outside, Turks are looking for them, and suddenly a baby among them begins to cry. Someone says, "We'll have to strangle that baby before it gives us all away!" The mother cries, "No, strangle me first and then the baby!" As the footsteps outside come closer, two hands reach out in the darkness and kill the baby. The soldiers pass by, and in the morning the Armenians escape. The last scene is of the crazed mother wandering through a village, crying, "I've killed my baby! Won't anyone strangle me? I have no more strength to do it!"

Though impressed with Astghig's delivery, I was shocked as I listened to the words. I didn't see how it fit with what Astghig had said she was looking for. But clearly the poem did fit with a popular theme of personal sacrifice for the greater common good. It is not accidental that in this poem and others, the image of family ties being secondary to those of the nation is used to show the importance of being and remaining Armenian. In fact, on a day-to-day level there is nothing in the Armenian world more important than the bonds between parents and children (and still, to a degree, those among members of an extended family). For many young people the message of the massacres is a commission to do well in this world to honor the memory of those who died.

In Cyprus another kind of sacrifice continues to be made several times a year. In a combination of religious ritual and community celebration, sheep donated by members of the community are killed, with the meat cooked and served to all who come. The ceremony (*madagh*, "sacrifice") is usually held at the community church.

One of these ceremonies traditionally had been held at Surp Magar, a monastery in the Kyrenia Mountains, to honor that saint's name day. Following the division of the island in 1974, Surp Magar was lost, and this *madagh* was not held again until May 1983, when it was transferred to the grounds of the Melkonian Institute and the celebration revived.

In 1985 the *madagh* ceremonies I observed were short, held outside on the Melkonian grounds or in the church courtyard, where the sheep were tied. The priests said a prayer and sang the service with deacons standing beside them. Children usually stood in a line, staring at the sheep. The sheep and the crowd of people listened quietly as salt was blessed and put into the sheep's mouths.[4] The ceremony ended very quickly, and a professional butcher, waiting nearby, began his work.

As the Surp Magar service ended, a group of women in the Melkonian kitchen began cooking and preparing for the next day's feast, washing vegetables and boiling chicken and wheat to make *heriseh* (a savory stew). A huge cauldron was heated in readiness for the sheep, and the large room filled with steam. Men came in and out, helping to carry pots, vegetables, and water. The cooks worked until late at night, returning early the next morning to finish their preparations by noon, when a large crowd was already sitting at tables set inside and out around the club.

In November, while helping with the preparations of the *madagh* for the Nicosia church's name day, several people mentioned that they thought that in the past the feast of the *madagh* had been distributed to the poor and not shared among the whole community. During a visit the next week, Mrs. Alice, a Protestant, said that she and her neighbor, an Apostolic (a member of the Armenian national church), had been discussing the *madagh* and its meaning. The neighbor, Mrs. Zabelle, had told her that in Sunday's sermon the priest explained that the *madagh* custom was a carryover from pagan times. In the Armenian Christian tradition it was changed to an offering by the rich to the poor, first blessed in a special service. Now it is a meal of fellowship for all. Mrs. Alice added that though all of this sounded good, she was still troubled by the idea of the sheep as a sacrifice, and she noted, "Didn't Jesus say that he himself was the last sacrifice?"

Later the priest added, "It is a tradition in old societies. But during the Christian era, Christ said, 'I'm not looking for sacrifices.' So why do we do it, if Jesus says this? Because in the old days you couldn't eradicate anything overnight. Today it is a way to take part in the religious activity of the church—the old *agape* system of eating together. In the liturgy we mention the forgiveness of sins, blessings from God. Well, it is a holdover from pagan times, but given a Christian aspect."

Whereas some people wonder to each other about the specific meaning and even the "correctness" of such an act, most, including the priests, are content to accept it as a tradition that should be continued for the sake of tradition and, if necessary, reexplained in terms that make sense today. The combination of sacrifice and sense of community is a major part of the learned experience of Armenians in Cyprus and London and grows in a somehow symbiotic way alongside its twin of display of wealth (or would-be wealth) and pride.

In 1986 the April 24 commemoration in London was a cooperative event, sponsored by a number of different clubs and organizations. Following the introductory remarks by a retired Melkonian teacher ("Our cause, the Armenian cause, is a holy one, and it will persevere because of that") and a dramatic recital of the poem about the baby in the cave, the main speech was given by an Armenian Iranian. The points were familiar and the themes generally acceptable to all in the audience. Toward the end, however, the speaker endorsed a point of view not held by all.

"The most important thing is our Armenian language," he said. "Without it we don't have our songs, our poems, our literature. Without it we don't have Armenian culture. Armenian schools and families are also important, mothers who raise the children to speak and to be Armenian. The church and the clubs must also be supported. As we don't have a government, these are the institutions that in turn support us." The speaker concluded that the Armenian cause was the return of the Armenians to their homelands and that the solution of the problem of the lands depended on the politicization of the Armenians.

A poem about Ararat, the holy mountain, was read by a young woman. Songs about Armenia were sung by a community choir. Finally the bishop rose to end the program, saying, "Ours is a history of blood spilled over three thousand years. But we don't have a day of mourning in all our history. If we are the true descendants of those who were massacred, we must vow to keep our church, our language, and to work for the Armenian cause. We have been a visionary and artistic race. April twenty-fourth must live on in the memory of our cherished dead, but we will work rather than mourn for them."

EMERGING THEMES

The memories of the massacres and deportations of the early twentieth century are the most striking part of the Armenian shared background. The subject is internalized, absorbed from family attitudes and schooling. The external, organized reminders, such as the commemorative services, lectures, and events described earlier in this chapter, interact with the internal aspect; their stridency is sometimes irritating, sometimes inspiring. Donald Miller and Lorna Miller, who worked with Armenian survivors and their families in Los Angeles, observe that communal conversation revolves around these traumatic events, adding that when such stories "include moral contradictions, we may reject them because they paralyze and threaten us, or we may seek to correct our past in an effort to achieve personal wholeness and healing" (Miller and Miller 1991, 35–36).

Armenians speak of feeling both a collective debt to the past and an individual one. The feeling is that the loss should not be forgotten and that those who have survived should achieve as much as possible as a way of trying to fill the hole left by the loss of so many people. This includes the notion of sacrifice for family, for nation. Frequently those who are most active in Armenian politics, education, or cultural affairs speak in terms of sacrificing their time and energy for the nation. Similarly, attending weekend classes in Armenian is very time-consuming for parents, children, and teachers alike, yet it is done in order to ensure that some part of the national heritage will continue. A sense of moral duty pervades many of the organized activities.

At the same time, life is to be enjoyed and lived to the fullest. Sacrifice is not necessarily monetary, and the well-dressed, stylish Armenian in Nicosia or London is not obviously a person touched by the memories of deep personal and collective losses. Instead, members of other ethnic groups who are their neighbors in Cyprus and England speak of Armenians as a group known for their hospitality and gregariousness, business acumen and shrewdness.

Both sacrifice and enjoyment of the moment relate to insecurity, a word frequently heard in conversations concerning the physical uncertainty of the future but used also to explain the psychological scars of the past created by the earlier deportations and by more recent losses in Cyprus during the conflicts between Greeks and Turks. The barricades along the Green Line in Nicosia are constant reminders of the old homes that lie just beyond and of the time when they were lost. Though there is a longing for the old neighborhood, there is also a concern that current negotiations to reunite the island could lead eventually to more disturbances. Armenian Cypriots want to believe that a united Cyprus would remain a peaceful one, but their own experience leads to great anxiety. People ask, "Will we be forced to move again? Should we move now to avoid losing everything?"

Concurrently, another kind of insecurity influences Armenians in Cyprus and even more so in London: the question of assimilation, of losing the Armenian nation not through bloodshed but through *jermag chart* ("white massacre"), a general drift into the surrounding cultures. The question of intermarriage also enters here. Intermarriage is perceived by many as the biggest threat to the nation and, more immediately, to the continuation of closely interwoven family ties. Jenny King Phillips, who worked with Armenians in the Boston area, has described this combined fear of physical danger in some countries, assimilation in all, as the "root paradigm" for Armenians, "the endangered nation, endangered people," a concept that informs their beliefs and actions as individuals and as communities (Phillips 1979, 15).[5]

Insecurity, both individual and communal, in turn encourages a sense of urgency and a need to achieve as much as possible while the opportunity is there. For many this takes the form of earning as much money as possible—to make up for what was lost and provide for future contingencies. Others push themselves, or their children, toward further education and the various professions, both of which are seen as ensuring mobility if that should become necessary. Another problem emerges as higher education introduces students to many job possibilities that the Cyprus community cannot support—and to a number of interesting and attractive non-Armenian students, at an age when many are beginning to think of marriage. Parents who encourage their children to achieve in education often find they develop interests and a circle of friends quite outside the community. Putting the children's interests first is also called sacrifice, though sometimes children speak of sacrificing their own wishes for those of their parents—giving up the foreign girlfriend, choosing a job close to the family home.

In practice it is the rare person who puts nation above family. In many ways nation does mean family and is often thought of in those terms, but on a day-to-day level the needs of family life are first. Though both family and nation are spoken of in terms of duty and responsibility, informally it is only when nation overlaps with family in psychological terms that nation is spoken of with similar affection. When people complain that there is a "missing generation" in Cyprus, skewing community life and boding ill for its future, they very frequently add that this includes a personal loss, a son or daughter who has moved away. Family is the axis of activity, the first priority in loyalty and in all practical terms.

Hospitality, the constant visiting and keeping in touch, is a basic part of Armenian family life.[6] It includes one of the most powerful and most discussed but least acknowledged symbols of Armenian life: food. Armenian food is taken for granted at home, and it is really noticed only when it is not there, as when students arrive in London. Then especially, the smell of a good pilaf or the taste of a crisp, sweet watermelon brings with it all the memories of home and other Armenians.

Food is not taken seriously as a symbol because the dishes are so similar to those eaten by the neighboring peoples and because hospitality is thought of as a Middle Eastern or Cypriot custom, not only Armenian. When it comes to passing on Armenianness to the next generations, community leaders, teachers, politicians, and priests would all agree that while family, food, and hospitality are important, they are not sufficient to carry on ethnic (and especially nationalist) identity.

In the early part of this century the Cypriot Armenian community had come from many different places and encompassed a large variety of habits, customs, and dialects; people's primary identity was with their extended family, village, or town. This was seen as a weakness by clerical and secular nationalist leaders, who led the way to a conscious consolidation of themes and symbols throughout the diaspora, emphasizing unity and trying to build the future of the Armenian people as a nation. This led to a reification of culture in nationalist terms on the level of public discourse, an ideology of Armenianness that was preached, taught, and written about in ever wider circles as mass education became more common.

The term *ideology* is used here in the sense of a conscious, focused attempt to create contemporary sense out of historical confusion. Kapferer defines ideology as "a selective cultural construction whereby certain significances relevant to experience are systematically organized into a relatively coherent scheme" but emphasizes the "relevance" and the grounding of the dismembered pieces selected (Kapferer 1988, 80). The experiences and conditions that formed the background to the initial formulations of Armenian nationalism have changed considerably throughout this century and vary now between different diaspora centers, but the continued significance of nationalist ideology remains founded on the resonance it has in the experiences of members of the oldest generation, the collective memory passed on within family circles, and the shared symbols and beliefs of the people. The "Armenian cause," as it is called by some—"the fate of the Armenians," as others refer to it—has taken on a sacred quality for many who are committed to working for it. For others this remains a poetic metaphor, but for them moral fulfillment is found in working for the cause through the organizations and political parties.

LIVING IN DIASPORA

Often Armenians asked me, or each other while we were talking, if they really had a culture. This was nearly always a rhetorical question, and the same person would answer, "Yes, but we in Cyprus are watered-down versions of the real Armenian. And it's worse in England." When people spoke of "traditional culture," I noticed, they meant the vague but powerful and often idealized memory of the customs and habits of Armenians before dispersal and modernization. An important part of the current culture is the contrast it is felt to have with "traditional culture."

Culture is popularly understood as a certain conjunction of traits and customs, and when these are seen to have changed, the culture is lost or in danger of being lost. Nationalists take this further, as Kapferer points out, by reifying an idealized culture, extracting it from the "flow of social life," and establishing it as an object of devotion (Kapferer 1988, 2). Here I am defining culture as a learned system of ideas and ways of communicating and behaving, a set of shared symbols and associations that is at the very base of everyday experience. Culture is constantly changing, as will be evident in the following chapters. Particular relations or sets of relations between people, along with certain dominant traits or ideals, are transformed or even abandoned as physical, emotional, and intellectual circumstances change.

At the same time, as Renee Hirschon has observed, there is continuity in the core "values and perceptions which people hold about themselves and the world about them, the ways in which their relationships are organized" even through the most disruptive times (Hirschon 1989, 14). Continuity should not be confused with stagnation, though, and culture is recognized to be in flux, always changing.

How does culture change? Individuals make choices within the realm of possibilities known to them through family, community, and collective memory; those choices in turn transform culture. Cultures have many strands, including certain dominant ideals, though these ideals or images of culture are not always carried out in practice. In addition, societies contain much individual variation.

In the case of Armenians in Cyprus and London, this process must, of course, be understood within the wider context of sociopolitical affairs of the host country and the region as well as world events. Given the crises that have disrupted Armenian communities in the past, it is tempting to see cultural change as imposed, as a consequence of outside circumstances. I do not deny that this aspect of change exists, but it should be made clear that even within the most dramatic events, choices were being made from a complex assortment of possible alternatives, with people selecting one strand over another from the culture; this will become evident through the personal stories in the following chapters. As Susan Harding points out in her book *Remaking Ibieca,* in many cases choices are made with the hope that traditional life and especially traditional values might continue and prosper (Harding 1984, 200). People often cannot foresee that their decisions—for example, those concerning their children's education—will irrevocably change the fabric of their own lives and that of the community as a whole.

Individuals choose, but choices have certain limits, and the results are far from guaranteed. Sherry Ortner further clarifies the role of the individual actor in culture as one "who is 'loosely structured,' who is prepared—but no more than that—to find most of his culture intelligible and meaningful but who does not necessarily find all parts of it equally meaningful in all times and places" (Ortner 1989, 198). She adds that what is felt to be meaningful at a given stage of one's life may be less so at another stage (and vice versa). This becomes especially pertinent in diaspora, as the actors are living in both their home and host cultures and are often mobile, both physically and socially.

The differences between levels of identity within diaspora—community, ethnic group, and nation—are slim and can be viewed as variations on a theme. But each has its particular resonance, and at times individuals will find themselves more attached and committed to one than to another, again depending on the situation and their own "prior text." A community is a group of people who share a certain geographical area, institutions, interests, and conversation; Francine Markowitz (1993, 247) suggests that community is formed and held together by talk, a characteristic shared in more formal ways by the ethnic group or nation. Here I use the word *community* as Armenians do, to mean the local entity, whether that be a city or a country. Anny Bakalian traces *kaghout*, "community," from *ghariboutiune*, "living as strangers," the root borrowed from the Turkish word *gharib* (Arabic *garib*), "stranger" (Bakalian 1993, 145). Referring to the "wider Armenian community," linking these local bases, Armenians speak of the Armenian people or nation.[7]

Glenn Bowman (1993) suggests that the Palestinian people occupy three "discrete locales" in diaspora, allowing and encouraging the development of different kinds of national identity. He cites Israel and the occupied territories, Middle Eastern refugee camps, and the bourgeois diaspora. The corresponding Armenian world would be Hayastan (formerly Soviet Armenia), the Middle East and Cyprus (lands inside or closest to the old homelands), and the rest, mostly Western diaspora. Though not entirely discrete, each of the areas has its own distinct priorities and variant of the shared culture; as a result, as Bowman points out for the Palestinians, ways of imagining the nation (and thus the aims and methods of nationalism) differ widely between them.

Ethnicity is a more appropriate term to use in the Western diaspora, as Khatchig Tölölyan suggests (1988, 62), while Armenians in the Near East, including Cyprus, probably view themselves, in relation to the rest of the diaspora and the homelands, as a nation in exile. This has as much to do with the political organization of the host states, such as Cyprus or Lebanon, as with the physical closeness of the homelands. Both the concept of ethnic group and that of nation connect local people to other related communities, and with this shift in emphasis comes an increased interest in the more theoretical and more readily observable aspects of identity, drawing away from the practical, everyday functioning of community. The idea of ethnicity is a conscious one—but less so than nationalism, a more politicized term, which requires belief and a certain amount of dedication to it as a cause (Deutsch 1963; Armstrong 1982).

Community, ethnic group, nation, and culture all involve the boundary marking and maintaining suggested by Fredrik Barth (1969). This also serves to mask (or draw attention away from) the many internal differences within the group, which in turn provide the fodder for cultural change, new forms of community life, and new views of ethnicity and nation. What makes a person Armenian or a group of people an Armenian community? In both cases I am taking the self-ascriptive approach: those who consider themselves Armenian are Armenian. This then leaves the discussion of how Armenian someone is to the nationalists. In this study I am more interested in the many different ways of being Armenian that exist within a certain community.

I think of the Armenians as a long-standing "ethnos" (Smith 1986) with shared characteristics and institutions (and also many differences), which has come to view itself as a nation in modern times. The time period covered in this book is just after the transition from ethnos to self-aware nation, but from the stories and memories described here it should be clear that there was indeed considerable variety in traditional Armenian culture and a very concerted effort through education, the clergy, and popular literature to create a modern Armenian nation.

Clearly Armenians see themselves as a group distinguishable from others in a number of important ways. As stated earlier, today this is believed to be due to a shared language, church, and history.[8] That history includes a shared descent, traced through family ties and connections but also through an assumption of ancestral ties to a much more ancient past. For most Armenians this is the myth-symbol complex that Smith describes as the underpinning of ethnic polity, the transmission of which, he says, must be examined if one wishes to understand "the special character of ethnic identities" (Smith 1986, 15).

This transmission does not follow a smooth course. Michael Fischer, looking at autobiographical works that focus on ethnicity, observes that ethnicity is dynamic: "It can be potent even when not consciously taught; it is something which institutionalized teaching easily makes chauvinistic, sterile, and superficial, something that emerges in full—often liberating— flower only through struggle" (Fischer 1986, 195).

This struggle is most often a personal, relatively hidden one, but early in my research I found that a related (though very different) kind of struggle was frequently in the news and in people's conversations and thoughts: that of the armed Armenian "freedom fighters" or "terrorists" (see chapter 3). In her study of the London Armenian community, Vered Amit Talai points out that the small group of activists sympathetic to the armed struggle received an "ambivalent response" from the larger community (Talai 1989, 138). As with other conscious aspects of ethnicity, their aggressive dedication to a specific cause had the ability to both inspire and repel, and in the mid-1980s changes in international politics and the groups' own internecine warfare left them splintered and relatively quiet.

Writing in the context of the Jewish experience, Jack Kugelmass notes that the myths and stories that all cultures provide to make sense of the chaos of their experience are themselves "all subject to considerable dispute" (Kugelmass 1988, 11). Jews, like Armenians, disagree among themselves about interpretations and the relative importance of different components of the myth-symbol complex. One of these is the notion of homeland: where and what it is, how central it is, whether the myth of return is a sustaining dream or a practical if distant reality. In the 1980s and 1990s several Armenian Cypriots did "return" from London, but not to the historical homeland of the present Republic of Armenia nor to Anatolia. They have returned to the space most meaningful, resonant, and practical for them—Cyprus.

In *After the Last Sky* Edward Said illuminates a Palestinian perspective, asking questions that concern all peoples in diaspora:

> All of us speak of *awdah,* "return," but do we mean that literally, or
> do we mean "we must restore ourselves to ourselves"? The latter is the
> real point, I think, although I know many Palestinians who want their
> houses and their way of life back exactly. But is there any place that fits
> us, together with our accumulated memories and experiences? Do we
> exist? What proof do we have? . . . When did we become "a people"?
> When did we stop being one? Or are we in the process of becoming
> one? (Said 1985, 33–34)

A people are always in the process of becoming. New ties and attachments are formed and re-formed at personal, communal, and national levels. Living in diaspora includes a constant reconstruction of a sense of place, where the past is woven into the present on new territory and the new space made meaningful. The space itself changes.

Chapter 3

Armenians and Cyprus

Melkon

Father I have your rug.
I sit on it now—not as you
did, but on a chair before
a table, and write.

It is all that is left of
Adana, of us, of what we
share: in this life, in
your death.

In my nomad head I carry all
the things of my life,
determined by memory and love.
And on certain distant nights,
I take them one by one.
And count.
And place them on your rug.

—David Kherdian

Hayastan, the Republic of Armenia (formerly Soviet Armenia), is
one of at least three parallel constructions of Armenian homeland. For those who live there—and, increasingly, for many diaspora Armenians—it is the homeland today. It is a place where Armenian is spoken on the streets and heard in the opera and on television.
Armenian schools and the university, dance troupes and choirs are all
pointed to with pride. As Mr. Shant made clear, at the beginning of the
century this land, in spite of its own troubles and poverty, was regarded as
a haven, a shelter, and this image continued in many people's minds
through the following decades.

A second homeland is also called Hayastan: the ancient kingdom, the
old territories embedded with the 2,500-year-old history, lands reaching
from Dikranagert in Anatolia to Karabagh in the Caucasus. These have
not been together under sovereign Armenian rule since 95 B.C.E. but en-
compass the ancestral homes of most of those now in diaspora.

The third is a related but more intimate vision. In diaspora the homeland is, or at least includes, an Armenian's own town or village of origin.
Now, of course, that means the village of their ancestors' origin. This includes personal and collective memories of towns such as Kharpert and
Adana, now in Turkey, and villages such as Kessab in Syria, places that
people wonder and care about and long to see. The varied customs and
dialects found in different Armenian towns and villages of the Ottoman
Empire have translated today into new differences of outlook, style, and
linguistic ability in a more widespread diaspora. As in the past, Armenians
often say they feel most comfortable and have to explain less when they
are with Armenians from their own diaspora countries.

Cyprus is not considered a homeland but has become a well-loved
home to its Armenian community. In Cyprus, as in other places, Armenians have had to create a new community, and many elements, material as
well as nonmaterial, go into this creation. Rugs, for example, are one part
of this process. As rugs have been passed on to new generations, they have
been moved from tabletops to floors and have gone from covering walls
to beds to floors and back to walls. Some people have lost their rugs
through wars and displacement, and others have thrown them away; then
one's possessions, the "things" of life, are taken out and counted and
placed on a new rug. All of this—the old rugs, the new rugs, the knowledge of the old rugs, memories and love of the "things" of life—mix together in the creation of the people and their communities.

Both Cyprus and the Armenian people have known the rule of foreign
empires and peoples for centuries, and today both still struggle with the
consequences of those years. This chapter briefly outlines events, people,

and institutions in the history of Cyprus and the history of the Armenian people that have helped form the self-image of Armenian Cypriots as a community.[1] These are an important part of the collective memory, which Armenian Cypriots use to understand their contemporary world.

CYPRUS

Located in the eastern corner of the Mediterranean Sea, Cyprus has an area of some 3,572 square miles with a population of 702,000 in 1990, approximately 80 percent Greek and 18 percent Turkish. Today it is divided between the Turkish Cypriots, who occupy the northern 38 percent of the island, and the Greek Cypriots in the south. The position of Cyprus has always been of great interest to powers competing in the region. The island is the site of strategic ports, and now airports and listening stations; it also had valuable copper and other mineral deposits, now depleted. The earliest colonists were Mycenaean Greeks, followed by the Persians, Romans, Mamlukes, Byzantines, Arabs, Crusaders, Venetians, Ottomans, and British. The population remained primarily Greek in orientation, language, and culture, but each invading force left its mark on the island. In *History of Cyprus* Costas Kyrris notes that the Byzantine emperor Justin II brought some 3,350 Armenian settlers to Cyprus in 578 C.E. "as Guards and smallholders" (Kyrris 1985, 169). Throughout the following centuries other Armenians were brought to help the Byzantines hold Cyprus against Arab attacks.[2]

Much later, in 1191, King Leon II of Armenia acted as best man at the marriage of Richard the Lionhearted to Berangaria in Cyprus. Beginning in 1080 Cilician Armenia had declared independence from the Byzantines and sought the protection of the Crusaders and alliances with the Lusignan dynasty of Cyprus, but in 1375 the title of King of Armenia was finally passed to the reigning king of Cyprus, a cousin, when the Cilician royal house ended.

The Ottomans were welcomed by the native Cypriots after Venetian rule, under which there had been attempts at forced conversion to the Roman Catholic Church. The Ottoman *millet* system of governance not only tolerated the Orthodox and Apostolic Churches but delegated authority to them. During this time, Turkish settlers came from Anatolia to colonize the island, and that minority became well established.

It is assumed from these pieces of information and from the existence of several contemporary Armenian ("military") villages (Kyrris 1985, 206) that Armenians remained on the island throughout these centuries.

Probably most of them gradually became assimilated into the main culture, but periodically new groups appeared, and a distinct presence there was maintained. This can be assumed from other information as well, for example, the Armenian church of Famagusta, built in 1346, and the church of Nicosia and the Surp Magar monastery in the Kyrenia Mountains, both given to the Armenians by the Turks in the sixteenth century.[3] From the year 1179, with few interruptions, a record has been kept showing a continual residence of Armenian archbishops and primates in Cyprus (Gulesserian 1936, 241–47). Links with other Armenians in the Ottoman Empire were informal, usually through trade, government service, or family ties.

The Ottomans leased the administration of Cyprus to the British in 1878 in return for their assistance against Russia. In 1914 Cyprus was formally annexed by Britain when Turkey joined the Central Powers, and in 1928 it became a crown colony. From the time of the British arrival there were numerous appeals by Greek Cypriots, led in great part by the church, demanding *enosis,* or union with Greece. Public education continued to be entirely separate for each of the ethnic groups and was administered by those groups under the supervision of the British.[4] Cypriot children were thus encouraged to identify with the ideals and accomplishments of their respective mainland compatriots (Loizos 1974). At the same time the British promoted minorities (Turks, Armenians, Maronites) in their civil service and, in a move that later would prove most harmful to interethnic relations, in the police force. The minorities in return supported the British as their guarantee of maintaining the status quo and preventing *enosis.* Greeks, Turks, Armenians, and Maronites were neighbors throughout this time. The groups were easily distinguishable among themselves, and homes were loosely gathered within ethnic quarters rather than completely intermingled or rigidly separated.

Mr. Nazar, born in the early 1920s, commented on relations between Greek and Armenian Cypriots and how he believed that earlier incidents still color people's perceptions. "They [the Greeks] say we [Armenians] are pro-British. Not correct. It is correct that we are usually on the side of the government, whatever government it is. Now that it is Greek Cypriot, we are pro–Cypriot government. We are law-abiding citizens, with the government. Why blame us for this?

"Usually they mention the 1931 uprising.[5] There was an Armenian constable on duty at Government House. When Government House was burned, he put the governor on his shoulder and took him down, saved him. Exactly as Makarios was saved years later. He was made a sergeant, Kaspar *Chaush.*[6] The governor was Ronald Storrs, who was pro-Cyprus.

But many Armenians went to jail for that thing, too. An Armenian from Limassol had followed the crowd to Government House and saw them trying to burn a government car with no matches. No luck. So he showed them how to do it with his handkerchief, dipping it in kerosene. He was a really simple man, he had no idea of what he was doing. A judge later tried to prove that, tried to lead him to say that he hadn't taken part. But he couldn't tell a lie, so he went to jail for twelve years."

The campaign for *enosis,* and later for independence, grew quickly beginning in 1950, led politically by Archbishop Makarios. The EOKA (National Organization of Cypriot Fighters) movement, led by General Grivas, began in earnest when the British continued to insist that there would never be independence for the island.

Other Armenians who were adults or teenagers during that period echoed the thoughts of Mr. Nazar. One man said, "Three or four Armenians did go to the mountains to join and fight for EOKA, but Armenians try to be law-abiding. Generally they don't participate in upheaval. It's not fair to ask for protection from the British, for example, and then revolt. Now it's the same for the Greek government. They have given us a school, church—just imagine plotting against them. We are more trustworthy than that."

Turkish Cypriots joined the police force in growing numbers and were used by the British in antiterrorist activities and curfew enforcement. Conferences between the various parties involved met with no success, and the Turks began their own demands for *taksim* (partition), having little trust in Greek plans for independence. Armenians found themselves in between.

A man who had been a teenager at the time remembered how he and friends had overstayed a visit to Kyrenia, returning after the curfew. They were stopped by a British soldier. "He asked how old we were, who we were. We said we were Armenian. Well, the soldier knew that EOKA was Greek, and VOLKAN was Turkish, but what was this 'Armenian'? He asked us to repeat it. We said, 'Look, you are English, we are Armenian!' He was still confused. Finally he asked his sergeant. The sergeant says, 'Let them go. They are Christian Jews!'"

Finally, in 1959, a conference in Zurich on the status of Cyprus ended with a constitution, a proclamation of independence, and a treaty of guarantee signed by Great Britain, Greece, and Turkey. Though the constitution was not considered satisfactory, it was agreed upon as a means of achieving independent statehood without further delay. According to the requirements of the constitution, a Greek Cypriot (Archbishop Makarios) was elected president and a Turkish Cypriot (Dr. Fazil Kuchuk) was elected vice president, both taking office upon independence in 1960. Ethnic quotas were established for the armed forces, civil service, and administration, while communal legislatures were elected along ethnic lines. During the few years of outward peace that followed, much political maneuvering went on behind the scenes. Greek Cypriot leaders protested that the constitution was not balanced and favored the Turkish community, while Turkish Cypriots feared that their communal rights, outlined in the constitution, were not being upheld, in spite of their power of veto and the fact that Turks held various important offices.

In 1963 President Makarios issued a list of objections and thirteen proposed amendments to the constitution. The proposals were rejected by Vice President Kuchuk, and soon afterward fighting broke out between members of the two communities. As fighting continued and the Turkish Cypriots pulled out of the national government, Nicosia was divided by a Green Line into sharply defined and more secure Greek and Turkish sectors. There was still freedom of movement at that time, but travel was difficult and there was considerable uneasiness.

Following these events, President Makarios began to back away from forceful demands for *enosis* and attempted negotiations with the Turkish side. At the same time, his drift toward the center and the left wing, his detachment from the hard right, his overtures to the Communist countries, and his aspiration toward a role of leadership in the Third World served to alienate old and powerful allies in the Western bloc.

In July 1974 a coup was staged against Makarios by right-wing, pro-*enosis* elements of the National Guard, led by mainland Greek officers and engineered by the junta in Greece. Makarios escaped assassination but was forced to flee the country. He was replaced by Nikos Sampson, a well-known anti-Turkish guerrilla, and this, added to the instability of the new regime and its pro-*enosis* platform, caused great alarm in both mainland Turkey and among Turkish Cypriots.

Having consulted with both the British, as coguarantors of Cyprus, and the Americans, Turkey went ahead with the long-threatened invasion of Cyprus to protect the Turkish Cypriots (Birand 1975). A narrow corridor was taken between Kyrenia and Nicosia, quickly ending the brief civil war between coup supporters and opponents. Glafkos Clerides, an experienced nationalist leader, replaced Sampson on the Greek side and negotiations began. Stalemate and then a second, more expansive invasion by Turkey followed, leaving the island divided. The initial corridor had clearly not been large enough to be viable, but the new territory, some 38 percent of the island, was vastly disproportionate to the Turkish Cypriot population. Soon afterward mainland Turks were brought to live in northern Cyprus. Cypriots on both sides of the new border lost their homes, which in many cases had been in their families for generations and even centuries, and moved to the side held by their respective ethnic group.

The popular view is that Sampson, the EOKA-B fighters (the follow-up group to EOKA), their supporters, and the junta in Greece were all puppets in this scenario, the strings manipulated by the United States with British support. Having been denied NATO bases in Greek-dominated Cyprus, the United States arranged to have a more cooperative Turkish side to Cyprus.[7]

Peter Loizos, in *The Heart Grown Bitter* (1981), gives a moving account of the experience of Greek villagers in 1974 and their adjustment following the loss of their homes. He also discusses attitudes toward local and international politics, which are not dissimilar to those heard among Armenian Cypriots—for example, the search for scapegoats in large- and small-scale politics, or the balance sought between passionately held political views and the more fundamental ties of family and friends.[8]

Since 1974, protracted negotiations have yielded only further talks, and more than two decades have passed with neither full acceptance of the status quo nor any substantial changes. That is not to say, of course, that time has stood still on either side of the Green Line. Both north and south have rebuilt, and the Greek south in particular boasts a booming economy. The relative stability of these years has even led some to consider that the division may, after all, be the least bad of any number of worse possible scenarios. However, even without the nightly television spots picturing villages lost to the Turks (Ladbury and King 1982), Greek Cypriots have vivid memories of the north, and politically it is impossible as yet for Greek leaders to accept the situation as it stands. In this way life continues.

The Armenians still in Cyprus watch and wait. They are not detached bystanders, for they have developed a strong sense of being Cypriot as well as Armenian, but they feel just as strongly their position as neither Turkish nor Greek. Those who have stayed are hopeful and even optimistic but still have serious concerns about the future of Cyprus and their own security there. They say, resignedly, that the real Armenian story is that of moving and rebuilding.

ARMENIANS

Several points are always raised when Armenians describe themselves as a people: the length of their 2,500-year history; their particular language and early alphabet; the national church; the hard circumstances of Armenian history, culminating in the massacres and dispersion of the early twentieth century. These interconnected aspects of the Armenian self-image are seen today in the light of another concern, that of assimilation into the modernized Western world. A brief background on each of these follows, giving an idea of the changing but continual sense of Armenianness.

The Armenian genesis begins with speakers of Indo-European coming into Anatolia, mixing and settling with the Urartian peoples there. Archeological and linguistic evidence points to an Armenian presence predating the first historical reference to those people by name, which is found in Herodotus's writings in 520 B.C.E.

Language

The Armenian language is Indo-European, branching off early on the family tree from its relatives. Today vernacular Armenian has two main divisions, eastern and western, an old split stemming from the geography and history of the area. Classical Armenian (*grabar*) is maintained in the liturgy of the national church. Both classical and vernacular Armenian use the alphabet developed in 404 C.E. by St. Mesrob Mashdots, a priestly scribe.[9] This provided increased autonomy, reducing Armenian dependence on Greek and Syriac alphabets and languages, and the following centuries saw a great flowering of literature and art, alongside architecture, in both eastern and western Armenia. The church, in the monasteries and ecclesiastical centers, sponsored this growth, as did princely families (*nakharars*) and kings.

Early History

The name used by Greek, Persian, and later outside commentators to describe the people of ancient Armenia was Armenian (*Armani, Ermeni*), while the people themselves used the word *Hay*, as they do today. The land is called *Hayastan*. Historic Armenia included much of eastern Anatolia, including Kayseri and Kharpert in the west and extending into the Caucasus to Karabagh in the east. Walker (1980, after Gibbon) refers to this location as a "theatre of perpetual war." Others have likened the territory to the intersection of two busy interstate highways. It is a mountainous region, in places green and fertile but mostly very harsh. Following the defeat of Tigran the Great by the Romans in 95 B.C.E., Armenia became a buffer zone in the battles between the kingdoms and empires of the

East and West. In turn, Persians, Byzantines, Arabs, Seljuks, Ottomans, and Russians competed for the territory and fealty of the inhabitants.

Armenian kingdoms and princely families continued under these outside powers, a system that itself contributed to the fragmentation and thus possibly to the longevity of its people. At various points several kingdoms existed at the same time, the mountainous geography encouraging these separations and parallel developments. From 387 C.E. on, Armenia was divided between its eastern and western portions, the former dominated by Persia and much later also by Russia, the latter by the Byzantines. Conflict arose between the Armenians and the governing powers over the practice of their national religion, as the Byzantines demanded submission to the Orthodox Church while the Persians periodically tried to force conversion to Zoroastrianism. The Byzantines also forced the migration of small Armenian settlements to Cilicia (and to Cyprus), which later became the base for the many refugees who fled Anatolia from the Seljuks.

In Cilicia, Armenians made their last independent kingdom, from 1080 until 1375, allying themselves not with their neighbors and old enemies but with those farther afield. They made diplomatic contact with Karakorum, hoping for protection on the northern front, and gave considerable aid to the Crusaders. The latter link led to alliances with the ruling Lusignan family of nearby Cyprus and intermarriage between elite families. The network of princely families gradually became obsolete, though the framework of the national church remained. Successive nomadic invasions proved especially debilitating until the establishment of the Ottoman Empire, when the Armenians were more fully incorporated into the workings of an empire and the balance of power shifted from the now defunct princely families to the church.

Church

According to Armenian tradition, the first Christian missionaries to the Armenians were Thaddeus and Bartholomew, two of Christ's apostles, thus giving the name *Apostolic* to the church. Further contact continued with the Assyrians and later the Greeks, but fire worship remained the dominant religion for some time. In 314 C.E. King Tiridates was converted by St. Gregory and made Armenia the first entity to officially adopt Christianity as its state religion, a source of great national pride today. Though the old temples were destroyed and pagan holy days co-opted into the Christian calendar, certain customs and beliefs persisted and, as elsewhere in the world, found a way to coexist with the new.

The church developed an ecclesiastical hierarchy, the upper echelons of which were originally hereditary but today are celibate. Like the princely families, the clergy had different centers of power and learning, which evolved concurrently with one another. The oldest of these centers, Etchmiadzin, in the Republic of Armenia, is today the seat of the "Catholicos of all Armenians."

The doctrine of the Armenian church is based on the first three ecumenical councils: Nicea, 325 C.E.; Constantinople, 381 C.E.; Ephesus, 431 C.E. The Council of Chalcedon, in 451, coincided with Armenian involvement in a major battle with the Persians on their eastern front. In their absence, the council debated the ongoing question of the nature of Christ, agreeing that in him, divine and human elements are united. The Armenians did not accept this interpretation and became known as Monophysites, thus further distancing themselves from the majority of churches, which came to be known as Chalcedonian churches or Dyophysites.[10] Armenians today discuss whether this difference of opinion was indeed over the interpretation of Scripture or was rather a prime instance of political opportunism, the early Apostolic church fathers recognizing their chance for more independence from an increasingly centrist, western-based Church.

The Armenian defeat in the Battle of Avarayr in 451 proved a pyrrhic victory for the Persians. Though the Armenians lost their commander, Vartan Mamigonian, and most of their soldiers, Persian losses were proportionately heavy, and Armenia was allowed to remain Christian. Vartan and his warriors became heroic martyrs, celebrated up to this day. While the language of the historical texts describing this event, called Vartanants, is heavily religious and the battle's purpose portrayed as the continuation of Christianity, the subsequent interpretation of its importance in annual celebrations became the preservation of the Armenian race or nation. Vartan and his soldiers prevented assimilation into the neighboring Persian empire.[11] This change in emphasis is part of the view that the church has been the main instrument of union among Armenians and of their continuation as a people through dispersion and lack of central government.

Since the fifth century, the Armenian Apostolic Church has continued to perform its liturgy in the classical language. In both eastern and western Armenia church liturgy remained the same and the ecclesiastical hierarchy bridged and connected wide areas. Later, under the *millet* system of the Ottoman Empire, the church was given unprecedented political power over its people, and its social role correspondingly increased. This proved to be a mixed blessing. The right of Armenians to worship in their own church guaranteed the continuation of the liturgy, classical language, and a tangible connection between Armenians in the empire, but at the same time it encouraged new possibilities and depths of corruption as clergy and lay people vied for control of the offices of power.

Rise of Secular and Nationalist Movements

In the nineteenth century a number of factors combined to contribute to the current, more ambiguous status of the church and to a transformation of national consciousness or ethnic identity. These included

1. the rise of secular intellectuals and relative decline of clergy in the realm of ideas
2. the rise of nationalism in Europe, which influenced the beginnings of Armenian political parties, and efforts at reform within the Ottoman Empire
3. an increase in education, including the founding of American Protestant mission schools, which encouraged an increase in Western orientation for some
4. major massacres and deportations in the Ottoman Empire in 1895, 1909, and 1915, and the upheaval of World War I
5. the establishment of a secular Armenian state in 1918 and a rapid change to a secular Soviet Armenian state

The corruption of some of the clergy and the alliance of ecclesiastical with state power was but part of the picture. Priests were also active in encouraging the education of lay people (men only, until the mid- to late nineteenth century) and in the revival and publication of secular, historical texts for a wider audience. This laid the groundwork for the much more radical secularization and spread of learning that were soon to follow. Lay intellectuals began to publish secular works, both original pieces and translations, in vernacular Armenian, causing a major upheaval in lay-clerical and progressive-conservative relations.

The ideals of nationalism began to attract Armenian intellectuals as they pursued further education in Europe and in Russia. Whereas previously Armenians had identified most closely with their kin group, village, or town (and church, under the *millet* system), some Armenians became influenced by the German and French romantic movement and began to organize small groups of activists. A variety of newspapers as well as a considerable amount of vernacular poetry and literature were produced, much of which was aimed at spreading the ideals of nationalism to fellow Armenians.

The first major Armenian political party began in 1887 in the Russian empire: the Social Democratic Hnchakian ("bell" or "clarion") Party, Marxist in outlook. This was followed by the Armenian Revolutionary Federation (Dashnaktsoutiune, or Dashnaks), founded in Tiflis in 1890. Both these political parties were concerned with the ideals of socialism and with reform of the imperial governments of the Ottomans and Russians as well as with an awakening of secular nationalist feeling among their fellow Armenians. Most clergy, leading merchants, and civil servants were more interested in the maintenance of the status quo, which they believed would result in stability and their own protection. The vast bulk of the Armenian population carried on with their daily lives with no interest and little awareness of the various policies and plans of these groups.

By this time, at the end of the nineteenth century, American Protestant missionaries had opened a number of schools and several colleges in western Anatolia and Cilicia. Some Armenian families became Protestant themselves, but many of the students at these schools remained Armenian Apostolic. The opportunities for Western-style education and further contacts with the United States and Europe were welcomed by many, increasing the Western orientation and (in spite of the mission approach) the secular outlook of educated people.

Intellectual identification with Europe and with fellow Christians also lay behind the earlier welcome of the Russian annexation of eastern (Persian) Armenia. Ironically and tragically, the same advance of the Russians had two unforeseen consequences for the Armenians. First, the Ottoman government suspected Armenians of aiding the Russians against them, and retaliation against the Ottoman Armenians was brutal. Second, later years showed that the Russian tsar could also be ruthless in his suppression of Armenian institutions and emerging nationalist interests (Walker 1980; Shahgaldian 1979, 24).

In spite of this, Armenians more and more looked toward Russia, Europe, and America for intellectual and spiritual inspiration. This connection was later revealed to be as much a curse as a blessing, in that these countries were the enemies of Turkey in World War I and therefore identification with them proved to be a liability within the empire (Hovannisian 1967; Nassibian 1984). Some politically active Armenians looked to Europe to help bring pressure on the Ottoman government to improve its treatment of minorities, while within the empire itself many Armenians, including the Dashnaktsoutiune, worked with Turkish groups toward general reforms. But in 1895, the same year that Sultan Abdul-Hamid agreed to certain reforms, thousands of Armenians throughout Anatolia were being killed.

Death and Dispersion

Further devastation followed in 1897 and 1909, as Armenians increasingly were cast as scapegoats for political unrest and other problems. Still, substantial hopes remained pinned on the promised reforms of the Young Turks. These too were shattered as the Young Turks began to formulate plans for a new nation of their own, built in place of the crumbling empire and based on Turkish or Turkic identity. This new outlook proved disastrous for the Armenians, especially as World War I began and powerful alliances were cemented. When Turkey joined the Central Powers, Armenians found themselves in the unhappy position of being not only a minority but also one suspected of sympathy with the country's enemies—Russia in the East, England, France, and later the United States in the West.

At the same time, expected reforms within the Ottoman Empire had not significantly materialized, but Armenians, still including the Dashnaks, continued to support the Young Turks and began joining the army. A small number of Armenians began to organize for an armed struggle against the Turks. Some crossed the eastern border to join the Russian troops, and the Hnchakian Party issued a statement against the Ottoman Empire (Walker 1980, 198).

Though constituting a very small number of Armenians on either side of the east-west border, the armed revolutionaries were and are significant. It is clear that at the time, Ottoman authorities saw the existence of Armenian insurgents as an additional and important threat to the crumbling empire. The possibility of cooperation between Ottoman Armenians and the Russians was equally disturbing. Today the Turkish government still uses this as the excuse for the devastation of Armenian life that followed.[12] And as Armenians in the armed forces were disarmed and sent to hard labor, men gathered and killed in town centers, and women and children transported out of their homes, more people began joining in the resistance when able, or sympathizing with its aims. The Dashnaks changed their direction from one of support of the Turkish government to organized opposition.[13]

The actions of the Ottoman government against the Armenians during the last years of the empire, through World War I, have been discussed and argued in numerous books, articles, and meetings. There is very considerable and authoritative documentation to show that between 1 and 1.5 million Armenians, out of approximately 2.2 million living in the Ottoman Empire, were killed and that orders to carry out the killings and deportations of whole villages into the Syrian desert came directly from the top of the government.[14]

As pointed out in chapters 1 and 2, the memory of this tragedy and the issue of its denial by Turkey is today the most discussed and prominent concern in the public life of every Armenian diaspora community. For many decades following the pogroms, stories of pillage, rape, murder, and starvation were passed on within families or were kept in silence, but recent years have seen a proliferation of popular and academic writing by Armenians on the subject and increased attention to the annual public commemoration on April 24 of the genocide. Political action has also been organized against Turkey's efforts to convince the West of its very different version of events.

Diaspora life today is a legacy of these pogroms. Armenians first escaped to Syria or the Caucasus, then to Lebanon, America, France, Egypt, Cyprus, and other points. Some families returned to their homes in Cilicia (to towns such as Adana, Mersin, Marash, and Zelifkia, for example), believing that they would be protected under the French Mandate and would be able to rebuild and remain in their old homes. When the French withdrew and the British also were unwilling to safeguard Armenian interests, Armenians began to leave Cilicia again as they faced renewed violence.

The Establishment of a Political State

While some western Armenians were attempting to re-create their lives in Turkey, a related struggle was taking place in the Caucasus. There an independent Armenian state was formed in the brief power vacuum following the regrouping of Russian troops during the revolution of 1917 and the ensuing civil war; at this time the attention of the new Turkish leaders was set upon the start of a fresh nation. In 1918 the Republic of Armenia was declared under the leadership of the Dashnak party. Western powers promised assistance to the fragile Armenian state and recognized its status, but when it was necessary to implement the conferences and treaties signed to that effect, none was willing or able to do so.

Instead, as Western nations considered their own agendas, Kemalist Turkey and Soviet Russia, the two countries most immediately interested in Armenia, reentered the scene (Suny 1983, 31–32). With few resources of their own, and bowing to military pressure on two sides, the Armenians signed a new agreement in December 1920 in which they were ensured protection by the Soviet state, thus paving the way for a sometimes brutal incorporation into the Soviet Union. The early years of the Soviet Republic of Armenia were very difficult, and later the people also shared the hardships and persecutions of the Stalin years, but under Soviet protection from outside forces a gradual rebuilding took place.

Neither the establishment of the republic nor the surrender of its sovereignty have been without controversy in the Armenian world from that time until today. Only the Dashnak party and organizations sympathetic to it regularly celebrated the establishment of the early independent republic, mourned its demise, and continued to wave its tricolor flag (red, blue, and orange). They were skeptical of the amount of freedom possible under Soviet rule and suspicious of Russification. Ramgavars, Hnchaks, and those clubs friendly to their objectives saw Soviet Armenia as the more practical and, for some, more ideologically sound alternative. For them, Hayastan was the center of Armenian life: Its artistic and literary products were much admired, its dialect was seen as the purest, and its people were thought to be fortunate to be there.

With the advent of the cold war, the differences in these two basic views became exacerbated and entrenched in East-West antagonisms. In recent years attitudes on both sides began changing, though not entirely, and young people, those born after the 1950s, say they are bored by talk of these schisms. As tourism increased generally, more Armenians of all political persuasions visited Soviet Armenia, and most were deeply touched by their encounters there. Exchanges also took place regularly through students and teachers invited to workshops and tours in Soviet Armenia and visits by musical, dance, and other artistic groups to diaspora communities.

In spite of increased contact and admiration, very few western Armenians have tried to settle in the Republic of Armenia since the 1960s. In this respect even those most sympathetic to Soviet Armenia changed their outlook. In one sense this could be seen as an acceptance of the reality of diaspora life, of the rooting of the new generations in various lands outside of Armenia and the reluctance to split families further by insisting on an ideologically founded move. The visits themselves also pointed up problems; as one person explained, "We are Western people now. They are not exactly Eastern, but they are very different. They think differently. I couldn't get along there."

Visits to Soviet Armenia revealed the extent of the material, political, and social differences between life in the West and life in the Soviet Union. The complaints of old friends and relatives were treated with sympathy by some, impatience by others. At the same time some of the idealism with which Soviet Armenia and the Soviet Union had first been admired was tarnished by the realization of the extent of Soviet mistreatment of its citizens under Stalin and then the corruption that increased losses from the 1988 earthquake in Soviet Armenia and made reconstruction more difficult. By the 1980s Soviet Armenia was recognized by most Armenians as a small corner of the old homeland where Armenians could survive and, some would say, flourish. The demise of the Soviet Union and the independence of Armenia was received in diaspora with a confused mixture of elation, amazement, and concern. The Republic of Armenia is called Hayastan by Armenian-speakers, and that name will be used throughout the rest of this study.

Diaspora communities, including Cyprus and London, still bear the marks of political rifts, though these are sometimes difficult to distinguish from social divisions. The main parties today are the Dashnaks and Ramgavars, both of which are active in Cyprus and London. The Hnchakian Party also became very visible in London in the mid-1980s. It is difficult to attach conservative or liberal labels to these parties, though until recently it was generally believed that the Dashnaks were Western-oriented and the Ramgavars and Hnchaks Eastern-oriented (inclined toward Hayastan and, by extension, the Soviet Union). This orientation seems to have little to do with one's personal economic activities or ideals, as Armenians of every political stripe participate fully in the financial system of their host countries. Few people active in the party-associated clubs seem to have a clear idea of the differences in ideological doctrines between the major parties. Extremely few act out the revolutionary ideals of the parties. Instead, affiliation currently appears based in kinship, though there are many exceptions. Originally the Ramgavars and Hnchaks included wealthy merchants and educated men, and their outlook was considered conservative by contrast with the *fedayeen* or the Dashnaks. In that sense the conservative label is still applied to the Ramgavars by the Dashnaks, who accuse them of compromise and accommodation.

The church has also been affected by political divisions, and a major split has divided the Armenian world between the authority of the Catholicos of Etchmiadzin and that of the Catholicos of Cilicia in Antelias, near Beirut. The Dashnak party supported the promotion of the Antelias Catholicosate at a time when it was widely suspected that clergy in Hayastan could be used by the Soviets and that the church needed a base where it was free of outside interference. The Ramgavar and Hnchakian parties and their affiliates backed the side favoring Etchmiadzin, because they were distressed by the Dashnak influence in Antelias and because this stance was consistent with their policy of working with the status quo in Hayastan. In recent years much effort has been directed at repairing that split, and there has been talk of reunification.[15] The churches of Cyprus fall in principle under the autonomous jurisdiction of the Catholicos of Cilicia, while those of England are under that of Etchmiadzin. This has to do with the traditional geographic division of Armenian churches in the world.[16]

Political and religious issues and events have touched all Armenian communities. Currently the most important issue is that of coming to terms with life in diaspora, home to more than half of the world's Armenians. Before World War I, customs, dialects, and attitudes did differ between towns in Anatolia and Cilicia, and certainly between village and city. But the variety was not so pronounced as it was to become when local influences shifted to places as diverse as Los Angeles, Boston, Cairo, Marseilles, Beirut, and Tehran.

Diaspora Life

Somewhere in the original diversity lie clues to the pattern of dispersion following the massacres and deportations. Who chose to go where when there was a choice? By 1914 certain families had ties with or interests in different European countries or the United States. Many of those coming to Cyprus were attracted to the security (both physical and symbolic) they felt was provided by the British presence and saw Cyprus as a place to wait until they could return to their real homes. Others arrived and did not continue on to other places simply because they couldn't afford to do so.

Once in Cyprus, the influence of the British became noticeable, and many Armenians looked to them as ideal bearers of education and civility. To Armenians outside of Cyprus, the island was a slow, quiet outpost, and the dignified stance affected by the English and by their Armenian admirers was seen as lifeless and dull. As years passed, Armenians looking outward from Cyprus, and later from Britain as well, came to view their compatriots in other communities as being overly frantic, flashy, and boisterous. Other diaspora centers, though, have been and are important to Armenians in Cyprus and London in terms of influence and resources as well as self-comparison. As both the Cyprus and London communities are relatively small, they are perhaps especially aware of their links with and debts to the larger centers.

Recently the geographical balance of the diaspora has been shifting toward the United States, Los Angeles in particular. Large numbers of Armenians are immigrating there from Hayastan[17] as well as from Lebanon, Iran, and other Near Eastern centers. While America is admired as "the land of opportunity" and as a place where ethnicity is encouraged ("everyone is a foreigner"), there is also a fear that the language and way of life and values particular to the Near East, the old homelands, will be permanently lost there.

During the 1970s several groups of Armenian "freedom fighters" emerged and began an active campaign of assassinating Turkish officials. This was understood as having two basic goals: bringing the Armenian question before the public, and extracting an admission of Ottoman guilt from Turkey. Further goals varied between the groups but included motives of revenge, retribution for those who suffered, the restoration of land, and establishment of a "free Armenia." Ignoring the possible international implications of revolutionary alliances, political ideology, and funding of the freedom fighters, most Armenians were willing to see this development as a natural one, considering the sense of frustration felt in the face of official Turkish denials of the massacres.

It has been suggested (Tölölyan 1987, for example) that a major objective of the revolutionary groups may have been to stir Armenian rather than Turkish consciences and arrest the drift of the comfort-seeking, Westernized third generation. Real support for these groups is impossible to gauge, but Armenians seem impressed with the publicity value of their work and give them credit for reopening the Armenian question. "Our boys" (who are sometimes girls), "our heroes," "the martyrs," or—to others—"those who have ruined the good name of the Armenians for nothing" were the subject of many heated discussions. The most frequently heard comment was "I don't believe in their methods—two wrongs don't make a right—but who had heard of the Armenians or cared about them before they started making all this noise?" Others disagreed and felt that no publicity at all was better than having Armenians in the news as murderers and "terrorists."[18]

The revolutionary scene has been outwardly quiet since the mid-1980s and appears to be in disarray. The pros and cons of the groups' methods and goals are still discussed among Armenians in London and Cyprus, however. The idea of the return of the western homelands is tantalizing but somewhat unreal. This becomes ever more so with increasing trouble and tensions within the former Soviet Union and the Near East.

Outside Hayastan, diaspora life is reality for Armenians. The community of Cyprus, though a small one, has a longer history than most.

When the British arrived in 1878, there were few Armenians in Cyprus (179 in the 1881 census), but the population began to grow quickly as the century closed and a series of major changes started taking shape there, as elsewhere in the Armenian world. The western homelands were emptied, and Cyprus became a new home in the growing diaspora where, as in Kherdian's poem, old "things" and memories mixed with new ones. People sat on old rugs and created new lives.

Chapter 4

In the Beginning

"How did your family come to Cyprus?" This was one of the few questions I asked of nearly everyone.

Mrs. Yeghsabet sat on a sofa in her son's home and told us stories she had heard as a young bride about the transition to the British occupation of Cyprus.

"When the British first came to Cyprus they were altogether lost . . . they couldn't communicate. So they sent a letter to Smyrna and Constantinople: 'Please send us some new men who know Turkish and English!' So my father-in-law, he was in Roberts College . . . and after that he taught Turkish to the personnel in the British Consulate. They said, 'Look, we have an offer like this.' He was twenty-two and he said, 'Well, I'll risk it.' And he came.

"And so he came with others, a young man, an adventure, to see the world, see something. But it was a desert, a desert. Some of the young men saw the land: 'Are we going to stay in *this* place? Everything in ruins, everything broken or in terrible condition!' But he said, 'I've come all this way. Let's try it.' And they were received like angels from heaven because they could communicate with the Turkish authorities. Instead of [staying] two or three months, he made all his career in Cyprus. He was called a translator of state documents."

DEGHATSI LIFE

When the young translator arrived, he found other Armenian families already there, those who would be called *deghatsi* ("native") in contrast to the later-arriving *kaghtagan* ("refugee"). The origins and the exact date of arrival of these families is unknown, but *deghatsi* families have traced their ancestry back as far as the early nineteenth century, when Boghos-Berj Artin Eramian arrived in Cyprus with his family. Though his daughter died early, his son married a descendant of the Latin Cypriot families, Catharine Luigi Carletti, and they had eight children, seven of whom married Armenians and had children of their own. Thus the *deghatsi* community began to grow.

Where were Armenian spouses found? Most seem to have come from Constantinople or Cilicia, as arranged through family or friendly connections. Some men came for work purposes and stayed. One, for example, was sent by his parents to Cyprus—perhaps to increase the family business interests, perhaps to escape conscription into the Turkish army, his descendants surmise. Once in Cyprus he bought a farm north of Nicosia with an enormous mansion and asked for one of the Eramian daughters in marriage. (In this generation the family tree shows twenty-six children, five of whom died without marrying, two who married Carlettis, two "others," and seventeen who married Armenians.)

This family became wealthy through the farm, but their own children did not continue the parents' interest. The farm was sold and the family moved to Nicosia, where the older son entered the Ottoman civil service. Later, as a judge, he was sent to Boursa, where he noticed a beautiful Armenian girl on her way to school. He wrote immediately to his younger brother, urging him to marry her, and so it was arranged. It is a legendary wedding in Nicosia, remembered as a fantastic spectacle, with Persian carpets laid out all along Victoria Street for the arrival of the bride and groom.

With Cyprus being part of the Ottoman Empire, and because of this constant influx of new brides and grooms from the mainland, customs and language remained decidedly Turkish-influenced. Older informants remember being told that their grandmothers in Nicosia had dressed in the Turkish fashion outside the home, covering themselves with a veil (*yaşmak*). Men wore a fez. In the church, it is said, there was a section for women, as can be found in some mosques, separated from the main room by a screen of fine wooden latticework.

Armenian was not proscribed in Cyprus, as it was in some parts of the Ottoman Empire, but Turkish seems to have been the first language of most families up until the end of the nineteenth century and even later. Certainly it was the lingua franca. By the 1890s, as the community grew somewhat larger and as nationalist feelings increased, various attempts were being made, especially by the local priest, to introduce Armenian to all the community. One way was to organize theatrical productions, teaching the children just enough Armenian (that is, their lines) to put on plays. Some plays were by well-known Armenian authors; others were originals written by the priest to educate the relatively sheltered community on matters of Armenian concern. One man, now in London, remembered, "Later a workmate of mine, an older man, who wasn't Armenian, kept repeating, '*Absos kez vor zavagt uspanetsi!*' ['Woe unto you, for I have killed your child!'] And I kept wondering why on earth he would keep saying such a thing, until finally the man, he was a Carletti, said that it was from a play by Raffi, which he and my father had been in as boys. It was the only Armenian he knew, so he would say it all the time!"

The priest also pursued other ways of increasing knowledge of Armenian on the island. As another older man recalled, "Father was from Banderma, near Bolis [Istanbul]. He was orphaned at ten or twelve and sent to Bolis to live with a rich man who later sent the boy to Jerusalem to study at the seminary. But Father didn't want to become a priest because he didn't like the lifestyle. Meanwhile, the priest in Cyprus was always asking the Jerusalem people for a teacher who could also sing in the church. So the Patriarch said, 'If you're not going to be a *vartabed,* be a *varjabed!*' ['If you're not going to be a priest, be a teacher!']. So at nineteen he went to Cyprus [1893?] and a year later got married there. Then everybody spoke Turkish. And my mother learned Armenian from my father as well."

And parents learned from their children. One woman remembers that her mother would punish them soundly if they spoke a word of Turkish at home once they started learning Armenian at school. The mother learned as they did, as did the father.

Families lived in Nicosia, Famagusta, Larnaca, on farms north and south of Nicosia, and around the Armenian monastery in the Kyrenia Mountains. Bearing in mind the difficulty of transportation and communication at that time, even such a small distance as that between Nicosia and the farms outside it must have hindered daily contact between families. The Nicosia church and monastery would have been meeting points, as were weddings and other special events, but daily life centered around family (especially for the women), neighbors, and business contacts.

South of the town was another farm of approximately six hundred *donums*[1] where a wide variety of crops and livestock were raised. The men of the family enjoyed hunting hare, partridge, turtledove, quail, and pigeon, as did many in the village. About thirty to forty villagers worked on the farm, some Turkish, most Greek. Lunch was served to all the workers on the farm, and there were cooks and other servants to help with both this and household chores.

Though this family also used Turkish within the home, Greek was spoken with the villagers, and the family is remembered by other Armenians for their early proficiency in Greek. Another family, in Kyrenia, also encouraged use of the Greek language and sent the children to a Greek school there for a time. The father came to Cyprus from Constantinople, soon after the arrival of the British. Trained as a teacher, he began to work at the Armenian school in Nicosia but fell out with the church council and instead found work as a civil servant and was posted to Kyrenia, a long distance from friends and family in Nicosia.

The father spent his spare time writing poetry and stories and keeping extensive diaries. In Turkey he had written patriotic songs; in Cyprus he tried to write poetry that would help the Turkish-speaking *deghatsi* to learn their "mother tongue." His own children and wife became his students, as he gave them lessons in both vernacular and classical Armenian and insisted on Armenian being spoken at home. The mother, her children recall, learned to read the language by reading the Bible. A *deghatsi* herself, she remained close to the "Latin" side of her family, the Carlettis, after marriage and eventually became a Catholic.

By the last decades of the nineteenth century girls were being sent to school, both Armenian schools and foreign ones (English, French, or in rare cases Greek if the others were not available). To be well educated and literate was desirable, and girls as well as boys were encouraged to learn English when Cyprus came under British occupation. Though a woman's work was almost entirely within the home, people remembered women who were admired exceptions to the rule—for example, one who supervised the running of her farm upon being widowed, and others who were teachers.

One man of ninety-two recalled that Armenian society at the turn of the century was divided between the "school people" and the "shop owners." The school people, meaning especially those who had gone to the

English School with an eye to becoming civil servants, centered their activities on church and home, their entertainment consisting of visiting each others' families. It was a quiet life, he said. The shop owners attended Armenian school for some time but apprenticed themselves in their early teens to learn a trade or run a store. These men and their families also found church, home, and visiting relatives and friends most important in their lives, but the shop owners also enjoyed the coffee shops (*tavernas*) where they could sit and sip a coffee, smoke a *narghile*, and have a chat. For a school person, he said, this was shameful (*amot*). For a woman, it was out of the question.

In the summer those families who could retreated from the heat of Nicosia, on donkey-back or in carts, and made their way to the Vank, Kyrenia, or even farther, to the Troodos Mountains. There the women and children would stay for a month or longer, the men visiting as often as their jobs in Nicosia permitted.

The people called *deghatsi* at the beginning of the twentieth century were not a homogeneous lot. Because they differed from each other in such areas as trade, education, location, and even religion and language, interlocking family ties and a general awareness of being Armenian were most responsible for any unity felt between them. As with other peoples, the most effective reinforcement of their own identity came through contrast with the other groups around them: Turks, Greeks, "Latins," and then British. At this time, however, community relations, organization, and Armenian consciousness began to change quite drastically as a result of several external factors. These included increased political activity in the Ottoman Empire and in eastern Armenia, news of the massacres and deportations there, and the arrival of Armenian refugees in Cyprus.

THE FIRST WAVE OF REFUGEES

The census of 1891 shows 280 Armenians living in Cyprus, but by 1901 that figure had nearly doubled, to 517. Armenians escaping pogroms in Diyarbekir, Aintab, Kilis, and elsewhere began arriving in Cyprus in 1895 (Kurkjian 1903). Between the two census dates it is clear that many more Armenians passed through Cyprus but, as with later waves, did not stay. In 1897 the Scottish sociologist Dr. Patrick Geddes and his wife raised funds and set off for Cyprus to help in the resettlement of Armenian refugees there. He also hoped to demonstrate a hypothesis he had developed: "Solve the agricultural question and you solve the Eastern Question. . . .

Give men hope of better land, of enough food for their families and you remove a main cause of bloodshed."[2]

Though the Geddeses apparently achieved some considerable success initially, they were disappointed that after several years little remained of their projects. While Geddes cited as a cause the strained communication between the refugees and the Eastern and Colonial Association, Ltd., which had taken over the management of the Geddeses' projects, the main reason noted for this decline was the relocation of the refugees themselves. Geddes had not anticipated that the newly arrived Armenians might not want to stay in Cyprus permanently. Once able to travel, many left to join family and friends in other countries. In fact, many of those who came to Cyprus may have originally intended the stay to be a temporary one. The attachment to the old lands and villages where families had lived for centuries was strong. Later refugees also harbored hopes of returning, but by then political circumstances had changed too radically. Also, Cyprus was seen as a poor and backward country where it was difficult to earn a living in some trades (for example, goldsmithing) and opportunities were not so obvious as in the United States or Europe.

While the Geddeses were arranging the resettlement of families, Vahan Kurkjian, a former resident of Aintab, raised money in Paris, Cairo, and Manchester and opened an orphanage in Cyprus in 1897 for boys made homeless by the same troubles. In the winter classes were held in Nicosia, and in the summer they were held at the monastery in the mountains. Documents show there were twenty students in the fifth month and thirty-seven in the fourth year, but even though enrollment was small, the school and its director made an impact on the community at the time and through the later work of its students (Kurkjian 1901). It is significant that during my interviews and conversations, no one mentioned (or when I asked, had heard of) Geddes and his work, while Kurkjian and the orphanage were frequently brought up as an important part of Armenian communal history.[3]

A few boys from *deghatsi* families also attended the orphanage to take advantage of classes there, and though most of the funding came from outside Cyprus, reports show that Armenian Cypriots also actively supported the school.

> From the list of donors one can see how the Armenians of Cyprus care for the Orphanage established among them. Many show charity according to their capacities. They show hospitality with Armenian sensitivity and they give a share of their "grain" (production or wealth) to

the pupils of the Orphanage. Especially, they consider the Orphanage as
their favourite national institution of the island. (Kurkjian 1901)

Included in the appendix of this 1901 report is a list of these donations,
which included sheep, geese, fruit, baklava, and a "feast" (often given by
a family on the occasion of a child's baptism or a holy day).

Kurkjian was a well-loved and respected figure. A leader of the Ramgavar party and later of the Armenian General Benevolent Union (AGBU),
an Armenian cultural organization, he exerted a great influence on the
politics of many of the boys. In spite of his popularity and significant local
support and participation, though, funds ran out, and the orphanage
closed within ten years. At the same time, however, the Armenian population there was steadily increasing. Events outside Cyprus continued to
have an indirect effect, as men such as Kurkjian made the *deghatsi* aware
of their part in a larger Armenian diaspora. Thus while Armenians in Cyprus were gradually building their community, they became aware that
others were being destroyed. But there was no such conflict in Cyprus,
and, devoid of direct experience, many *deghatsi* found it difficult to com-
prehend events they had only heard of at second hand through the papers,
in letters, or from the refugee families who came to Cyprus. This gap was
not really bridged for some time, and some claim that it is still significant,
but each person's national consciousness was strongly jolted as they
learned of the massacres and deportations.

LIFE IN NICOSIA IN THE EARLY TWENTIETH CENTURY

Nicosia was the center of Armenian life in Cyprus, and by the early twentieth century enough Armenians had made their homes there for community life to begin emerging. Armenian families were clustered in the
Turkish quarter, near the church and school. Their lives were largely
separate from those of their Turkish and Greek neighbors, and there was
little or no intermarriage. Yet the groups continued to interact through
children's play, business matters, and shops. Through this friendly contact in the streets, Turkish and some Greek continued to be learned and
used alongside Armenian. Inside most homes, both Turkish and Armenian
were used.

In Nicosia, most homes were inside the walls of the old city. Victoria
Street meandered past the church, school, club, and many homes and
businesses. The streets were narrow and lined with two- or three-story

mud-brick and sandstone houses; the whites, beiges, and browns of the walls and road contrasted with the blues and greens of the painted wood-work around doors and windows. Balconies on the upper levels, either protected by shuttered windows or open and connected to the main house with a shuttered door, provided shelter from the hot sun and dust while inviting cool breezes. Occupants could keep abreast of comings and goings on the street below by peering through the raised slats of the shut-ters, or they could open the shutters entirely for a conversation with neigh-bors across the way. Passersby were on foot, mounted on donkeys or mules, or occasionally riding in a horse-drawn cart. Peddlers pushed their two-wheeled carts, shouting the praises of their wares. And children often played in the dried-up moat nearby.

The moat around old Nicosia is approximately a hundred feet wide, a flat, open space ideal for children's games (soccer, cricket, marbles, tag) and also for slightly more adult activities such as parades. Families whose homes were built on the Venetian wall itself had a much sought-after view of these events and would call their family and friends to come and share their windows. The monarch's birthday and other such occasions brought out the full splendor of British pomp and circumstance in the colony. Chil-dren watched to see if a soldier would faint from the heat this time. Parents were impressed by the display and by the security they felt it exemplified. And then the moat would empty again, the dust would settle, and the little boys drifted back.

"I remember when I was five or six and Queen Victoria died," a ninety-year-old man born in Cyprus recalled. "It was 1901. We were play-ing in the moat and we heard that Queen Victoria had died, so we ran and told the *jamgotch* [watchman] to ring the bells! And he did—all that eve-ning and all the next day. I can still hear those bells. *Dong . . . dong . . . dong . . .* And they hung a black cloth from the church tower.

"Earlier there were no bells to ring, as they were outlawed by the Ottomans. Instead the *jamgotch* would go from house to house, announc-ing the services. With the change of government, bells were allowed, and Mr. Hagop Guevezian of the church committee was sent to choose them.

"In the evenings boys of eleven or twelve ran back to the church to sing in the evening service. They were about half-hour services. It was very strict. We had to drop our footballs and run when we heard the bells ring! But we didn't mind at all. We felt it was an honor to do it."

The boys took turns singing for the morning, evening, and Sunday services until their voices changed. Boys also assisted in the celebration of extraordinary events. Mr. Aram, now in his nineties, remembers walking slowly with his brother down Victoria Street as the candle bearers in the procession leading Sahak Catholicos to the church.

Gradually the Armenians began to look toward Britain and the local representatives of that colonial power, rather than the Ottoman government. Most shop owners and farmers had little contact with "the English" at that time, but other families were increasingly drawn toward them. Of course, civil servants met them at work, but there was also some reciprocal entertainment.

Movses Soultanian, a *deghatsi* and one of Kurkjian's graduates, owned a tall building on Victoria Street, the ground floor of which was a hotel that housed numerous English guests over the years. Once a year the hotel would host a large ball and invite the governor and his entourage. People wore white gloves, danced quadrilles, and were given a lavish feast. In return, some Armenians were entertained at the governor's palace. Descendants of these *deghatsi* families suppose that the British found the Armenians interesting and rather cosmopolitan, as most spoke several languages and many were well traveled. These initial contacts and friendships led later to needed favors and also pointed toward the future orientation of the Armenian community in general until well after the independence of the island.

Around this time Armenians began to solicit funds from wealthy *deghatsi* to build a new church in Larnaca, a fine archway to the Nicosia church, and a club, which were all completed around 1905. Later, in 1920, a donation by the Melikian family in memory of Artin Bey Melikian enabled the construction of a larger primary school. The oversized Melikian Varjaran seemed a white elephant to many at the time, because initially it had so few students, but only a year later the school was filled with the children of the refugees from Cilicia.

SAFE HAVEN IN CYPRUS

Following the 1909 and 1915 massacres in Adana, a number of Armenians visited Cyprus with the thought of moving their families there. Few actually settled then, but the flow of refugee families began to increase. One woman remembered her parents later telling her how they had decided to come and why.

"In 1909, during the massacre of Adana, they lost all their possessions. They took refuge in Tarsus at the Greek Embassy, where they were saved. The ambassador had been very kind and said to the Turks, 'If you kill this man, you will kill me as well.' So they left. Until 1913 they felt unsafe. Slowly they began to feel safer, but still worried and always thinking of safety. Both my parents were born in Hadjin but had grown up and married in Tarsus. They had five children.

"During those three years [between 1909 and 1913] Father started work and thought things were getting on well. But he had an obsession about moving. Eventually Father had a dream that he should go to Cyprus. He tried to persuade Mother. They had no idea of what it was going to be like. Mother said, 'If God, through a vision or a dream, lets me know that I should go, then I'll go with you.' That same night she had a dream. Both of them were pious people. In the dream she was in a room where the women were praying, and at that very moment they hear that Jesus is coming, and he does appear at the door. He blesses them all. His clothes look like a military uniform. He leaves them and moves away, and Mother goes after him to ask him her question. She finds him in a field beside a pool of water, looking thoughtful, head in his hand. Mother kneels before him and says, 'Lord, where shall we go? Hadjin or Cyprus?' He tells her that Hadjin will be completely destroyed, not a stone will be left upon a stone. It will become like a field. And he says, 'Obey your husband, take your children and follow him to Cyprus.' She awoke in a sweat and woke up her husband and told him what she had dreamed.

"When they came here there were so many hardships! Five children and a baby. Larnaca was the first stop. Then they traveled by carriage, about a day's travel [to Nicosia] because of the bad roads. They stayed awhile in the courtyard of the church and then settled down. Mother and Father, working together, managed to get one shilling a day, which was enough to keep the family going."

At the same time, many others who had escaped or survived the deportations went back to their old homes and farms in Cilicia as soon as they were able and began rebuilding their lives, thinking that the French and the Allies were their safeguards against further troubles. When the French left and the area was awarded to Turkey, however, villages again were threatened, and some came under attack. Many Armenians feared further confrontations and fled their homes once more. Anjar (near Beirut), Egypt, Greece, and Cyprus received thousands of these refugees. Many also followed the earlier exit of family members to America, Soviet Armenia, and France.

Why Cyprus? For some it was simply chance—that is where the first available boat took them, and they had no money to go farther. Approximately three thousand stayed only temporarily in Cyprus. Others made directly for Cyprus for two main reasons. First, it was under British rule and therefore thought to be safe and stable. Second, it was near Cilicia, and they could more easily return to their homes when a more peaceful time came, as surely it would soon.

"Why did your family come to Cyprus?" I asked one man of eighty-one. His parents were from Gessaria but had emigrated to Mersin and then been evacuated to Zelifkia.

"Because Cyprus was very close," he replied. "We came in 1922. The Turks told us that there was a certain place where those who were Christian could stay [unharmed], but we had heard that people were being massacred elsewhere. So . . . my uncle decided that we should leave that country. I was eighteen then and the head of my family, though I had an older sister. We came in small boats to Cyprus and went to Nicosia, where I wanted to begin leatherworking, making shoes and later purses and other things."

"How did you pay for the trip?"

"We'd saved some things and sold them before leaving. That paid for the boat, and then we sold other things in Larnaca and lived off that for a while. When the money ran out, we had to find any kind of work possible. Some had to go to the mines."

"You see," his niece told me when he had finished speaking, "they left, but not everybody wanted them to go. Their neighbors and friends loved them and wanted them to stay. But the government's policy was to get the Armenians out. We were the intellectuals and they figured there would continue to be trouble and again later if we were left to stay. It was the German idea. They advised the Turks."

A number of people recalled a long boat trip to Larnaca in 1922. The ship was initially refused entry due to a smallpox scare on board. The overloaded ship sailed to various Mediterranean ports before finally being accepted back in Cyprus. Some said that as they grew increasingly frustrated, the refugees threatened to throw the ship's cargo into its engines if they were not allowed to disembark. Finally, toward the end of December, this group was allowed to land, and the people were quarantined at Dhikelia, east of Larnaca, for forty days. Families staked out corners of single-room houses near the seashore, were inoculated, and waited for the time to pass. Baghdasar Nshanian, a deacon in the Larnaca church, and his wife often prepared food for the refugees and took it to them in a hired car, covering all the expenses themselves.

Conditions were difficult, but most people who remembered the arrival and quarantine days were children at the time, between five and fifteen years old. Their memories are mostly of excitement, the thrill of coming to a new country, the pleasures of having so many playmates all around. Food appeared, mothers cooked in their corners on primus stoves,[4] *vermaks* (blankets or quilts) were laid on the floor for sleeping. The children didn't ask where any of these supplies came from. And after the quarantine and a strict check by the British authorities, the children followed their families from Dhikelia to Larnaca and from there mostly to Nicosia.

Some families stayed on in Larnaca, which at the time was a rather sleepy port town. A few Armenian families had already settled there, and Surp Sdepanos, the church, had been built in 1913. Earlier, other churches had been borrowed or rented for services. The church was served by a *kahana* (married parish priest). By 1924 a national primary school and kindergarten had also been built next to the church, with the assistance of the Watertown (Massachusetts) Adana Education-lovers Association, the church, and later Garabed Melkonian (Gulesserian 1936, 112).

In between their arrival and the opening of the school in Larnaca, many families sent their children to the Protestant mission school. The Reformed Presbyterian Church of the U.S.A. had begun a mission there in 1890, and when the refugees arrived in 1922, there were at least three Armenian teachers already working in their school. Both boys and girls attended, and its former students remember "a missionlike approach" and Protestant hymns taught in Armenian. But they also learned some Armenian there, and when the Armenian school opened and children were asked to read a little in Armenian in order to determine class assignments, those who had been attending the mission school were placed ahead of the others. Thus, at first, children of different ages could be found in each classroom.

Armenians in Larnaca settled in both the Greek and Turkish sections of the town, near the church and school. The Greek neighborhood was apparently in the center, bordering on the sea, with Turkish quarters to the east and west of it. The Armenians lived in homes in the east-central side of the town.

FINDING WORK

The early years of settlement were taken up with finding or creating viable ways to earn a living. Some had brought along gold jewelry or other valuable items and sold them as needed for living and setting up new businesses. Many Armenian men had practiced specialized crafts or trades in the old country, and they slowly set up workshops and produced these goods again in Cyprus. Some found good opportunities, as their particular trade was not yet widely developed. These people began to prosper and train others as apprentices. Mr. Kegham, for example, had had a foundry in Turkey. In Cyprus he spent his savings on the beginnings of a small machine shop, seeing that there were so few then in Cyprus. To supplement this he also started an ice factory with a secondhand ice machine.

Shoemaking is one skill that many people believe Armenians improved greatly in Cyprus. Some say they introduced the trade. "In the early years the Cypriots were all wearing those heavy black boots, or else imported shoes if they could afford it. Maybe there were a few Greek shoemakers then, but the Armenians came and were able to make shoes cheaper and faster."

Armenians also came as copper- and tinsmiths, potters, bakers, carpenters, jewelers, mechanics, soap makers, and leatherworkers. Others found either too much local competition or not enough demand for their skills and began other work. Some came without any portable skills, having owned farms or worked on another's land. Agriculture both required too expensive an outlay and was too permanent for those who hoped to eventually return to their original land. Thus many men began with a simple retail business, buying in quantity and then loading the goods on their backs, selling them not only around Nicosia or Larnaca but also in various villages throughout Cyprus. Wives and daughters as well as sons often helped in these businesses. In addition to being responsible for the running and care of the household, a number of women crocheted, made lace, or crafted other items that were sold with their husband's goods or to order. Others took in laundry, cleaned houses, or worked as cooks.

Few of the newcomers spoke English at first, and so jobs in the civil service were not options initially. Some of the teachers among them found work in the Armenian school. Dentists and doctors were also among the refugees, most educated at Tarsus, some with further training in Beirut or America. The asbestos mines of Amiandos, high in the Troodos Mountains, offered both skilled and unskilled jobs, drawing a number of families initially. They traveled there on big carts, pulled by mules, over two or three days. The work was heavy and difficult, the village cold in winter and far from the Armenian communities. But the small income enabled families to get started in the new country.

One family had owned extensive farmland in Cilicia and had sent the oldest son to Europe to study agriculture. When those farms were lost, he changed his course of study to engineering. Meanwhile the family reluctantly left their village and came to Cyprus, where the father tried several times to start over. As he became progressively more discouraged, his son joined them and found work as the head engineer and electrician in the Amiandos mines, supporting the family. Later the father and older sister set up a general store in the nearby mountain village where they lived.

Some single men also chose to work in Amiandos. One such man's son later asked me in London, "Have you heard my father's story yet? Well, he came from Tarsus, but the family was originally from Gessaria. From Tarsus he went to Smyrna with his family, where they were evacuated with the Greeks on Greek ships. His whole family. Everyone on their ship was dumped on one of the little Greek islands. And no one there was prepared to receive a shipload of refugees! What was to be done? The villagers pointed the refugees to an olive orchard and assigned each family to a tree. That was to be their home until mainland Greece gave them other directions. My father's family sat under their tree and wondered. They weren't farmers, anyway. They were metalworkers. What could they do with an olive tree? So they decided to pick all the olives and take them to the town to sell them. With that money, and with some credit, they managed to buy the rudiments of metalworking equipment and materials and very slowly began to build up a business. Then they moved to Piraeus with other Armenian refugees and set up shop there again.

"They set up a metalworking shop in Piraeus in that souk-like area that the refugees built themselves. But when my father was eighteen, he decided to leave. One business couldn't support the whole family well. And he wanted his independence. They had family in Cyprus, so he decided to go to Larnaca.

"But from the boat he could see minarets on the shore. 'What's this?' He told the other Armenians on board the ship to tell his relatives there that he wasn't landing anywhere there were minarets and Turks. His relatives took a small boat to the big one and persuaded him—'It's okay. These Turks are friendly and there aren't very many of them.' So he agreed finally and went to Amiandos, where they were building the mines.

"When he got to the mines the boss asked him if he knew how to fit out all the ducts and how to build the machines. After all, he was only eighteen years old and looked very young! So my father said, 'Give me the blueprint and I can do it.' They were skeptical, but they didn't have any choice. There was no one else around to do it. So he was given the job on probation, shown all the parts to use, and given people to work under him. They were all big, huge men, gray-mustached and brawny. There was a mini-rebellion. 'How can he teach us anything? This little guy!' At least he could speak their language. He spoke Greek well. The boss said, 'It's up to you to convince them.' Dad said to himself, 'There's no way I can order them, convince them . . . I have to prove by doing, by actually doing it myself.' Gradually the men started joining in, following his directions. And it all went well and he earned a lot of money. He was very well paid.

"When the Amiandos project was finished, during which he made and spent a lot of money, he went down to Nicosia. He could have stayed there in Amiandos for maintenance work, but he was fed up. He enjoyed the good life in the city, and Amiandos was too quiet."

HOME LIFE AND MARRIAGE

The mining town was not ideal for families, either. A small Armenian school operated there for some time, but many children in nearby villages went to the local Greek school, while others were sent to live with relatives in Nicosia. Transportation was not easy, but people did keep in contact with friends and relatives in Nicosia and Larnaca either by post or through visits. As they were able, and especially as they felt the need for Armenian schools and further contact with other Armenians, families moved away from the mines and to the cities.

Most people chose to settle in Nicosia, the government center and the largest town on the island. Some went directly to the courtyard of the church, where they stayed until they were able to settle in rented housing. Others found a large home to rent, keeping one room for their own use and subletting the others. Thus it was not unusual to find four or five families in a home during their first years in Nicosia. Nearly all found homes or rooms in the Turkish quarter, near the old church or school, inside the old walls of the city.

Today it strikes many as unusual that people fleeing from the Turkish mainland would then settle beside other Turkish people. At that time there were a number of practical reasons for doing so. Rent was cheaper; the church and school were there, as were some *deghatsi* families; the language and customs of the neighbors were familiar; and it was thought that it would be easier to set up new businesses there. Moreover, Cypriot Turks had clearly been in Cyprus at the time of the massacres and deportations and were therefore not involved. People also remembered the Turkish friends they had left behind.

With whole families living in one room, the space was organized to provide maximum economy. Quilts or bedrolls were rolled up each morning, stacked on one side of the room, and covered. Some homes had electricity and running water, but many did not. One woman described how her family first stayed with relatives who had arrived two years earlier and then rented a home nearby that was owned by a Turkish *hodja* (cleric or teacher)[5]—"a very kind man," she said. Entering from the street, there was a main, large hall with a white stone floor, the eating room to the left, and the kitchen to the right. Water was brought in from a well outside. Upstairs there were four bedrooms and a little enclosed veranda. One married sister and her family occupied one bedroom, her father and younger brother another, four sisters another, and the oldest brother was given his own small but private room. Outside in the courtyard were mandarines and jasmine.

Victoria Street was at the center of Armenian activity. It wound past the church and school, to the Kyrenia Gate in one direction and toward the center of the old city in the other. Armenian homes lined this street as well as a parallel street bordering the wall itself and other, smaller streets adjacent to these. The new shops and workshops were also here, and thus people were constantly meeting each other during the course of the day.

The occupants of an Armenian house were usually members of an extended family—parents, children, and possibly grandparents, unmarried aunts or uncles, and frequently a cousin or more distantly related (or unrelated) orphan. These configurations changed as households grew through birth, marriage, or new arrivals or found more room through emigration, death, or a new house. A grandmother, for example, would live with whoever had room or whoever needed her help the most. It seems that rules of residence, if they existed in practice in the old country, gave way entirely to pragmatic decisions in Cyprus. Newly married couples, for instance, might share a home with the family of either spouse. As young couples became financially able, however, they usually set up their own households, either separately or on a different floor of the same house.

One afternoon while I was visiting Mrs. Shakeh, she pulled out a large, well-worn book on the Armenians of Gessaria (*Hayots Gessariatsi*), published in 1937. She had read there, and also remembered being told, that in Gessaria it was very uncommon for the man to marry into the woman's house.[6] Rather, the husband's mother was "the boss" in the old family home, and all the sons and their brides would live together in the same home. Mrs. Shakeh and her cousin then told the story of an aunt who every night, like other young brides of her time, had to follow the custom of sitting with her arms and legs crossed, waiting for the father-in-law to fall asleep. One night she was so tired that she fell asleep first and toppled right onto his bed. That custom, Mrs. Shakeh and her cousin added, was never a problem for them. By the time they were married, in the 1940s and afterward, that practice was only a memory.[7]

The 1920s were an especially difficult time for making marriages, for the old order was gone. In the old country many towns and villages had long histories of mutual distrust or disdain; for example, someone from Adana would not think of marrying a person from Zelifkia. But in Cyprus family circumstances were altered drastically by the deportations, and differences of background and status were less easily distinguishable. Family histories were not known. One woman remembered that when the refugees arrived, Armenian couples wishing to be married were required to have a civil marriage ceremony first, after which their names were posted for fifteen days to see if there were any objections from anyone. This was to ensure that they were not third cousins, were not already married, had no criminal record, and so on.

As mentioned earlier, *deghatsi* families chose spouses from other *deghatsi* families or from wealthy, educated families in the Near East, rather than from the unknown refugees. One *deghatsi* recounted how he had first seen his future wife when she was sent to Nicosia to study Armenian. Her family, also *deghatsi,* lived in Larnaca.

"I saw her but I couldn't talk to her. Our family knew her family's standing, because if you came to Cyprus, the next day we would know everything [this was the case before the bulk of the refugees arrived]. When I came back from military service, I told my mother, 'I want Haroutunian's daughter,' and they sent a cousin to Larnaca to ask for her. We couldn't talk to each other at all because it would be a great risk for the woman. The wedding was in Nicosia at the church with the reception at the club, and because we are *deghatsi* we must invite everybody or they would be insulted. We would give a small boy a fiver and he would deliver the invitations for you. You just write the name because you don't know all the addresses. But the boy would know.

"There was no fraternization between the *deghatsi* and the newcomers," he went on. "Because you had to know who they were before you could get married. These people were *tursetsi* [outsiders], as we called them, and you couldn't know who they were. There were extremely few marriages between these two groups, and no visits between houses, either—for about fifteen or twenty years. The *deghatsi* held everything in their hands."

In the first twenty years after the refugees arrived, there was a gradual mixing between the two groups, beginning with the professional, "church," and "school" families, and some intermarriage. The two groups were still quite distinct after that time, however. The following stories give some idea of the ways and reasons why marriage choices were made in the early and mid-1920s. First, one from a refugee family: "My mother came from Zelifkia, but the family was really Gessariatsi. When they came to Cyprus, as refugees, they landed in Larnaca and . . . they were put into quarantine. From there they went to Amiandos in big carts, driven by mules. . . . They were so shy that on the road the girls and women covered their eyes and heads so that no one could see them. She was thirteen and she came with her sister and brother because their parents had died in the massacres.

"My father had also come to Amiandos. There he knew a fellow villager who was older and already married who was friends with my mother's sister and her husband. He first asked the family for my mother to be his wife when she was only fourteen, but she didn't want to get married then. Meanwhile other men asked also, but the brother-in-law didn't approve of them. When she was seventeen, my mother's sister thought, 'Since she is alone, let her get married.' The mother-in-law was difficult to live with, too, and already my mother was sometimes sent to Nicosia to spend time with her grandmother, who had come with them as refugees and stayed in Nicosia with cousins. One time, while she was in Nicosia, my father came to the sister and her husband and again asked, through a matchmaker. They agreed and had an engagement party while she was gone, with the sugared almonds and everything, and then they sent some of the almonds to the Nicosia cousins, too, and to my mother to announce her engagement.

"She was very surprised and felt rejected by her family, and she cried and cried for days. My father then came to Nicosia with a family party, but Mother wouldn't enter the room to see him. But finally her grandmother persuaded her. She was a pious woman, and for her sake Mother didn't resist anymore—because otherwise she'd have no one left. So she went in, made jokes with everyone (she could tell very humorous stories), had chicken, and broke the wishbone. Gradually she got used to the idea, and after a few months they got married."

A contrasting story was told by someone who had married into a *deghatsi* family during the same period.

"My family lived in Egypt. But we didn't live in the capital, Cairo. Papa had some lands, some farms. Then in 1919 there was the revolution. Papa and my uncle were afraid, and they decided that we had to go—to go to Cyprus. I was ten years old, well educated, knew everything—but in my time—when they told me we were going to Cyprus! Oh! I had such nightmares! Because I'd learned at school that an island is a bit of land surrounded by water. Imagine my thinking, eh? I said to Papa, 'What if we fall into the water? It's a scrap of land!' Now a little girl of three years old wouldn't think like that!

"So we came here. My sister, and my cousin too, who lived in Cairo. We came by boat and were staying in Famagusta. Then my uncle said to Papa, 'Let's go see Nicosia, what it's all about.' So the first thing Papa did when we got there was to put our feet inside the church. So we went to the church to light a candle. Our house, the one in which I was married and lived with my husband, overlooked the courtyard of the church, and it seems that the brother of my husband saw my sister, who was then nineteen, from a window. And they came to ask for her in marriage. And that is how we met.

"So we rented some rooms nearby, and soon I went to school. Then we went back to Egypt, but my future husband and I had developed a certain *sympathie* for each other, and a bit later he came to visit some of his cousins there. My father invited him over, as he was the brother of our *pesa* [son-in-law], and he spent a few days with us. While he was there, he proposed. Nobody knew that we had feelings for each other before that. This was more than fifty-nine years ago, but it was a marriage *très à la mode*, very modern."

Once a couple was married, children were considered a blessing. The average number of children in the 1920s and early 1930s was four. The physical closeness of family life meant that children were rarely dependent only on their parents for either affection or discipline. While young parents could share the responsibility of child-rearing, they were, at the same time, limited in their own efforts by the interventions of grandparents, aunts, or uncles. Children were to show respect for their elders and would always kiss the hands of adults when they visited.

Visiting, formal and informal, was the main form of entertainment for everyone. Some men met at *tavernas,* coffeehouses, or the Armenian club. Women received their family and friends at home and drank coffee together in the courtyard or garden of the house. As soon as they were financially able, families designated one room as the guest room (*hyiuranots*) and decorated it with special care—if not with the furniture of their choice, then at least with handmade doilies, shelf covers, tablecloths, cushions, and probably a kilim or rug. In the winter the *mangal* (charcoal brazier) stood in the center, and families and their guests gathered around it to talk, play cards, and sip coffee.

"Our family shared a large house, and we had two *mangals,* one in the guest room and one in the *amenoria* [everyday room], but it was still cold all the time in winter. My grandfather would ask our friends and relatives to come and visit awhile. He would send my cousin down the street to tell them to come. And, do you know? Pinar Mama, she knew it was cold there, and so she would pick up their own *mangal* and carry it down the street with her, just like that! Imagine."

Someone from the visiting family added, "We would tell stories, laugh, joke, and have a wonderful time together. And when the fires went out, we would go home again."

In the early years after the refugees' arrival, only coffee was offered to visitors, unless the guests had come at mealtime. Later various sweets were included. People visited most often with relatives, but they also visited fellow villagers (people from their original town) and others, including neighbors.

EDUCATION

In Nicosia in 1922 there were the Shushanian kindergarten and the Melikian Askayin Varjaran (Melikian National Primary School). Bishop Saradjian was the head of the school, and a committee of lay people administered it. As in Larnaca, children were asked to read a passage in Armenian to determine their entrance level, and so older refugee children who had missed their first years of school were mixed with the littlest ones. Some were fortunate and had been tutored by parents or had been in one place long enough to have had some schooling. Others had to start at the beginning. Teachers were faced with an enormous range of competence in their students. Some children could read Armenian, while others had never even heard it. Somehow all these young people had to be evaluated and organized into classes.

One man was fourteen when he arrived and had spent some time at a French Jesuit school in Adana. He told me that his Armenian was very poor but through his father's friendship with Bishop Saradjian it was arranged that he should start Armenian school in the top class. "How did I manage?" he said. "Not easily. But I must say, fortunately my father knew good Armenian and he, the poor man, spent—or suffered—with me a lot of hours with a petrol lamp, studying and getting ready. Furthermore, our class was, I think, about twenty-four, and there were eight to ten books only."

When the refugees arrived, some of the *deghatsi* families took their children out of the Melikian school and sent them to a convent school, Terra Santa, or the American Academy. They received private tutoring at home in Armenian and were discouraged from mixing with the refugee children on the grounds that the refugees spoke Turkish rather than Armenian with each other and would be a bad influence on the *deghatsi* children. It was not only the language, *deghatsi* remember now, but the customs, slang, and coarseness of some of the refugees that their parents said they wanted to avoid.

THE UNKNOWN BECOMES FAMILIAR

The wedge between *deghatsi* and *kaghtagan* was a deep one. However, as individuals or through the church board, *deghatsi* did help the refugees in many ways to settle in the new country. Educated, Armenian-speaking refugees did have social contact with the *deghatsi*, but this was limited at the beginning. The great majority of the refugees were ignored by the *deghatsi*, and thus two separate Armenian worlds existed side by side, overlapping at church and, increasingly, at the Armenian clubs. While this might have been due, as some tried to explain, to class differences and related snobbism (see chapter 6), the turbulence of the era and the divisions among the refugees themselves point just as strongly to a cultivated fear of the unknown. Little was known about the background of the refugees. This also helps to explain the continued ties of Armenians with Turks, whose customs, attitudes, and language were known, rather than a shift at that time toward ties with the Greeks, who were relatively unknown.

Language was singled out as part of the reason for division, but in spite of this it also became a powerful cohesive force. First the drive to teach and learn Armenian spread to all in the community. Before long, speaking Armenian became not just an ideal but a reality and a standard marker of being Armenian in Cyprus. This did not mean that all other languages disappeared, but rather that Armenian became part of the natural panoply of words and linguistic styles available for Armenians to use. (See chapters 11 and 12 for more on the use of multiple languages.)

When the refugees arrived, they viewed Cyprus very much as a safe place to wait. They would surely go back soon to their ancestral homes, farms, and towns. This remained a preoccupation of older and middle-aged people for some time, but as the younger refugees grew up, they, like the *deghatsi*, began to see Cyprus as home.

Chapter 5

Settling In

In the evening after work Mr. Bedros used to walk out into the fields beyond the old city wall, his daughter told me years later. The air was still quite warm from the day's sun; the bougainvillea cascaded from trees he passed. There was a light breeze, but otherwise all was very peaceful and calm. That was what they had come for. That was most important. But the soil always caught his attention, she said. "'Look at it,' he would say. 'Look at this gray dirt! *Aman!* Look at it! I have looked everywhere, and there is no good red earth like we had in Adana. Red it was, and just like bulghur. Here we have nothing but this gray, rocky, hard dirt! This won't do for our son.'" And with a mixture of contempt and resignation, Mr. Bedros would gather up a small bagful of the gray dirt and take it home, where it was used as absorbent filler in babies' diapers.[1]

Though he was vexed by the lack of soil for his son's diapers, almost certainly the frustration of the evening ritual, as remembered by his daughter, stemmed primarily from a desire to see Adana itself. Mr. Bedros was not a farmer, but he and many others told their children over and over about the fertile soil, "red like gold," that they had left behind. Many refugees followed the news from Turkey, read letters avidly, and planned how they would one day return to that good red earth, to their old homes and farms, when "things calmed down." Some pinned their hopes on the expansion of the Soviet Union, which would someday include their lands. Others waited for a clear affirmation by the new Turkish government that Armenians would be safe back in their old homes. Looking forward to that day, they kept their deeds to those properties in a safe place. Meanwhile, the refugees began to settle into a new life in Cyprus.

DAILY LIFE

Families who had been sharing space eventually found homes of their own. Some rented entire houses of their own, but more often they would wind up sharing a house by floors rather than by rooms. Some of the houses had fireplaces in which wood was burned in the winter, but many refugees had to find other means of heating their rooms, including purchasing charcoaled olive pips from bakers, who used the pips as a means of economizing on wood for their ovens. In the summer men and women could sit on their verandas overlooking the street or in their courtyard gardens to escape the heat of the town.

Most of these homes were still in the same neighborhood, close to the church and school. At that time men were usually responsible for the shopping, and they went to the Turkish market nearby. But the streets themselves were full of commerce and activity. Mountain water was sold from the back of mule-drawn carts, as was cow's and sheep's milk. Villagers brought vegetables, fruit, and wheat in season and sold them from baskets piled on their carts. Donkeys laden with stacks of dried grass to be used as fuel were led through the streets. Prepared foods were also sold by vendors passing by.

A woman in her seventies remembers, "*Sahleb* [a sweet, milky beverage] was my brother's favorite drink. In winter, very early, at sunrise, a man used to come down the street with a giant copper thing on his back. The drink inside was heated—it was a kind of samovar with a few pieces of charcoal burning inside it. Every morning Stepan used to ask for some money from our father and take a tray with glasses for each member of the family and stand by the door. The vendor would come by and pour out the hot drinks and sprinkle some Oriental spices on top. It was really very delicious. We all loved it. Later my mother-in-law came and she said, 'There's nothing easier to make!' So she got all the ingredients and we made it. But it was never the same."

Other favorite foods sold by the vendors included roasted corn, *ganaouri* (roasted hemp seeds), and *melengich* (roasted seeds). The bakeries provided breads and also warm ovens for cooking family meals. People brought their foods, prepared, to be baked in the oven after the baker had finished for the day. Shops lined certain commercial streets and were scattered between the houses in others. Craftsmen and shop owners passed each other several times a day, going to work, home for lunch, and back again. In the evenings people visited with friends and family, rested, or went to the club.

THE CLUB AND POLITICAL PARTIES

By 1925 the Armenian club had been functioning in Nicosia for twenty years and was an important part of *deghatsi* life. Later arrivals also began frequenting the club, which was directly across from the church on Victoria Street. In the library/reading room were numerous books and periodicals from around the diaspora, and news of Hayastan. There was also a large room used for dances and meetings, and a small canteen from which coffee and food were served. Upstairs was a space for backgammon and card playing; above that were more rooms, where a few poor families lived. Unless there was a special gathering or meeting, women usually did not sit around in the club, but men enjoyed the convivial atmosphere, where they could argue politics and discuss the future of the world.

Some mentioned that during this time at least one woman, a young, unmarried teacher at the Melikian Varjaran, did read and talk with the men at the club, but this was apparently rare. A ladies' auxiliary branch of the club was formed in 1916, primarily to raise money and organize donations for Armenian survivors in Cilicia.

In a short time the refugees were contributing to club life, and one of them became its chairman around 1930. An Adanatsi, Setrag Guebenlian had edited and published newspapers in Adana and Aleppo, and at the club he continued his journalistic bent, giving weekly talks on current world events and happenings in the Armenian world. He also arranged for a cultural hour at midday on Sundays, after church. These were attended by both men and women and included poetry, music, dramatic recitations, and lectures. People from the community played instruments or sang, and occasionally artists or speakers would come from outside. Theater productions, evening lectures, wedding receptions, and tea dances all took place at the club as well.

All the older people who mentioned the club (and most did) added that it was a center for everyone, of any political persuasion. Young people, looking around at the physical separateness of club life today, find this hard to believe. Political divisions did indeed exist in Cyprus, as they did elsewhere in the diaspora, and the club itself seems to have been founded and led by men who leaned toward the Ramgavars and sympathetic organizations. However, the club appears to have hosted more general activities for all the community, while political groups and associated cultural organizations met in separate facilities or in private homes.

The number of politicized organizations and associated activities increased in the first years of the twentieth century in Cyprus, as was the case throughout the diaspora. The most basic division of the community was, and is, between pro- and anti-Dashnaktsoutiune or, until recently, between proponents of Soviet Armenia and those who were pro-West. This distinction also entered into the making of friendships and family ties, though there are always degrees of interest and passion, of course. At times the distinctions became an open disturbance as feelings were aroused in both public and private. Most often these disturbances reflected the interests of diaspora communities and thus world politics, but the issues also became mixed with feelings about particular prominent figures in the community, especially when opposing political points of view were involved.

There are no divisions with clean edges. Armenians who had come to Cyprus in the early twentieth century had done so because they felt safe under a British flag. Many of these people also looked to Europe and especially to Britain as the center of power and culture, learning and style. Some of the same people also felt sympathy toward and even admiration of the new Soviet state and appreciation of its role as savior of a remnant of Armenia. Dashnaks, on the other hand, resented the Soviet interference and looked to Britain and the United States for eventual restitution and possibly a change in those nations' policies toward Turkey as well.

At the same time, for both sides, Armenian nationalist rhetoric, poetry, and learning were increasingly becoming of great importance for the average person, not just for intellectuals, as it had been before. This was an effect of mass primary education as well as political emphasis and church aims, all of which were interconnected. However, the conflict between the political parties oriented toward the East and those oriented toward the West increasingly polarized the community. Another dimension was also emerging, that of the growing strength and appeal of wholly secular activities, ones outside the control of the church.

EDUCATION

This mixture was further complicated in Cyprus by the choice of educational programs on the island. In the 1920s and 1930s, with the exception of some of the *deghatsi,* nearly all Armenian children attended either the

Melikian primary school or the school in Larnaca. Following that, young people's choices included apprenticeship to a craftsman or craftswoman, working in a shop, or attending secondary school. There was the English School and Terra Santa in Nicosia for boys, the American Academy in Nicosia for girls and the one in Larnaca for boys and girls, or St. Joseph's convent school in Nicosia for girls. In 1924 the ground was laid for a future Armenian secondary school, one that affected the community from its beginning, although it was originally intended for orphans.

Having made a sizeable fortune from tobacco in Egypt during World War I, the brothers Garabed and Krikor Melkonian were persuaded to found an orphanage for survivors of the pogroms. They bought a large plot (18.7 hectares) of land south of Nicosia and began construction of the massive pair of sandstone buildings that became the Melkonian Orphanage, later the Melkonian Educational Institute. On its completion in 1926, children were brought as boarders from Syria, Lebanon, Egypt, Greece, and elsewhere and divided into classes ranging from kindergarten onward.

Mr. Vahan went to Cyprus as a child with his grandmother and uncle, having lost his parents. Sitting in his living room in London with his wife, Mrs. Sylvia, he recounted how entering the Melkonian had been a major turning point. His story also contains many details about life then.

"At that time we heard that Melkonian, a great benefactor, was building a school and they were gathering orphans like me to come to Cyprus and be part of that school—to look after them, educate them, to make men out of them. My grandfather's son was a tailor and I was helping him, working in the shop. I was about twelve. I did some ironing, cleaned the store. And we used to live in that way—good or bad!"

He told me that one day a friend stopped in the store and suggested that the uncle send Vahan to be enrolled in the Melkonian. That day Bishop Zaven, the new director of the orphanage, was staying in Larnaca, and the friend wanted Vahan to see him. The friend asked Vahan what he thought about going to the Melkonian. "'I want to study,' I said. So he took me inside."

There was a long pause, and I mistakenly wondered if Mr. Vahan had forgotten something.

"In order to go, you must have something"—a longer pause—"to wear." Mr. Vahan began to cry very softly and stopped altogether.

"*Heideh* [come on], continue," said Mrs. Sylvia gently. A teacup clattered down on the table.

"I'm getting ready. It's nothing." Another pause. "Whatever, I needed a haircut, so I went to the barber. I asked the barber if I could have his jacket—because you needed a jacket to go see the priest." He stopped again.

Mrs. Sylvia continued. "That is, the barber dressed him [in his own clothes] so that he could go and meet the bishop. When he arrived at the hotel, a young lady showed him into the bishop's office. He called the bishop 'Der Baba' [Reverend Daddy] because he didn't even know Armenian! He [the bishop] thought he was a nice boy. 'Der Baba,' he said, 'I want to study.'"

"I'm ready now," Mr. Vahan told me. "You weep again when you think of that period. I had to see the bishop. The girl took me upstairs and told him, 'Srpazan, this little one wants to see you.'

"'What is it, my son?'

"I said, 'Parev [hello], Der Baba.' I didn't know what to say!" We all laughed.[2] "I said, 'I want to study, to go to the Melkonian.' He said, 'All right, my son, tomorrow we'll send you to the Melkonian, find a teacher who will test you, and you try it. If there is a suitable class for you, we'll take you.' But the shoes weren't mine. I'd borrowed them. The jacket wasn't mine. Now we laugh about the boy in the outsized, borrowed clothing.

"Now at that time, when I helped in the tailor shop, we went to school at night. There was a night school in Larnaca. There were a lot of boys on their own like me. And there was an Armenian Literature-lovers Society, an Armenian organization that gathered us together and gave us lessons—in Armenian, English, geography, maths. Those four classes. Voluntary. We wanted to learn Armenian. We didn't know Armenian. We were Turkish-speaking because we were from Adana. The language of our house wasn't Armenian. What I learned [at the night school] was very helpful to me [at the Melkonian]! They did an interview to see which class I would be put in.

"So the teacher took me inside and handed me a book to read. 'Read,' he said. And if that wasn't the same book we had been studying in night school! I was really lucky and did well. 'Eh, good, my son,' he said. 'What do you know about geography?' he asked. 'How can you tell that the world is round?' [I told him] whatever I'd learned. 'Who wrote your book?' he asked.

"'Someone named Mahdessian,' I said. And if that wasn't Mahdessian himself! The author of the book! The teacher. He was amused. He closed his books and said, 'You've passed! You are accepted.' He was so happy that we were reading his book and I had learned something."

Mr. Vahan had trouble continuing because he was laughing so much. He explained that he studied at the Melkonian for six years and then stayed on to teach for a time.

The Melkonian had an impact on the community in several ways. First, the collection and arrival of children orphaned by the massacres was a constant reminder of those years. The Armenian General Benevolent Union (AGBU) took over the administration of the orphanage, which meant a considerable workload and commitment but also an increase in status and prominence for that organization in the community. From its early years, the Melkonian teaching staff included well-known Armenian intellectuals and writers (such as Hagop Oshagan and Vahram Mavian), many of whom lived on the grounds of the school. At that time it was a long bicycle ride from the center of town, but they often visited the club, church, and certain Nicosia families. This, the later acceptance of Cypriot Armenians to the secondary school, and the opening of the teachers' training school and the trade school there all influenced Armenian thought and expectations of Armenian intellectual development in Cyprus.

At first the school was known as a place for the homeless and very poor, and most *deghatsi* families were reluctant to be branded as indigent by sending their own children. This gradually changed, and five or six years after its beginning, the Melkonian began accepting a few Cypriot Armenian students to its secondary school classes, but still as boarders.

The English School attracted boys who could be spared as wage earners at home and who were aiming for jobs in the civil service or other office work. While the Terra Santa school and later the Melkonian were other options, the education provided by the English School gave its students wider opportunities in the colony. Elementary English was taught at the Melikian primary school, but the older children who arrived with their families as refugees in 1922 were in a difficult position, as one man, now in his seventies, relates.

"I went to the English School. Now, that's very interesting as far as I am concerned. I had some classmates who went with me at the same time, who knew some English. I did not know any English at all, so the teacher who examined me put me in the bottom class. I went home, honestly, I went home and I was crying. Because my classmates at the Armenian school—" He paused, and I asked, "They were ahead of you?"

"Two classes up. Above! Some of them are here. And once a week the headmaster of the school used to take our class, the bottom class. It so happened that, when he was teaching us, he knew good French. Excellent French. So when he was explaining to me or to the class things in English, there were Armenian boys and Turkish boys, and [I had gone to] the

French school in Adana run by the Jesuits, which was an excellent college, excellent teachers, and I was to translate from French what he was explaining, and when he found that I did it correctly, he asked me to translate the same thing in Turkish to the Turkish boys and the Armenian boys. This went on for a short while, and then he moved me up, two classes up, where I reached my old schoolmates. That was sheer luck."

The American Academy in Nicosia and the one in Larnaca were mission schools. Classes were conducted in English, but the Armenian students also received instruction in Armenian (the Greeks were taught in Greek and the Turks in Turkish) in addition to their literature, math, French, science, and various homemaking courses. Religious studies were part of the curriculum at the English School and at the Academy, but the flavor of the latter was decidedly conservative, reminiscent of the American Midwest. For example, girls were cautioned not to play musical instruments on Sunday and to behave decorously at all times, especially when in their uniforms.

Women remember now that they treated their studies seriously, especially as they were made aware that their families were making a sacrifice to send them. Like the Melkonian and the English School, but in a very different way, the American Academy had a profound and long-lasting effect on the community at large. It was the only English-speaking secondary school for girls at that time, giving a critical advantage to any young woman who wanted to find work in the public sector. This also must have been true for Greek and Turkish girls. For the majority, who did not work outside the home, the English-language secondary education was an important link to understanding the world outside Armenian circles. This influenced them as individuals and in their roles as wives and mothers. A few attended the French convent school, but girls did not attend Greek or Turkish secondary schools. Thus until the Melkonian was opened more widely to Cyprus students, and later more English-language schools were started, the American Academy represented the main opportunity for any secondary education for girls.

Through the girls, a strong Protestant influence was extended throughout the community. Some families had been exposed to this American Protestant approach in Adana and Tarsus before their arrival in Cyprus. While very few girls or their families converted, the school's Bible readings and study, short daily sermons on Christian ethics, biblical interpretation, and particular moral stance made an impact on the way the girls thought about their own religion and how they later organized their own lives and taught their children.

As we left church one Sunday, Mrs. Anna, a former boarder at the Academy in the late 1920s and early 1930s, took my elbow and said, "In our church, if I didn't read the Bible, I wouldn't understand when he read the Scriptures in classical Armenian. During our school days, the head-mistress insisted that we girls go to the Protestant church on Sundays. 'Why?' I asked. She said, 'Because there isn't a sermon during your ser-vices.' So I went to the Srpazan and asked him why there weren't any sermons, and he promised to preach every Sunday. So the Protestants al-lowed us to go as long as we brought back weekly reports on the service and especially on the sermon. That worked three or four times, but then he stopped preaching again."

The girls were not quite passive in their reception of these Protestant ideas and values. One of the early classes at the Academy was nicknamed by the French teacher *"ma classe Bolchevique."* A member of this class, who later became a teacher herself, remembered that the girls were pun-ished for misbehavior or for speaking a language other than English by being made to memorize Bible verses. "Sevan was a fanatic Armenian and used to get angry about this rule. 'It's not fair!' There was a ticket that was given to whoever spoke another language, and then it was passed on to the next offender. One time it stayed with the Bolshevik class for a week. Sevan always insisted on making the sign of the cross when we prayed at school, and when they assigned too many Bible verses, she would shout, 'Are they trying to make Protestants out of us?' "

In Larnaca the curriculum and aims of the Academy were similar, but the staff included several influential Armenian teachers, among them Ma-nuel Kassouni, himself a Protestant. Born in Aintab, Kassouni graduated from the American College there and then went to eastern Armenia to teach, later serving as director of the Protestant High School in Adana. He arrived in Cyprus in 1921. Kassouni was mentioned many times with af-fection as someone who had made an impact both on his students' ideas of Armenian patriotism and on their ethics and values. Former students remember that he organized the Armenian-speakers Club (Hayakhos Mi-youtiune) "in order to inspire our Turkish-speaking youth into speaking and writing Armenian." He also acquired a printing press and Armenian fonts so that the students could publish a monthly paper of their own, *Lousaper.*

Kassouni's efforts again point up the importance given to learning Armenian (mentioned also in chapter 4 and in Mr. Vahan's reference to the evening classes, and visible even in the defiance of the young girls at the Academy). The Academy was an English-language institution, and this was seen as an advantage for future employment and connections. It was learning and improving one's Armenian, however, that became the basis for a new Armenian identity, both individual and communal.

Studying and learning in general were important to many. Miss Emma had come as a small girl to Cyprus in 1922 and was raised in Larnaca. After the Protestant nursery and Armenian elementary school, she set her sights on the Academy. "There was a great yearning for education and learning. This we understood as children. I used to cry so that my father would send me to the Academy. But our family had six children. So I had to stay at home for three years while my older brother finished the Academy, and then there was money for me. My sister had already started learning to be a seamstress, and so she didn't go to secondary school."

Her brother tutored Miss Emma in English, and she was able to skip two of the four years of schooling, thus saving money for the family. Miss Emma also mentioned national meetings and events organized by the Armenian primary schools and the church, often together, to celebrate or commemorate events or holy days in the Armenian calendar. A particular kindergarten teacher was well known for arranging assemblies at which she played her mandolin, and the children sang and recited poems as families and friends watched.

"Miss Kohar prepared a gathering at Christmas every year. It was a great highlight, and everybody would go. During the year there were other high moments—there were special events for Vartanants, and great nationalistic fervor was aroused. And April twenty-fourth was very important in those days, remembering, mourning. In the 1920s it was only ten years after the massacres, so it was close to many people's hearts.

"Because all the Larnaca people went to the church and school and knew each other, whenever there was a death and funeral, the whole community went. Everything was shared. There was only one [elementary] school and one church."

In fact, there was also a Protestant church, and a few children went to the American Academy's elementary section as well as the high school. But those families today also remember the closeness of the Larnaca community. Mr. Kassouni, mentioned earlier, was an active member of the Protestant church but frequently helped in the Apostolic Church—for example, in the training of the choir. Even for these families, the Apostolic Church was a significant part of community life, both in Nicosia and in Larnaca.

CHURCH LIFE

Armenian Protestants and Catholics made up a small percentage of the larger Armenian communities, and while in some ways they were considered part of the group, in others they were thought to be outside of it. This feeling seems to have been mutual. The Armenian Protestants worshiped with Greeks and others in the Larnaca Evangelical Church but also took part in many of the Armenian school and church events. The same was true in Nicosia. In both places there was some intermarriage between Apostolics and Protestants.

Apostolics were more critical of their Catholic compatriots. Intermarriage was undesirable because Apostolics had learned that neither baptism nor marriage ceremonies performed in their church were recognized in the Catholic Church. One would have to become a Catholic to marry a Catholic, they said. Catholics went to services in Larnaca and Nicosia with the Cypriot Maronites and "Latins" and intermarried with these groups.

Church and religion were interwoven with daily life on many levels. Services were held on Sundays, beginning with the morning service, or matins (*aravodian jhamerkoutiune*), and followed by the Mass, or Divine Liturgy (*badarak*). Short morning services continued throughout the week, and these were attended by a core of older women and by men on their way to work. Some of the schoolboys served as candle bearers and acolytes, and laymen served as deacons (*sargavaks* and *tebirs*), choirmaster, and warden (*jamgotch*).

Men and women sang in the choir during Sunday liturgy, the service being a continuous three-way exchange of statement and response between the priests, the deacons, and the choir. Members of the congregation sang, chanted, or spoke along with some parts of the liturgy as they felt moved. Women were active in the design and creation of clerical vestments, crocheted or lace altar ornaments and curtains, and flower arrangements for the altar.

During Lent and especially Holy Week, the number of services increased, as did the number of those attending. Children became more involved as well, in their religious education and participation in the services. In Larnaca, children sang with the adult choir, as it was a small church. A retired teacher now living with her extended family in London recalled, "During Lent [Medz Pak], the seven weeks before Easter, every Wednesday and Friday morning we used to start school with a church ceremony. And we also sang in the church choir. Practically all those who could sing in the school also sang in the church choir with the adults. Mr. Tossounian was the choirmaster and also the math teacher at school. We looked forward to church. We used to sing and wear the *shabig* [choir robe]. Girls were not allowed to go up on the altar, but we used to sing on Friday evenings, special church songs, which we still know by heart after all these years. And the entire school would confess and take communion. During Holy Week it was like having real festivities from the children's point of view."

Special services and holy days were not confined to biblical events; they included the celebration of particular Armenian occasions and saints' days. Schoolteachers often helped, and children presented appropriate songs, drama, and poetry recitals at an assembly or gathering following the church service. The name days of the churches were celebrated by a *madagh* (sacrifice and memorial meal), which became a community meal.

Religious education was given in the school as part of the curriculum. Most remember this as lessons in church history with some Bible stories. The organization of the church was then, as it is now, a combination of lay and clerical power. Laymen were elected to serve on the church councils and oversee the administration of the church, school buildings and grounds, and general finances. The clergy were answerable both to the local council and to their own clerical hierarchy, the Catholicosate in Cilicia. But a charismatic and forceful bishop could accomplish much of his own program through persuasion and other tactics. Bishop Saradjian later became the Catholicos of Cilicia, and thus his influence continued to be felt in Cyprus even after his departure. The bishop had friends among the more educated refugees and wealthy *deghatsi,* and also among powerful foreigners, as demonstrated in the following story.

My mother-in-law, Sirvart Chilingirian, arrived in Cyprus as a young girl with her family in 1922 and had many vivid memories of those times. One day as we sat talking and looking through photographs, she showed me one of the Cyprus Orchestra. Everyone was arranged with their instruments around a big bass drum that had Armenian writing on it along with the year, 1926. "How did the Armenians gather together so many instruments so quickly?" I asked.

"Well, there are Greeks and Turks also in this orchestra picture," she replied. "And I think they already had their instruments. I don't know exactly about that. My uncle had brought his violin with him. But the drum was part of a donation by the King of Arabia!"[3]

"The King of Arabia?" I asked. "Why?"

"Well, you see, the British had made a deal in Saudi Arabia and replaced the king with someone. It had something to do with Jordan and Palestine. And they forced the old man to retire to Cyprus. There he became good friends with Bishop Saradjian. He used to come to our school and we would go and kiss his hand. And, of course, a king makes a donation. My uncle asked him for money for the band, and he gave fifty pounds, which was a lot in those days. And they bought many instruments.

"Later he donated much more—between two hundred and three hundred pounds—so that a narrow road could be built to the monastery from the nearest village. Before that, people had to go by donkey and cart. But then some people were getting cars, and this made travel easier. Bishop Saradjian wanted Armenians to make it their summer vacation spot. Some did, but most went to those Greek villages in the Troodos. The monastery was too primitive, too secluded for most people for an extended stay."

The *kahanas* (parish priests), who were married men, usually with children, were responsible for carrying out weekly services, for general pastoral duties, and often for teaching at the school. The *kahana*'s family and the nature of his duties increased his attachment to and immediate involvement in the particular community and ensured regular contact with a wide variety of people. With their intimate knowledge of the community's various families, the *kahanas* also were often active, or at least important sources of information, in the arrangement of marriages.

Outside the church itself, other connections between religion and daily life were present—for example, in the celebration of name days, especially for men. Throughout the year Armenian saints are commemorated at church on their feast day, and boys and men with those names are also feted by family and friends at home. The name Vartan, for instance, is celebrated at Vartanants along with all other names that do not have a particular day. (It is assumed that because so many died in the Battle of Avarayr, there must be heroes of every name who should be honored that day.) On a saint's name day families go from house to house, wherever a man with that name lives, and congratulate the saint's namesakes. On the bishop's name day, students from the Melikian lined up to congratulate him, kiss his hand, and receive an orange in return.

Birthdays were usually not celebrated, and their gradual evolution as a time for parties and presents, still primarily for children, is seen as a result of "the English influence." Name days were and are celebrations shared with others in the community and around the Armenian world who share the same name and with the saint whose name one bears.

Some homes hung portraits of churchmen and saints; most had a print of the Lord's Prayer. Some also hung the "holy eye" (*surp achk*) over a doorway, either as a print or a glass bead, to indicate that God was watching over the household. This was separate from the "blue eye" (*gabouyd achk*), used as an amulet against the evil eye, which also was displayed prominently throughout homes, on babies' clothing, and elsewhere. A cross was often hung on the wall. At homes and in bakeries, loaves of bread were often marked with a cross before baking.

The speech of Armenians also included many references to their religion, and expressions such as "God willing"[4] and "with God's help," which prefaced the making of plans, were part of everyday discourse. "*Astvadz loosahoki*"[5] ("May God light his or her soul") introduced the name of a dead person in conversation.

At the same time, the primacy of Christianity in Armenian identity had been fostered throughout the years of the Ottoman *millet* and even before that by contrast to their neighbors: Greek or Russian Orthodox, Persian Zoroastrians, Muslims. With the demise of the *millet,* the church remained the focal point of the community for a long time. In diaspora, identity as Christians continued alongside growing secular nationalist feeling; in Cyprus this was encouraged by the perception of neighbors as contrasting groups in which religion coincided with ethnicity or nationality (Greek Orthodox, Turkish Muslims, English Anglicans, and American Protestants).

RELATIONS WITH NEIGHBORS

During this time Armenians' relations with others in Cyprus operated on several levels. On the surface, the most paradoxical were those with the Turkish Cypriots. While history lessons and various programs at church and school emphasized past struggles and troubles with the Turks, Armenians made their homes among them, established businesses beside and with them, made friends with their neighbors, and exchanged visits with some. Adults had cordial but mostly reserved and formal relations, it is said, meeting outside on the street, in shops, and chatting from their doors and windows. Children played together in the streets, the moat, and later in their gardens. They also became acquainted with Turks and Greeks through the English School and the American Academy. These friendly relations continued (albeit with limits) into adulthood until the interethnic troubles began in later years.

Most Armenians continued speaking Turkish to be able to converse with the neighbors, carry on business, and speak with older people in their own families. While a number of families put a ban on speaking Turkish within the home, many others continued for years to tell jokes, anecdotes, or Hodja stories[6] in Turkish, even if the rest of the conversation was in Armenian. Armenians did most of their shopping and carried on their own businesses within the Turkish quarter and at the Turkish market.

The few larger businesses and some individual *deghatsi* had begun to establish ties with Greek Cypriots. But though the Greeks were the vast majority in Cyprus, most Armenians had little contact with them in the early years of the twentieth century. Few Armenians spoke Greek, and initially most felt there was no need to do so. The island was British, the neighbors were Turkish, and the most important language was Armenian. After that, one could learn more European languages for the sake of business or culture. It is important to remember that most did not expect to stay in Cyprus for long. Adults were focused on being prepared for the return to the homelands. At secondary school, when Armenians met Greeks and, through them, their families, English was usually their common language, not Greek.

Gradually, however, more Armenians became aware of the need to learn Greek and to extend their ties in that direction. This happened as the next generation grew up in Cyprus with only vague memories of the homeland; their immediate interest was in their present surroundings. At the same time, the Greeks themselves were becoming increasingly vocal; eventually their growing demands for independence or union with Greece began to affect the Armenian perception of life in Cyprus. That is, as Armenians began to envisage a possible future in Cyprus, there was a dawning awareness that the Greek majority would be a very important part of that future. This may seem rather elementary in retrospect, but it should be remembered that Armenians at the beginning of this century were used to the rule of empire, not local rule. The return to the homeland that they dreamed of privately was almost always seen as taking place under the umbrella of a much larger power: France, the United States, the Soviet Union, or Britain.

The British in Cyprus, in particular, were seen as protectors, an assurance of stability, but also as a model of civilization and culture, learning and education. The British were much admired, as were Europeans generally in spite of the bitter disappointment of many that Allied promises to the Armenians during and after World War I had not been kept. Civil service jobs had status, if not high pay, and children were encouraged to learn English for these jobs and others. Shop owners found English useful in attracting British customers, and as their trade expanded some used the language to buy textiles in Manchester. A few families socialized with the British, through work or as representatives of the Armenian community.

In addition to their ties with neighbors and coworkers in Cyprus, Armenians there were very much connected to another group: Armenians in the diaspora and Hayastan. Family ties extended to other countries, especially America and the Near East, and the exchange of letters and photographs meant not only that these ties were maintained but also that Armenians in Cyprus learned about other countries and what Armenians were doing there. Though many did not have close family in Hayastan, there was a great interest in its affairs, and a number of families seriously considered emigrating. News of Hayastan was regularly given at the club, and there was great excitement when someone would come from abroad, especially from Hayastan, with firsthand reports.

Armenian theater groups, musicians, and poets from the diaspora also performed in Cyprus, usually hosted by the club. Sometimes Cypriot Armenians would assist or take part in the performance. In this way, too, Armenians kept in touch with other communities. A few traveled to Europe or America for education, training, or business. When they returned, their houses would fill with friends and neighbors eager to share in the excitement.

Armenians continued to socialize and prefer marriages with those from their own group: newer arrivals associated with their fellow villagers from prerefugee days, and *deghatsi* associated with *deghatsi*. This extended to an interest taken in family and fellow villagers abroad. Perceived status continued to be affected by prerefugee status, but within Cyprus, education and work gradually began to replace geographical origin as keys to status. Those who had been wealthy once still thought of themselves as such, however.

After family and fellow villagers, then other Armenians working in similar jobs, the Armenian community generally was of greatest importance. Beyond this, most Armenians certainly met Turkish families and traders quite often, but at the same time Turks were taboo for marriage (though there are rumors of exceptions). Greek and British husbands or wives were not desirable but were accepted, especially later, when young people began making their own contacts and decisions. It was suggested to me that in some ways "life was easier for us with the Turks as our friends, because it was obvious that we couldn't marry them and they couldn't marry us. We could be friends without these worries."

For many of the refugees, life in Cyprus began with the island being thought of as a place to wait. During the first ten to fifteen years, however, community life had already begun to evolve. Though the divisions between *deghatsi* and *kaghtagan* remained, these too started to be bridged, gradually and in different ways. The refugees themselves were not homogeneous. Some arrived as orphans; others were part of relatively well-off, educated families that had managed to escape relatively intact.

Diversity in the community was not limited to degree of wealth or length of time in Cyprus. Political divisions were passionately and openly debated during this time, and divisions between the major political groups began to deepen. The diversity of education, both in length (primary only, secondary, or even university) and in kind (Armenian, American, English, French), points up the varying interests and financial statuses of the parental generation and also gives an idea of the different attitudes and influences that were to follow.

In spite of the variety of education and backgrounds, common threads ran through the community: the importance of learning the Armenian language, and the role of the church and club at the physical and moral center of people's lives. These played an important part in promoting a new kind of national awareness and a sense of the community as part of a larger Armenian diaspora.

Chapter 6

Scenes from an Armenian Community, 1930–1949

By the 1930s, growth in the Armenian population of Cyprus had stabilized. There were some new arrivals—a few families, but especially individual men—and others left, but generally the mood was that of settling in. The younger generation began putting down roots in Cyprus, and those who had come earlier were now in a position to help the few who later followed.

A woman now working in partnership with her sister in their father's old business explained how their family had decided in the 1930s to come to Cyprus. Her father had tried to find work in a number of different places, including Aleppo and Ethiopia, but with little luck. His own mother had been very instrumental in helping him get started in business, and she finally suggested that he learn shirtmaking, paying for the course herself.

"After that there were two Armenians from Cyprus who came to Aleppo for trade. When they came, they said, 'Why don't you come to Cyprus and try your luck? It's small, new—maybe you'll succeed there. It's still backward. Also, it's a British colony—more safe, more civilized.' So he came in 1935. Came without a penny—but he was a person who could make friends easily. He went to the Armenian church, the club, to meet people. People asked, 'What are you doing? No money? Don't worry!' So one man gave him a machine. Another, who had a soap factory, gave him some cash for material, and another was the guarantor for the loans. Someone else provided material. So he opened his first shop in Ledra Street with one machine and a few pieces of material."

Within a short time Mr. Armen had repaid his loans and gained the title of "Shirtmaker to the Governor" (of Cyprus). He, like the others in his generation whom he joined in Cyprus, saw the island as a refuge and an opportunity to raise his family in peace. The possibility of returning to the old lands gradually began to fade in most people's minds.

The theme of movement, displacement, and worry about the future was never completely allowed to rest, however. The final group of refugees to arrive came in 1948 from Palestine; many of these people had already been uprooted earlier in their lives.[1] Their concerns reflected an insecurity that was part of the general outlook of the Armenian diaspora community.

Mrs. Ashkhen, telling of her family's arrival in Cyprus at that time, vividly remembered what a difficult time it had been for her daughter, age four.[2] Nora had had an accident as a toddler, she explained, which had made her afraid. But things got worse afterward.

"She remembered what we went through in Tiberias," Mrs. Ashkhen said. "Because when they were bombing, we used to take them [the children] and lie on the floor. And every time there was the bombing, she used to [cry], 'Mummy! Mummy! It's started again! Come!' So she remembers all these difficulties. So when we went to Cyprus, she was so tense. As soon as she heard the aeroplane flying, she used to get scared. The bombings were by plane. And it came right near the house and they bombed and the house shook and it was all dusty. She turned to us, because we never lied to her. Always said the truth. When we went to Jordan [en route to Cyprus], we told her, 'Now we are not going to have any bombings nor trouble.' When this took place, the first thing, she turned around and said, 'You said nothing was going to happen here! What happened?' So she didn't trust us."

Mrs. Ashkhen seemed worried that somehow she and her husband had failed to protect their child from the stresses of war, though she knew that it was impossible.[3] In Cyprus, she said, Nora became weaker and tenser, and she developed a bad case of asthma. Though the family had intended to go on to Britain, where the father could carry on with his profession, the exigencies of earning money and settling into a more peaceful life for the children took precedence.

The people who came throughout the 1930s and later were most often skilled and had some education; they were able to adapt quickly to life in a British colony. By then the American government had also developed a monitoring station in Cyprus, and the linguistic skills of the Armenians were found very useful there.

WORK

In addition to the British civil service, employment with the American government, banking, and other office work, a great variety of jobs were held by Armenians. A number of men gradually built up their buying-and-selling businesses from the back of carts to small shops and later expanded again, to the import and export of textiles and other goods.

In the following passage, Mrs. Azniv explains how her own father made this transition. The family had begun in Amiandos, where he worked in the mines, but when the eldest daughter reached school age, the parents decided that, even without work, they must move to Nicosia, where there was an Armenian school.

"He was not educated—he had no skills," she said of her father.

I asked, "Couldn't you have stayed in Amiandos, where he had work, and gone to a Greek school?"

"No! My father was a very fanatic Armenian. He started by putting some clothes in a basket and he went around the streets selling them. Then he got a small cart, which he pushed around. My mother used to help him by making small bibs and knitting booties for children, which he sold. He also bought some material for dresses to sell. At the same time, with the things that Mother made, they used to make ends meet. That's what my mother used to say.

"Slowly, slowly, the cart grew into a big cart, driven by a donkey. We used to live in Nicosia between the wars. We had a house with a big gate so that we could drive through it. I was very embarrassed. Don't look at how the Armenians are now. Thank God it's different. Then we used to buy a new pair of shoes once a year. Not like now.

"Then my second brother was born, and Father had to work very hard. He used to wear a safari hat in the summer, and when he'd come home, we would pour a bucket of water over his head and the steam would rise. I loved my father very much because he worked so hard."

Craftsmen continued their trades in Cyprus, making shoes, smithing tin and copper, repairing machinery (and, later, cars), and so on. Photography, a new skill, became a source of employment, one that eventually attracted many Armenians, who took portraits and scenes of Cyprus, opening shops where photographic equipment and goods could be bought. Edward Vosgeritchian, of Limassol, was probably the first professional Armenian photographer in Cyprus; he learned his trade in 1920 from an "Italian" (Latin Cypriot?), passing it on later to his sons.

In many instances, fathers taught their skills to their children, and the business was continued into the next generation. In most cases the sons, and sometimes the daughters, were also responsible for adding new, modern techniques to the general family store of knowledge and were thus encouraged to take some responsibility for the growth of the business.

Women continued to help their husbands or fathers in their work where necessary and possible, sometimes taking care of the accounts at night or making things to be sold. Some unmarried women developed skills and businesses of their own, including hatmaking, sewing, and giving piano lessons. They also worked as teachers, secretaries, accountants, in banking, and at the Cable and Wireless as operators and receptionists. A few married women also worked in these areas.

There was a prevalent feeling that women should not do outside work in addition to running the household and raising the children. If they did, it indicated that their husband or father was not providing well for the family. In spite of this, it appears that many women did work outside the home, especially before they married, and this steadily increased as the first generation born in Cyprus grew up. Most unmarried women worked, and one, who began working alongside her father in his store in the 1930s and later took it over from him when he retired, is remembered as being ahead of her time. Much later other women opened their own shops, selling fashion and lingerie.

Though very few Armenians became involved in the growing of food for sale, some did create businesses out of its preparation, for example, bakeries, the making of *basterma* and *soujouk,* sweet shops, and so on. The restaurant of Mushegh Bichakjian was frequently mentioned. He had previously run a restaurant in Adana, sold baked goods from a pushcart in Beirut and Famagusta, and worked as a cook at the Melkonian Institute and the Armenian Hotel in Nicosia.

One of the *deghatsi* families extended their business to importing and selling cars, radios, agricultural tools, and other large items. The scale of a few such businesses grew quickly, and Armenians began to employ others, not only Armenians, and make business alliances with other successful Armenian families. Armenian craftsmen took on Turkish and Greek apprentices as well as young Armenians.

The years of disruption and emigration had somewhat leveled the economic differences between refugee families, but the *deghatsi,* because of the stability and potential for accumulation that resulted from years of work and contacts in one place, remained among the wealthiest families in the community. Those *deghatsi* who adapted their capital to businesses in the new postwar climate became especially well-off. Others preferred the tradition of civil service, some rising to high levels.

By the mid-1930s a number of Armenian doctors and dentists had established themselves and drew their patients from the various ethnic groups. A few women trained as nurses; only later did some study to be doctors. At that time women worked as midwives, some officially trained, others "by practice"; others dispensed home remedies and advice.

DIVISIONS

As the years passed, *deghatsi* and refugee families mixed through their trades (sometimes working with or for each other), at the club, and through the activities of the political and cultural organizations. Old divisions could still be distinguished, though they were more subtle and were subject to the overlay of the numerous other divisions and connections that existed. The very wealthy and the very poor had little contact with each other, but in between, degrees of affluence were only part of the story, along with village and family ties, education, career, and so on.

In fact, wealth and poverty, though clear in their extremes, were not the real basis for division. While in some cases people associated the *deghatsi* with wealth and the refugees with being poor, or extended that to being part of the upper and lower classes, respectively, this is not enough to explain the differences or the rejection of the newcomers by the *deghatsi.* Many refugees had been wealthy, especially in land, not long before. Others, not necessarily the same families, built up a solid income in Cyprus. But this was insufficient to overcome the gap. While the civil servants, "school people," and clergy regarded the shopkeepers and craftsmen as lower in status than themselves, the reverse was true to a degree as well; many people mentioned to me that there was a general scorn of salaried jobs ("You couldn't rise at all, and everyone knew what you earned— the worst thing for an Armenian!"). Furthermore, refugees were to be found at every economic level and in most kinds of work.

While *deghatsi* may have regarded the refugees as uncouth, uncivi-

lized people, there were those among the refugees who were equally dis-
approving of some *deghatsi*. Perhaps because of the pain of rejection, perhaps from a heightened sense of national and personal priorities at the
time, the display of wealth and lavish entertainment among the *deghatsi*
and some members of the clergy left bitter memories for some. A retired
shopkeeper in his nineties who had remained in Cyprus said, "When we
arrived in Cyprus, the *deghatsi* didn't look too kindly on the refugees. [At
one *deghatsi* house] they used to play cards and gamble all night. All those
families were wrapped up with the bishop. It was an unethical, dishonest,
debauched life that he led! Wasting the public money! But the [*deghatsi*]
clique kept him."

What would eventually turn out to be the most bitter communal divisions were gradually building up at this time, based on the different attitudes associated with the Armenian political parties and with the nomi-
nally apolitical cultural and social organizations such as the Armenian
General Benevolent Union (AGBU) and Armenian Young Men's Association (AYMA). Briefly, and at great risk of oversimplifying, the divisions
were as follows.

I list the political parties first, though relatively few in Cyprus actually
belonged. They provide a frame of reference and are often used by fellow
Armenians to indicate which side someone belongs to, whether it is official
or not and whether that person agrees or not.

Those of the Ramgavar party are pro-Hayastan (and in the past, by
extension, were accepting of the Soviet state). This was viewed as accommodation by the Dashnaks but as realism by their own people. The AGBU
(whose Armenian name is Parekordzagan), the Friends of Armenia, and
the Melkonian Institute were popularly considered to be within this
sphere.

On the other side were the Dashnaks, seen as nationalist, pro-West,
the party of resistance (and, in the past, anti-Soviet). The AYMA club is
considered to fall within this sphere. Seen as serving the entire community
were the Armenian Club, the Melikian-Ouzunian primary school and an-
nex, and the church. In a remnant of old divisions, more *deghatsi* were on
the Ramgavar side than the Dashnak side, while refugees were active on
both sides.

This division focused much attention on Hayastan. Those who supported it (and, with varying degrees of enthusiasm, its then parent nation,
the Soviet Union) were accused of being Communists. A few were, by their
own account; most probably were not, although many were sympathetic.

Some were accused of being spies. In return the Dashnak side was reviled for not supporting Hayastan and thus not being true Armenian patriots. Some were accused of spying for Western governments.

In most instances these divisions fostered a war of wit and words, gossip, and community theater. Occasionally, however, they had more sinister reverberations in the actions of some who were believed to have acted as informants for the British colonial government or for the Soviet government. The divisions reflected wider global rifts as well as Armenian diaspora politics and, not least of all, conflicts of personality. Mistrust and resentments built up within the community, and during the 1940s and 1950s, as the cold war began and then intensified, the split between the two sides became more and more a chasm, rather than differences to be argued over and discussed.

Later, by the early 1950s, the political struggle for power over the position of Catholicos of Cilicia had direct repercussions on the community as the anti-Dashnak side protested and many dropped out of church activities completely. Araxi, a schoolgirl at the time, remembers that her father, a member of AYMA, tried to bridge the gap between the two sides. He felt there should be unity in the community and wanted his daughter to have an Armenian education. He sent Araxi to the Melkonian (which was considered to be on the other side) after elementary school. She also sang regularly in the church choir, but she remembers that one day the choirmaster came to her and one other girl and said, "'I am very sorry, but you can't sing in the choir anymore.' He had been told to say this because we were Melkonian students. I went home and cried all day. My father said, 'What is this? Am I sending my girl to the cabaret?'" Araxi laughed at the idea of the Melkonian's being equated with something as shameful as going to a cabaret.

"And on the other hand, as many students at the Melkonian were from abroad, my father used to invite them home for evenings, weekends, or holidays and so on, and they used to have a good time and we would sing and eat and so on. But apparently one of the songs we sang was an AYMA song of some sort, and one of the boys mentioned this back at school. After that the school authorities wouldn't allow children to visit our home. My father was furious, and I didn't go back to the Melkonian the next semester."

Elections to the church board (essentially, the community governing body) exposed these divisions and also the ways in which people tried to manipulate and maneuver them in order to gain some degree of individual power. The Melkonian was governed by a board of directors, which ultimately answered to the central board of the AGBU, then in Cairo. The AGBU also had an active branch in Nicosia, which is the subject of the following irreverent passage, written by an Armenian journalist in 1945. The style of the meeting he describes is more generally Armenian than uniquely AGBU and gives a taste of the era.

> A General Meeting speaks to the soul of the average Armenian. The fact that he is invited to a General Meeting gives him great importance, and once he is invited, he can do two things: he can increase his importance by not condescending to attend, or he can decide to make full use of his importance by attending. In the second eventuality, he takes care that he should be at least one hour late, puts something in his mind to say at the meeting, whether the subject is raised or not, and proceeds to the Armenian Club Hall.
>
> The essential element of the Parekordzagan General Meeting is noise. All members are orators inside the meeting-room, and they invariably talk at the same time. There is no rule as to how many persons can speak at the same time, but the generally accepted notion is that five members can speak at once, provided that each makes an effort to be heard better than the other.
>
> As none of the members is an expert on anything, those present at the meeting speak about every subject that is raised—or not raised, whether they know anything about it or not. In fact, the less they know about the subject the more talkative they become.[4]

During World War II a club called Friends of Armenia (Paregamats, or Hayastani Paregamnerou Mioutiune) was established, dedicated to helping Hayastan in the Soviet war effort and generally to strengthening ties with Hayastan. Mrs. Arshaluis, a teacher who has remained in Cyprus with her husband, explained her perception of that time: "During the war years, when everything was so bleak, they started a strong movement called the Hayastani Paregamnerou Mioutiune. It wasn't Communist, simply for national heritage and culture. It lasted into the 1950s. It did a lot of nice cultural work in Cyprus—plays, lectures, theaters. Their aim was to let the new generation know about Hayastan and our culture. Because before the war, we didn't know much about Hayastan. Then, when Britain was allied with Russia, there was a chance to do something about our culture.

"The first division [in Cyprus] was *deghatsi / kaghtagan,* but after the war the division was more pro-Hayastan or not pro-Hayastan. Foreigners will not understand. Because on our side [pro-Hayastan] we had many rich people—so it was not left or right. Left or right comes only because Hayastan happens to be a Soviet country and it is our only hope. Whatever the regime is there, we would still be with Armenia.

"But we sincerely believe we have never had it so safe as we have it now, simply because somebody is protecting us. Can you imagine a small Hayastan with Turkey and nobody to protect them? I don't believe that the diaspora in any way protects the Soviet Armenians. Everything may not be ideal there, but at least they are safe. We want to give too much importance to us in the diaspora. We are nothing.

"And with Hayastan in the Soviet Union, at least our country has had some breathing space. We were packed and ready to go in 1946. But it didn't happen. In 1947 we were registered, but they didn't accept us. After that the times changed. We had our studies, a lot of things happened after that. A lot of Armenians would have gone then, but the quota was filled from Beirut and elsewhere, and Cyprus was considered a safe place."

With backing and funding from the Soviet Union, Hayastan issued an invitation to those in diaspora to join their fellow Armenians in the new "homeland." Some families applied to be part of this *nerkaght,* or gathering-in, which was to have taken place in 1948, but though many waited with crates packed, resources were limited, and Cyprus was bypassed in favor of poorer, more desperate communities in Beirut and Syria. Disappointed as they were, few had the means to emigrate on their own, without the assistance of the Soviet ships and the government apparatus to facilitate the move.

Such attachment to Hayastan and, by extension, to the Soviet Union was viewed by the other side as naive at best. They saw the Soviet Union with great suspicion as a foreign country that had imposed its own greater plan on Armenia, something that would eventually lead to assimilation within the Russian image. The Dashnak party and AYMA club continued to emphasize their revolutionary origins, praising the *fedayeen* and early freedom fighters, and remained anti-Soviet and anti-Turkish, waiting for an opportunity to re-create a free Hayastan. Their opponents, of course, considered this to be an idealistic impossibility. Both sides were susceptible to the wilder claims made by the propagandists of both East and West.

NEIGHBORHOOD

While few families left Cyprus between 1930 and 1950, people did move within the towns, changing houses as their income increased. In Nicosia more Armenians began to move outside the old city walls. A few moved south, to the Greek neighborhoods, while a large number moved to a new (largely Turkish) section called Naopolis, northwest of the center.

Mrs. Azniv remembered, "My mother had been given a pair of bracelets when she got married. Houses were being built in Naopolis then, and for about two hundred pounds you could buy a small house with a hall, dining room, two bedrooms. We later enlarged this by having a kitchen built outside. My mother sold her bracelets to buy the house. Father only earned enough to pay our rent and everyday needs. I was eleven when we moved there, so excited and happy! The houses in town had no running water. To have a house with running water in it was like going to heaven! Even now it is important to me, and I get upset when there are cuts."

Mrs. Azniv said that it appeared to the children that their mother had been the major decision-maker in the move, choosing the house and paying for it. In a number of other cases also, mothers had considerable power in the decision of where to live and when to move.

Though new homes, and some of the larger old ones, had running water, few had bathing facilities, and families continued an old tradition of going to the Turkish baths. Many people mentioned this as something that was very important but is altogether lost today (except in London, for some all-male stag parties—probably a rather different experience). Even some who didn't go mentioned it. The family of Mrs. Yeran, now in her fifties, came to Cyprus slightly later than the other refugees. "We were different," she began, by way of warning. "We didn't even go to the baths. We used to bathe at home [taking sponge baths]. I was so interested in the baths and everything that was new to me that my friend and I went on our bicycles by ourselves to the baths. We were in [high school] then. We just wanted to see those ladies and smell the pine logs burning. Such a wonderful smell!"

The majority of families did go—both shop owners and school people, *deghatsi* and refugees, people of all political stripes. Men and older boys went on Saturdays and specific evenings, women and children during the weekdays. The baths were not used merely for getting clean but to spend a relaxing time together, chat, and eat. Women mentioned that they would take picnics with them and spend hours in the steam, dyeing and washing their hair, cleaning themselves and their children, and getting a massage from the Turkish women who worked there.

There was little hidden in the baths, and from an early age girls were scrutinized as prospective brides. Their bodies, their hair, their behavior over the course of the day—all were subject to discussion among the older women as they scouted for future brides for their sons. "They even looked at her wet footprints on the floor because it was very important that she not be flat-footed!" said one woman. Children ran and slipped, were washed, ate their picnic lunch, and were sent back outside to play while the women continued their ritual.

The desirability of a new home's location was its proximity to Armenian institutions—church, elementary school, club. Even as the number of cars owned very gradually increased, people mostly walked or rode bicycles around the towns. Children who went to schools farther away from home, such as the Melkonian, the Junior School (an English-language primary school), and the English School, rode bikes or, much later, took a bus.

Within the neighborhoods, in the workplace, and in the market, there was an exchange of small talk, gossip, information, and help among Armenians, Turks, and Greeks. Women at home became friendly with their neighbors, sometimes meeting for morning coffee. Children played together in the streets and moat; teenagers met at secondary school. Men more often met at work or in the market. Very often these contacts overlapped, and whole families knew each other quite well. These interethnic contacts had limits, but the differences between the groups, the outsider aspect of the relationship, often meant that problems could be shared between them that would have been more difficult to share with people inside the culture. Mrs. Anoush, now in her seventies, remembered one such story from her young married life. "We had Turkish neighbors. The man was so gentle—he couldn't hurt anybody or anything. He was very timid, a musician. They had a son named Ali, who was nearing the age where he must be circumcised, but Hassan Bey, the father, was too afraid that something would happen to his son, and he kept postponing it! He had to travel to perform his music, and one time when he was in Turkey, the old grandfather came next door and said, 'We are going to do the ceremony for Ali while his father is away so that when he comes back he won't have any worries and it will be all done, finally. It's a shame that it has been put off so long!' The mother arranged everything, and they did it.

"Then that night there came a loud knocking at our door! 'Bedros *effendi*, Bedros *effendi*! Ali has a fever! He's in a terrible way! What shall we do? What will happen to us? Please go and get a doctor for us!' So my husband went off on his bicycle to find a doctor [an Armenian one] for the boy and brought him back to them. The fever passed, and Ali was fine by the time Hassan Bey returned."

In the same way, exceptions were made for the behavior of neighbors belonging to other ethnic groups that would not have been made for

people within the same group. For example, while Armenians were extremely critical of women's behavior that could in any way be construed
as "loose" or flirtatious, Nora recalled how one young Turkish woman, a
neighbor, was welcomed into the homes of Nora's relatives for afternoon
visits with the ladies. "Pembe *hanim* [roughly, "Madame Pembe"] was the
most famous of prostitutes. Her story was well known. Her mother had
been one before her and was stabbed to death. Pembe continued the
trade—in Tanzimat Street—with the others. She was said to be the most
beautiful of all, with gray-green eyes, peachy skin, [a] slightly plump [fig-
ure], dark hair. But then suddenly she quit. And she went to live with the
son—who was younger than she was—of a rich pasha. It was a great
scandal for the family until he later married an acceptable young woman.
Later he and his new wife lived near us, and we visited and the children
played. But Pembe *hanim* lived near to our relatives and she used to often
come for tea there, and I would meet her there frequently. She would tell
our fortunes by reading cards and coffee grounds. She was an extremely
nice woman."

Nora, now in her late forties, remembers how parents used to worry
about their children walking down Tanzimat Street, which they had to
pass on their way to school. "They used to say, 'Go quickly! Don't stop
and talk to anyone!' At first, I only remember the images of those women's
faces from the windows. But later we came to understand the situation
and then we would make a game of recognizing the bicycles of men that
we knew! But the women were very friendly. They were nice to us, the
children, and every afternoon as we returned home from school, we noticed that the houses had been freshly cleaned."

ENTERTAINMENT

The club continued as the focus for activities outside the home. It sometimes served as a place where Armenians as a community could serve as
host to other groups, introducing people and ideas to each other. The following anecdote, told by Mrs. Vartanoush, gives some insight into the
atmosphere at the club and also the gradual changes taking place in the
ways men and women met.[5]

"At one time [in the late 1940s] the organizers of one of the Armenian
balls invited some Royal Air Force soldiers to come, and the girls were
told not to turn their faces away from them when they approached us. We
were supposed to be polite. The girls who knew English were pointed out.

Everybody in Cyprus knew who spoke English and who didn't. And the soldiers were told that they must ask permission from the girls' escorts before dancing. My escort was my brother, who was younger but who was still supposed to grant permission!

"So I did dance with a young man, and afterward his officer came over and he asked me if I would go out with that man. Go out? Impossible! 'Why?' he says. 'Don't you have a key?' First he has to explain what he means, and then I have to explain that I don't have a key. Of course, I could have one if I just asked my mother—but I don't want it because I don't need it. And anyway, the door is not locked!

"He couldn't understand, and we talked a long time about this. 'You are twenty-one, right?' Right. And I was rather big and looked very grown-up for my age. 'Where did you go to school?' The Melkonian. 'Was it mixed?' Yes. 'Well, didn't you have any boyfriends?'" Mrs. Vartanoush laughed loudly, with her eyes wide open, at the memory of this. "Impossible! And it was impossible to make him understand that we didn't have boyfriends and we didn't go out. Of course, people did things like send letters between those who were interested in each other, but nothing else. You couldn't!

"Eventually he gave up—because he didn't have any choice. That is the way things were then. But we had a good time at the ball that night. These soldiers were well behaved, not like the Australians who came during the war [World War II]."

In addition to the family entertainment offered by the club, and later AYMA and the Friends of Armenia, *tavernas* and cabarets attracted many men for an evening out. For the most part, the split generally remained between those who regularly went to these places and those who felt it was shameful to go. But close extended families often contained both sorts and many degrees in between.

Many people, both men and women, spoke of the importance of the Armenian soccer team, Gaydzak. One year Gaydzak won the championship of Cyprus, playing against the top Greek team, Apoel. People remember this as a tremendously exciting event. Armenians enthusiastically supported the team and went regularly to matches. The Greeks were equally enthusiastic in support of theirs and found novel ways to mock the other side during the game, calling the Armenians "garlic-eaters" and waving bulbs of garlic in the air at them.[6]

One man, particularly sensitive to this insult because his living is made from garlic-flavored meats, remembered the famous championship match. "The Greeks brought garlic to the game and instead of the cup, they were going to give us garlic. But we won! Garlic was a way of making fun of us—but now they eat it, and Armenians are still afraid to."

Movies also became popular, and live performances of music became an important part of community life. Armenians in Nicosia enjoyed performances by the Melkonian Choir and choruses organized by the club and others. Small events took place at the club, while larger ones were held at the local theaters.

A band and an orchestra (the Cyprus Orchestra), each with Greek, Turkish, and Armenian musicians, were organized and conducted by Vahan Bedelian, who came from Adana in 1922. This was an extracurricular activity for Mr. Vahan, whose primary allegiance was to Nicosia's Armenian church, where he was choirmaster, but he also taught music and choir at the Melkonian, the Melikian-Ouzunian, and the Turkish schools, and he gave violin lessons to generations of Armenian, Turkish, and Greek children.[7] When we spoke about this time in his life, Mr. Vahan was most concerned that I understand that he had enjoyed working with all groups in Cyprus.

"It's all the same with music," he said. "Music is the international language. One time [in the 1930s] the new director of the Turkish *lycée* was taken for a walk around Nicosia. They passed Victoria Street, where our band [a smaller Armenian ensemble] used to play for the people on Sundays at three-thirty or four o'clock in the churchyard. There were no cars then. People stayed at home, and they came there to listen. The director heard us. 'What nice music! Oh, they're all Armenians—but they play nicely.' He entered and I noticed him.

"Then a week later the director wanted to see the bandmaster, so they sent for me. 'We need you in our school!' And they invited me to teach all the [instrumental] classes in the Turkish *lycée*—band, orchestra. The Turkish director was a poet also. And he wrote a prayer and asked me to put it to music." Mr. Vahan broke off here and sang it in Turkish. "The director changed, but I worked in the *lycée* for fourteen years. And every morning, before they would go to their lessons, they would sing and pray with this song. Every morning."

In addition, a group of women interested in classical music met regularly in each other's homes, played for each other, listened to records, and discussed the music. Other men and women in the community learned to play the mandolin and entertained each other with popular songs.

The most common form of entertainment remained the visit, whether it was a casual evening for close family members, an afternoon with neighbors, or a more formal gathering with distant relatives or other guests. Whereas previously only coffee or cold drinks had been served, as the years passed the table became increasingly laden with foods, fruits, and sweets as people were able to afford more hospitality. People emphasized that as there was no television and little radio, they entertained themselves with stories, songs, and their own instrumental music.

During World War II there was a partial evacuation from the towns to the mountains. Women and children, for the most part, were the evacuees, and new schools, both Armenian and English, were started in villages such as Lefkara. As there turned out to be little fighting in or around Cyprus, there remained considerable exchange between those who stayed in the towns and those in the mountains.

In some ways this wartime evacuation was a continuation of what many had been doing for years: spending summers in the cool mountains. During these summer retreats the men continued their work in the towns and joined their families on weekends or as frequently as possible. One of the favorite mountain retreats was Pedhoulas in the Troodos. Families rented a house of two or three rooms from the Greek villagers and set up housekeeping. The length of the stay, number of rooms, number of family members sharing, and frequency of visits from those remaining in town depended on the income of the family. Many families did not leave Nicosia at all, while others went only every few years.

The monastery in the Kyrenia Mountains continued to attract visitors, and some families preferred to stay there rather than in the Troodos. Boarders from the Melkonian were brought to the monastery to camp. Holy days, christenings, and the name day of the monastery (which was named after St. Magar) brought many visitors. People went for the weekend, walking in the woods and over the rocks surrounding the monastery, some going as far as the sea.

Even for people who did not go often, the monastery was an important presence, a distant but vivid part of the community. One man remembered, "I only went there one time, with my father and a visiting young priest. When the priest discovered that I liked music, he told me to go with him up into the forest, beyond the monastery. When we were by ourselves, he sang—beautiful old Armenian songs, there under the pine trees."

Looking at photographs of the 1940s, one often sees groups of teenage boys lined up by their bicycles, ready to set off or just back from an outing together. The boys went as groups of Scouts or simply as friends on an afternoon trip to Kyrenia, through the mountain pass, for a swim in the sea, a drink by the harbor, and back again to Nicosia.

In later years, some would talk of this time as one of increased "decadence" in the Armenian community there, referring to the bitter arguments, lack of firm guidance from the clergy, and increased friction between factions. Most, however, thought of it as the peak of community life, with a full range of activities, a steady increase in wealth and the standard of living, the easy availability of good education, and a generally peaceful environment.

Chapter 7

Disruptions and Disturbances, 1950–1974
"Everyone Has Left"

As World War II came to an end, part of the world looked forward to years of peace and stability. Cyprus and several other countries, however, began decades of turmoil mixed with tranquil times—insecurity and prosperity together. The refusal of the British to allow Cyprus to unify with Greece or, later, to become independent would mean a long and eventually violent struggle by the Greek majority. Turks and Armenians both were concerned that their own status quo would be damaged by either independence or *enosis*. Parents wondered what kind of future their children would have on a Greek island. Meanwhile, fighting, both between the British and the Greeks and between the Greeks and the Turks, became more frequent around them. Children had to pass through checkpoints on their way to school. Curfews were imposed, and people learned to be careful, trying to find some safe middle ground.

Mrs. Anoush, now living in London, tried to express the concerns and mixed allegiances that many Armenians then felt. "Our house was in the Turkish quarter, near the river and near the prison. During the EOKA troubles our family could hear the prisoners shouting when the young Greek men were going to be hanged for killing British soldiers. It was horrible. Our Turkish neighbors were rejoicing all around us, but we sat closed up in our house, quiet. We couldn't share in their celebrations.

"Later there was a rumor that the Greeks were going to come up the river and massacre the Turks in the neighborhood! One Turkish family that lived just on the river's edge came to us and asked if we would protect them for the night. We were Armenians and we wouldn't be attacked. They were very good neighbors. The mother had stayed with me when my father was dying, until my relatives could come. The boys used to play together. How could we say no? So we all stayed together that night, petrified that the Greeks would come in. How would we prove that we were all Armenians? We could show passports—but what could they do? Everybody stayed up all night. We couldn't sleep. My husband was the only one who wasn't quiet. He had to tell jokes, in Turkish, all night long, just to calm us and take our minds off it. But the Greeks didn't come."

Isolated incidents and increasingly tense intercommunal relations were followed by major violent incidents in 1958. Killings and ethnic cleansing of villages were perpetrated by both Greek and Turkish Cypriots. An older Armenian couple was murdered in their home in the Kyrenia Mountains, but the killer remained unknown, and connections between that event and the troubles were never established. Fear spread in all communities as a result of incidents witnessed and, almost as important, through rumor.

Armenians felt very much in the middle, with no stable ground of their own. They understood the Greek desire for independence but were suspicious of *enosis*. Turks were their neighbors, but the British had been their protectors and were perhaps their best hope for the future. It is said that some Armenian young men joined EOKA to fight. Many others supported the British, but mostly people tried to stay clear of the confrontations and began rethinking their future in Cyprus. By the 1950s Cyprus had become more than just a large, comfortable waiting room. Families had begun to buy property and feel that Cyprus was home, relying on the British to keep the peace and provide some jobs. As Commonwealth subjects during the colonial years, refugees had been given the opportunity to buy British passports, and many had done so, both for ease of future travel and because of the assumption of protection by the British government. Under the colonial government, the passport also allowed for emigration to Great Britain, but few had made use of the privilege until then. With the increasing unease and later violence, though, many Armenians began to consider the option of emigration again.

CONCERNS AND CHANGES

Why, if people were feeling settled and had established a vibrant community life, did so many consider moving from Cyprus in the 1950s? The

decision took into account many different factors for each family and individual. Those who did emigrate to England at this time most often mention an overriding concern for their children's future, in terms of better
opportunities for an education and a career. They also worried that Greek
rather than English would become the official language of the island, and
neither they nor their children were prepared to compete for work in a
language they knew only superficially. At the same time there was a sense
of danger, both immediate and impending, which some felt more intensely
than others.

Mr. Garabed explained how he and his wife decided to leave. "When
we bought the site for building the house, there was no trouble at all. Of
course, there was the *enosis* movement all the time—but not boiling
things. So that question was dormant until 1955, when they started the
EOKA movement and so forth and when the bombs started to go, and
everybody was frightened, especially those Armenians like my wife who
had seen these Turkish massacres and things."

"She especially wanted to leave?" I asked.

Mr. Garabed nodded. "She was the main cause, actually. She said
that we were living in an area where it is on the borderline. And, actually,
a massacre took place—about thirty Greeks were massacred by Turks
there. Now, the boys used to go to school, of course, and they used their
bicycles. There was the British Army trying to cool the uprising, and
EOKA was starting to become bold, and they used to put bombs everywhere. And it became dangerous to live in the quarter where we used to
be. My wife said that we either leave this area, sell the house or rent it, and
go and live in the Greek side, or we must leave this country, and we decided that the best thing was to come to England because [the boys] were
young at the time and we thought that their education would be inter-
rupted. The system would change."

Those who had been sending their children to English secondary
schools or even to the English elementary school had already primed their
children's interest in the British world and in life beyond Cyprus and the
Armenian community. Later some of these children, as teenagers and
young adults, made up their own minds about emigration, based as much
on personal interest and ambitions as on current political circumstances.

Mayda's father had been concerned that the family would lose their
British passports with the independence of Cyprus and thought that they
should consider emigrating. The children were teenagers then and had
their own ideas about this possibility. In her home in London, Mayda explained, "My father actually preferred Australia, and my older brother
ended up there. He didn't like the weather here."

"Why Australia?"

"Because it's English-speaking but the climate also—and economically it's a good place. But I didn't follow. Nor did my younger brother. And neither did my father and mother! Well, in my case it was a choice. I went and looked and I didn't really like it particularly. And I had stayed here. And I'd been to a boarding school for three years and then I went to university and then, when I went to Australia, it seemed like a bit of a wilderness culturally."

"You came over here initially to go to a boarding school?"

"That was my plan. It wasn't their plan! It was my plan and I had managed to get my way. They wanted me to stay in Cyprus and be educated in Cyprus—and perhaps have a year in Beirut doing domestic science! And I just didn't want that."

"So where did you get this idea?" I asked.

"I got it at school. I went to the Junior School, and a lot of my friends were coming to England anyway because they were British. They were all colonials, and they were returning. And I just wanted to go somewhere where I thought that the education would be good. It was very important to me."

Several other young women met and married English soldiers and went back with them after the war. Like the story above, the following account shows how traditions were changing, partly because of the unrest and unusual circumstances but also as a result of the ways parents were then raising their children.

Two sisters had been encouraged by their parents to learn the family business, tailoring, while they were still in school. Both girls enjoyed it and continued to help in the shop after their graduation from high school. A marriage with a Beirut Armenian was tentatively arranged for one of the sisters, Anahid, but after meeting him, she rejected this. Instead she met her future husband in a rather different way.

During the fight for independence, the area inside Nicosia's wall was off-limits to British soldiers. In order not to lose this clientele, the father opened a small shop outside the wall where the men could see the materials, get measured, and pick up their suit or shirt. The two sisters took turns working there.

Anahid continued the story. "One day, while I was working there, a British soldier came in asking about the hours of the pharmacy next door. He looked around a bit, saw the materials, and then decided to order a suit. He came back the next day to be measured and to choose the material. Everything was very normal. Then the next week he came in to find out when he could have a fitting—and he brought a box of chocolates and a box of cigarettes with him! But the first girl was gone! My sister was working that week. He looks and he says, 'This is strange. There is a resemblance but—you're not the same!' My sister said, 'It's okay, she's my sister. Can I help?' He says, 'Yes, I want to find out about my fitting—but also I wanted to give her these chocolates and cigarettes. And there is a ball next week that I wanted to ask her to, because I think she is very nice.' My sister said, 'Oh, no, that's impossible! We are Armenians, and that's not our custom. A girl can never go out with a man in that way!' He said, 'Well, tell her anyway.'

"So she did, when she got home—and I had the same reaction. We couldn't believe it. The next week I went back to the shop, and when he came back I told him the same thing. Armenian girls can't go out alone until they're engaged. 'Okay,' he said, 'let's get engaged!' Then I started to worry that he might be a little bit crazy, you know? I tried to explain that I can't go out with someone I don't know, let alone get engaged to him! 'Well,' he said, 'how are we supposed to get to know each other?' 'Oh. He has a point,' I began thinking. 'How are we supposed to get to know each other?' So I invited him to a tea party at our house a few days later. Family and friends would be there. But our house was inside the city wall, and he's not allowed to go. So I said, 'That's that.' But he said, 'Give me the address anyway and let me see.'"

On the day of the party a truck full of soldiers, with an escort, pulled up at the house, and the young soldier stepped out and was allowed to stay for an hour. He met the young woman's parents; they liked each other and talked awhile. Later, when he asked Anahid out on a date again, she told her father about her problem. "He said, 'Alan seems like a very good man. If you want to, you can get engaged. It's up to you.' So we did."

Though Anahid and her husband left Cyprus for a while, they returned to settle there later. Other mixed (British and Armenian) couples remained in Cyprus, at least for some time.

1960: THE REPUBLIC OF CYPRUS

When independence did come, the new constitution required that minorities officially be counted with either the Greeks or the Turks. Armenians became part of the Greek majority, with a nonvoting representative, Berj Tilbian, seated in the Greek Communal Chambers.[1] Some Armenians were relieved that the outcome was independence and not *enosis* after all and decided to stay. Others were suspicious of the clauses in the constitution that distributed percentages of civil service jobs between the Greek and Turkish communities (80 percent went to the Greeks, and Armenian civil servants were counted among the Greek percentage), feeling that this would increase competition and reduce chances for other minorities. The historic distrust of both Greeks and Turks was reactivated.

Through family memories and what they were taught at school, Armenians retained a distrust of Turkish authority, no matter how friendly they were with individual Turkish neighbors. Schooling also engendered a distrust of the Greeks, based much further back in history, when the Byzantines had periodically tried to dominate the Armenians and force submission of their church to the Orthodox Church. Many feared discrimination by both Greeks and Turks or that animosities between those two groups were only temporarily smoothed over by the recent negotiations and compromises.

Although few Armenians had been physically hurt by the troubles, many had been disturbed and shaken by the fighting, and between 1955 and 1960 469 Armenians left Cyprus, mostly for the United Kingdom.[2] This was a large percentage of the total 1956 Armenian population of 4,549, but at the same time this shows that many more decided to stay in Cyprus—to give it a try, as some have said. As before, it is difficult to pin down the key decisive factor for all. Ties to or sympathy with the British colonial government or Europe generally, the financial resources available to help the family move and become established in another country, memories of past losses and fighting—all these things appear to have influenced the emigrants. The same can be said, however, for those who stayed. Some who moved apparently had very little money with which to do so. Others with much more decided to stay and continue their business in the new Cyprus republic. Certainly lack of funds prevented some families who wanted to emigrate from doing so.

A few men traveled to England, the United States, or Hayastan during the 1950s and early 1960s specifically to see what the prospects were there for themselves and their families. Mr. Vartan, a shop owner now in his sixties, did this, and he remembered how he had reached his decision. "After I had made my trip and looked at many possibilities, I decided on Slough, near Reading, west of London. It was a small town then, which would grow as the family grew. So I came back to Cyprus and we had a family vote on the matter. We tried to have democracy in our family. Everything was decided that way, even when the children were young. And the family decided to stay. Many Armenians did leave, especially in 1959. They feared they would not be well treated. But they were wrong. It is even better than under the British, though the British did try to suppress the majority by helping the minorities."

Following independence came a time of peace in Cyprus, and though their numbers were diminished, Armenians generally continued as before in the old neighborhood, sending children to the old school, building up trade, visiting neighbors. In Nicosia a few families decided to sell their homes in the Turkish quarter or leave their rented homes and move to the Greek side.

NERKAGHT REACHES CYPRUS

Some Armenians continued to leave the island, however; nearly two hundred more settled in the United Kingdom in 1961. In 1962 the Hayastan *nerkaght* (gathering-in) reached Cyprus. Families who wished to emigrate would receive free passage and shipment of their possessions to Hayastan. Some of the families who had been ready to go in the late 1940s but who were passed over in favor of Armenians living elsewhere were among the 486 people who did go in 1962.

Nerkaght differed from emigration to Britain and elsewhere in that the ideal for Armenians was return to the homeland, not further emigration away from it. Though for many of the returnees Hayastan was not their specific part of the homeland (most had never been in the territory that became Soviet Armenia; rather, they were from Cilicia or western Armenia), it was still Armenia, more so than Cyprus and certainly more so than England. A few had family or friends already there. Those going to Hayastan were, with few exceptions, sympathetic to the Soviet state for its protection of that corner of the homeland. This emigration was thus motivated in great part by ideology, a desire to be part of an Armenian state. Whether that state was Communist or capitalist was not the most important consideration.

"I remember my father and others saying, 'Guaranteed, if you go there, you and your children will remain Armenian. Otherwise, anywhere else, it's assimilation. There it's secure, it's certain,'" recounted one man, whose father migrated to England, not Hayastan, because one of his children had already settled there.

But by 1962 family loyalties were severely divided. The decision was not an easy one for a large family. Hrair, who did emigrate to Hayastan but who later returned to Cyprus, remembered vividly that he and his married brother did not want to go but were eventually persuaded by their

father and other family members. "Two representatives came from Hayastan to organize the group. People gathered to ask questions. But the
questions weren't answered. Or sometimes they actually gave the wrong
answers to some things. How could we know? Each family took about
fifteen or twenty crates with them. Some people took their merchandise to
sell from the shops. These people became millionaires because there was
actually *nothing* in the shops there. Socks that were worth forty cents were
sold for eight dollars or so. We wrote back to tell the others, who were
going to follow later, not to come. We had to do this in a sort of code,"
he said.[3]

"People came to Kirovagan to welcome us, the newcomers. Nobody
had arrived since 1949. Children came with flowers. They had let out the
schools to greet us. But we saw that the people were dirty, they had beards,
no fashion as we knew it. We understood from those beards and the
clothes, their expressions, that they were very poor. We were afraid.

"The government arranged, by list, whom we would go with, in
which car. Actually they were big, open trucks and it was winter. On the
boat they had asked which place we preferred—north, south, and so on.
One good thing—Hayastan had central gas and there were none of those
dangerous gas cylinders like we had in Cyprus then. And it was very
cheap. And the house rent, water, heat—they were almost free.

"But it was very hard, very hard. The people who didn't go can't understand. They don't know what we went through there."

After ten years Hrair and others in the family began to try seriously
to return to Cyprus and eventually were successful. Once there they found
that, indeed, some people did not understand why they had come back to
Cyprus, were not willing to listen, and even cut off ties with them. Others
sympathized and welcomed them back. "We were blinded by our love for
Hayastan," said another who had left in the 1960s and later emigrated to
Los Angeles.

A certain innocence or naïveté marked a number of these émigrés to
Hayastan. They were thrilled by reports of progress, Armenian participation in all walks of life, and the care given by the state to all its citizens.
That is not to say that emigration to England and elsewhere did not have
its idealistic aspects. In the case of those who went to Hayastan, however,
it may have been the most important factor in the decision.

Some were also motivated by need. This emigration was affordable,
even for the poorest of families, and it is possible that some of those who
went to Hayastan would have emigrated to Britain or elsewhere earlier,
had they been able. The positive aspect of resettling in the homeland

mingled with the prospect of state care (which included guaranteed employment and pay) and with the fear of future trouble in Cyprus.

TROUBLES BEGIN AGAIN IN CYPRUS

By 1963 approximately three thousand Armenians were living in Nicosia, Larnaca, and Limassol.[4] On the surface, life was good and getting better. Three years of peace had encouraged Armenians to reestablish their social networks, visits, and celebrations and had allowed businesses to adjust and begin to flourish. At the same time Armenians were aware that tensions were building between the Turkish and Greek communities. They were well informed about the constitutional disagreements, remembered the antagonisms and rifts of the 1950s, and had frequently discussed the possible outcome of all of this, but they were still caught by surprise when the fighting broke out in earnest.

One older man said thoughtfully, "After 1902, in Adana, my family moved into a new house, which was built for my mother. She was the daughter of a rich man. But we had to leave. Here we also had a new home."

His wife interjected, "He used to sit on the balcony and say, 'If this house isn't taken from us, I'll be very pleased.' I said to him, 'Who is going to take it? You don't gamble or drink! Why should we lose it?'"

Another story comes from Avo, who is now in his late forties but who was a teenager during the troubles. "When I was a child, life in Cyprus was wonderful—everything was perfect. We were very happy. Then life became very difficult. I lost a few friends in the early fighting, Greeks and also a few Turks. They were close friends. And we lost two boys who used to work for us. The misery and the death you see all around you. Actually, we didn't see much as a family, but as a teenager, I used to go around and see quite a bit.

"I was out one night when the trouble started, and I had to cross town to get home. It was at night—at twelve o'clock—and I'd been at a party and now was going home, alone on the street. The lights went out and I found shelter in an empty coffee shop, the kind where the locals used to go to smoke *narghiles*, all stacked on the shelf for the night now. When things got quiet I sneaked out, walking in the street, trying to be very quiet. Then I saw the machine gun nest and there was a shout! 'Stop!' It was pitch dark; all the streetlights were turned off. 'Don't turn your head!' And there was a long interrogation. 'Yes sir, no sir!' 'Okay, walk straight home and don't turn your head!' Cold sweat reached my toes. I went home and could see the light and the door of our flat open outside and my mother was standing there in the open door, like an open target. Crazy! I threw myself on her and slammed the door and screamed, 'What are you? Crazy? People are killing each other!' And I piled up mattresses in front of the door. I guess I was a little crazy, too."

A couple who had been married only a short time when the troubles started remembered their last night in the Turkish quarter. "When the trouble started, we were at a wedding party at the club. It was after midnight and we were eating, drinking, really enjoying ourselves! And we heard *baboom! baboom!* everywhere! We had to stay there. We didn't dare to leave. Then from there we went to the Melkonian with a UN escort. We couldn't even go home. We went in the wedding dresses and stayed there for fifteen days, wearing the same clothes, day and night. After fifteen days we really wanted to see our house. We went and there were lots of soldiers, Turkish soldiers. They said that Mother must ask the chief of police. So we went to the Saray [Turkish government office] and stayed night and day, waiting. They said no but allowed it another day.

"We went to our house. The new carpet we'd just bought was already worn out by the soldiers, and many other things were ruined. We had just gotten married ourselves and had many nice presents. But in the end we could take only our photographs with us. The soldiers wouldn't give us our sheets. Our clothes, all our valuable things were gone. We had just bought new furniture, in installments, and even though we had to leave everything when we came here [to the Greek side], we still had to pay back what we owed! Before when we used to hear old people's refugee stories, they were like fairy tales. But after that, I understand."

A few older Armenians insisted on staying in their homes in the Turkish quarter during the height of the fighting and might have stayed longer if their children had not persuaded them to leave.

"We stayed ten days in that house while the fighting was going on around us in 1963," said one person. "Then we took a small bag and walked past the Ledra Palace to [my brother's house] and then on to a room at the Melkonian. Later the Turks phoned and said we could come back and take our things. So we went with the United Nations. We were able to save the piano, but we had to leave many important things because the Turks said they needed them. Never mind, we are all right. They didn't hurt us, and during those ten days they used to knock on the door and say, 'Hodja [teacher], we will feed you, don't worry! What do you need?' " Their house, like many others, was taken over as offices and living quarters for the Turkish Cypriot armed forces.

Many families were able to return at some point—two weeks or a month later—and load into a car what they could of what had not been looted, ruined, or confiscated. These visits were usually limited to one car or a specific amount of time. Others managed to arrange for Turkish friends to go to their old homes, collect important things, such as photographs, and take them to a spot where they could be retrieved—for example, at the workplace. But many people left quickly with very little and never recovered any of their possessions.

Within a few weeks almost every Armenian living in the Turkish quarter had moved or been moved to the Greek side. Besides the homes and businesses, also lost were the Melikian-Ouzunian primary school, the church, and the club. The Melkonian Institute, being south of Nicosia, was safe and was used as housing for many and as temporary quarters for the primary school. Families scattered throughout the Greek side of Nicosia, to wherever they could find housing with family or friends, and then rented accommodations.

ADJUSTING TO THE GREEN LINE

A dividing line, the Green Line, was drawn across the map of Nicosia, just south of the church, and the town was divided by barbed wire, blockades, and checkpoints. Movement across the Green Line was restricted but possible, and a few Armenians continued to work on the Turkish side while living on the Greek side. Fighting continued between Greeks and Turks for some time, but Armenians again tried to stay out of it. Emigration was not as easy in 1964 as it had been earlier, but a number of people, especially women and children, went for extended visits to relatives in England. As tensions remained high, more Armenians found ways to arrange visas for emigration.

One young couple in Nicosia faced these tensions daily, as both husband and wife crossed the Green Line to continue with their jobs, one in Kyrenia, the other at a British bank in the Turkish quarter of Nicosia. "At first the commute [to Kyrenia] wasn't bad, but gradually it became more and more dangerous, and one day it was reported that my husband and another man—they always drove together—had been killed! Fortunately it wasn't reported to me, or I would have died!" the wife, Armineh, recounted.

"Another time Hovaness called to tell me that he was starting out from Kyrenia. Our friend came by my office to take me home because it was a particularly dangerous day. After the phone call we thought everything would be fine. But then he didn't get home for six hours![5] We died a million times in between! There was a neighbor who had a tall roof and she could see the Kyrenia road from there. She used to go up every day and watch and then call down to me when she spotted his car off in the distance: 'Here comes Hovaness!' But this day she kept going up and seeing nothing. Finally he arrived. It turned out that soldiers had stopped him and insisted on using his car to take wounded men to a clinic or somewhere up by St. Hilarion."

Meanwhile, at her own job, Armineh had been working with three other Armenian women in their office. Then the British managers decided that it was too dangerous to keep crossing over the border and that they would be safer working from home. So the two men each took one of the secretaries and left Armineh to manage the main office with the other one. There was also a Turkish man who worked as a messenger there, and he had become very close to Armineh and Hovaness.

"We used to give the [Turkish man's] family lots of gifts at weddings, holidays, and so on because they were very poor. That man told me that he would watch out for me. Not to worry. Downstairs, by then, it was mostly Turkish people working in the bank. One day the bank was completely surrounded by people protesting the British. By then the Turks had also turned against the British. I let everyone go home and was left there alone in the big building with the Turkish messenger. People were throwing rocks and getting very angry outside! And I was getting angry and scared inside and wondering how I was going to get home myself! Everyone else who'd been there lived on the Turkish side, close to the bank.

"Finally I called the manager and told him that he had better help me. And he came with a police escort or an army escort, I don't remember, and they took me away. He gave me a ride as far as the checkpoint but he said that he wouldn't cross over to the Greek side to take me home because it was too dangerous! So I had to walk from one checkpoint, presenting my card on the Turkish side, and on to the Greek checkpoint to present my card again. Such a long walk. And then walk home. That was the longest walk I've ever taken. The manager told me to take the next few days off when he left me . . . and I was too numb to think straight then. But when I got home and thought about it, I called him and told him that I was not going back there at all. They could give me a job in the Greek division. So they did."

Those who had lost their jobs and businesses tried to retrieve what goods they could when allowed to cross over under escort to their old shops. Much had been destroyed or heavily damaged in the fighting; the old stores had been looted, and there was little to bring across to stock new stores. Before 1963 a few had already opened small branches of their shops on the Greek side of the old town or even outside the city walls. These had begun partly as extensions of family businesses as the new generation grew up. Younger Armenians wanted to continue the family business, but in many cases the old shops were too small for all to continue together. Also, the new generation spoke Greek and saw no reason to restrict themselves to the Turkish quarter. Others, such as Anahid's father, had opened branches outside the walls when the movement of their British clients had been restricted during the 1950s. These people were the fortunate ones when Nicosia was divided, as they were able to start again from a small but established base and could begin rebuilding immediately.

Others who had lost everything found work with relatives or friends, but this was not easily accomplished, as nearly everyone was hard up. Young mothers and other women who had not expected to work outside the home began looking for jobs as well. Some were able to use their multilingual skills to find secretarial jobs, radio work, or teaching. A few saw the turn of events as an opportunity to do something they had always wished to do: begin their own business. Their husbands could not provide money for the family for the moment, and it seems that in a number of families this meant that there was a general rethinking of what it was possible and necessary for women to do to help the family. Such activity by women followed in the footsteps of a few others who had made a similar move after the turmoil of the 1950s, and it was a precursor for those who would follow the same route later, in 1974.

Mrs. Azadouhie, now in her early seventies, still runs the successful business she began at that time. Her husband had had a successful workshop on the Turkish side of Nicosia, but during the troubles the business was damaged and lost. Her husband, older than her by some years, was crushed by the loss and hesitated to start something new. She told me of how, as she pushed her baby's pram, wondering what to do, she noticed an empty shop owned by a friend of the family. She went to him and asked him to rent it to her. Shocked at first, he said no, but eventually he was sufficiently persuaded to accompany her to their house and discuss it with her husband.

"Then my husband said, 'All Azadouhie knows how to do is *spend* money!'" She laughed as she remembered this and added, "It was true— I didn't know anything! But I wanted so much to try this."

The friend appealed to her husband's love of gambling and told him he should not be afraid to take a risk. He agreed to rent the shop to Azadouhie for a certain time and if it worked, fine; if not, he would take no rent money. Starting with very small amounts of merchandise, she eventually built up her business, losing heavily during the 1963 troubles, building again, losing again in 1974, and again rebuilding.

MAJOR CHANGES AFTER 1963

As they gradually settled into new homes and began to work and rebuild their lives, Armenians found that certain important aspects of their former community life had become completely transformed in their new setting. Some of this was perhaps an inevitable consequence of developments in modern taste and technology, such as in housing, or of the influence of concurrent developments in the diaspora (club life, for example).[6] But now, in addition to the still decreasing numbers of the community, there was a sudden and drastic break with the past. A whole way of life had been left behind on the Turkish side of the Green Line along with Armenian institutions, homes, and businesses.

Instead of a compact neighborhood with a central core of church, club, and school, there was nothing resembling a distinct Armenian neighborhood. Homes were spread around southern Nicosia, wherever it was possible to find space. The primary school was first housed at the Melkonian, just south of Nicosia, and then in a storefront on Makarios Avenue, closer to the center of town. Church services were held in a Greek Orthodox church, a mile southwest of the center, and later the vicarage and church office (*arachnortaran*) were set up halfway between that church and the Paphos Gate. The AGBU began meeting on the Melkonian grounds, and from that point there was no social organization as politically vague as the club had been. Formerly tacit connections now became open and clear. Each group held its own separate meetings and built up its own network of activities. At the same time, the geographic spread meant that arrangements and publicity for these meetings had to be organized in a different, more deliberate way.

As a means to pass information along the grapevine, the telephone began to replace the chance encounter, a conversation between someone leaning over the balcony and another person in the street below, or a chat in a shop doorway. The spontaneity of individual encounters was reduced, and people had to plan more to see each other. Cars and taxis were relied on more to get to work, to the clubs, to church. Many continued to use bicycles, but few were willing or able to walk to all these places. The scattered homes, use of cars, and lack of an Armenian center meant a considerable increase in privacy, which some may have welcomed; this was echoed by a similar increase of privacy inside each home. For the most part, the new homes were relatively recently built and were quite different in layout from the old homes in the Turkish quarter. The older homes had been built around a large central hall, and all doors opened onto this family room. Newer apartments and houses often used a corridor to connect bedrooms, kitchen, and living room (cf. Crawford 1985; Hirschon 1989).[7] Just as important, television became more common, encouraging the trend toward self-containment in the home. Ironically, television eventually became the only tangible link with the Turkish Cypriots and their language.

Meanwhile Armenians quickly began to improve their vernacular Greek as that language became crucial in their daily lives. School lessons in "proper" Greek, both *demotiki* (modern spoken Greek) and *katharevousa* (literary Greek), were taken more seriously, as children's future job opportunities were seen to depend on correct grammar in both informal and formal communication with their Greek peers. Turkish took on an added stigma. Children in Nicosia were no longer exposed to much Turkish, except from some grandparents and television. Their friends were now Armenian, Greek, English, or American, and their linguistic skills developed accordingly. Middle-aged adults struggled to learn better Greek, but many older people simply continued speaking in Armenian or Turkish and relied on their families to communicate with the world at large.

The most important effect was the very tangible feeling of insecurity and vulnerability that was left. Armenians who were born in Cyprus, whether *deghatsi* or those under forty, had not themselves been directly affected by war until then. The losses and the move were difficult and very sad, but more troubling was the idea that things were still unsettled. Emigration was reconsidered by some, although many preferred to stay in Cyprus "if possible." It seemed pointless to make plans for the future when no one had any idea how things were going to turn out, and yet it was necessary.

EMIGRATION AND REBUILDING

"My husband's family business was supposed to support five families by then," said one woman who left Cyprus around this time, "and his father said that somebody should go to London—because what if something happens in Cyprus? So we ended up here [in London]. It was a family, not a personal, decision. Otherwise, why would we have come? I still like Cyprus, the sweet smells, a lot of flowers, honeysuckle, pine and thyme in the mountains."

For many Armenians still in Cyprus, somehow neither emigration nor staying was clearly the right choice. A number of women reported that their doctors began giving them tranquilizers "so I could cope." The birth rate dropped drastically, undoubtedly due not just to the unsettled times but also to a combination of emigration, abortion, and the introduction of the Pill. People worried again about their children's future and immediate safety. For some, worry became a way of life.

Those who were children at the time now remember more of the adventurous aspects of the move to the Greek side and delight at the setting of the new school. A young professional woman recalled, "At that time, after 1963, the Melikian Varjaran, or Nareg School [the primary school was renamed after the move], was in what is now the AGBU club. It was nice there, near the Melkonian, a lot of woods, places for picnics. When we were there it was fun, like a different world. We would play a lot of games. I have very happy memories of those days. We also had Girl Guides there. We used to play war, girls against the boys. They would climb one tree, and they had a king and we had a queen."

Gradually the Nicosia Armenians rebuilt their community and their homes. Those in other towns, Larnaca and Limassol, had no physical losses and were able to help those in Nicosia. But these families were also affected by the turmoil of Nicosia and their own decrease in population. While political negotiations went on, working toward a settlement of the "Cyprus problem," Armenian life became more and more routine, again centering on family, work, church, clubs. As years passed, living in limbo became normal, and people took less notice of the soldiers and political talks, focusing more on daily matters: taking care of the family and home, providing and preparing food, planning the next meeting, preparing the next day's lessons for class, and so on.

1974 AND FURTHER LOSSES

In the years after 1963 there was increased talk of *enosis,* periodic threats of invasion by the Turks, and still much hope for a peaceful future. But the anti-Makarios coup in July 1974 brought back all the fear. Armenians stayed home and waited, but the next stage came quickly—and their nightmares appeared to be coming true. The Turkish army was invading. Many Armenians in Nicosia piled children and overnight bags into their cars and drove to Dhikelia, the site of the nearest British airbase, for protection. There they camped in their cars under trees, waiting for the fighting to end. Those who could manage it got on planes or boats and left Cyprus, at least temporarily. This time, though, Armenians in Kyrenia and Famagusta were the most severely affected, as they, like Greeks in the north and Turks in the south, were evacuated from their homes and allowed to take only a suitcase. In Famagusta an old church was left behind. Surp Magar, in the mountains, was also lost, a major blow to the community.

Still more Armenians left Cyprus, now spreading as much to the United States and Australia as to England. Those who stayed began once more the process of rebuilding. Some were able to be philosophical about the situation, as was Mr. Vartan, a shopkeeper in his seventies. "When I was young I read a story about a German philosopher whose family was very poor. When he was young he had to walk to school in the snow in bare feet! He used to ask God, 'Why?' and he would whine and cry until one day he saw someone with no feet. Then he said, 'Thank God, at least I have feet. I won't complain anymore!' In 1963 we lost our home, but I said, 'Thank God—the family is okay and the business is not gone.' In '74, though, I went to work after my thirty-second wedding anniversary. My son and family were visiting, we were all together. I went to work and found that my shop had been burned out by torches thrown from the other side! I said 'Thank God, at least my family is all right!' But it was much harder in '74. If you lose your home, it's nothing. But if you lose your livelihood, that's really hard."

Losing their home was the worst experience for others. Araxi's family had lost their home in 1963. By 1974 she was married and had two children. Having lost his first business in 1963, her husband had built up a new one and was doing very well until it was destroyed during the fighting that year.

"We had a very nice home, an apartment," Araxi recounted. "But it was very close to the Green Line. Hagop came home and said, 'We've got to move to a safer area.' My brother had just lost everything, my father had lost his shop, Hagop had lost his business. And he didn't want to lose everything in our house as well. But I didn't want to move—I liked our house. But he insisted, so we went out and looked. We found something very small, no cupboards, not nice. I started to cry, I couldn't even talk to the landlord. 'I can't move into this place!' But within two days we had moved in, with everything we owned. Hagop, my brother, my father, they all did it together.

"Then the night we moved in, Hagop came home and said, 'I'm bringing some UN people home for dinner!' So in that tiny kitchen I prepared something for them, and we ate!"

For others, the events of 1974 were politically galvanizing, as a community leader in his sixties told me. "1974 was a turning point for me— toward nationalistic chauvinism. A complete turnabout. It makes me very angry. I used to be against fanaticism of any sort. Racism, for example. And yet when it comes to Turks now, I'm one myself. I hate the Turks. And yet we made friends with them. As individuals, you can't hate them."

REBUILDING AGAIN

After 1974 there were no more individual Turks to make friends with in southern Cyprus. Relations between Armenians and Greeks became less ambiguous after the division of the island and the establishment of restrictions on crossing the border. Armenians became the "natural" allies of the Greeks, the two groups coming together in their misfortune. Armenians in the 1950s had not been able to rally themselves against the British, as the Greeks had. Throughout the 1960s and early 1970s intra-Greek fighting for and against *enosis* had clouded the situation. But the Turkish invasion and subsequent loss of territory redefined and crystallized the problem and left no doubt as to where Armenian sympathies lay. And at the same time Greek popular emphasis also shifted from *enosis* to an interest in Cyprus as an independent nation.

The relationship between Greeks and Armenians was helped by the Greek Cypriot government's decision to include Armenians who had lost property in 1963 with those who would receive aid for the 1974 displacements. Thus international aid for the refugees of 1974 was distributed to Armenian claimants as well. A few families went to refugee housing provided by the government. The government had already granted a sizeable piece of land (seven and a half *donums*) on the Acropolis for the construction of a new Armenian church, school, and priests' housing and offices. Expenses for the school, including salaries for teachers, were also paid by the government. In later years more aid followed, such as partial grants for tuition at nonstate (non-Greek) schools, an annual grant to the church, and another land grant on which a rest home was built in the 1980s by Aram Kalaydjian, then the Armenian representative.

Armenians as a group had turned their attention to Greek language and Greek affairs since 1963 and had begun making more Greek friends and contacts. But in the years after 1963 there had remained some hope of the return of Armenian properties and the reunification of Nicosia and the whole of the island. After 1974, as the months and then years went by, Armenians came to realize that "we are living on a Greek island now." As both Armenians and Greeks began to prosper again, some Armenians joined Greek-organized clubs, such as the Lions, Lionesses, and swimming and tennis clubs, and began to mix more than previous generations had. Teenagers continued to meet at secondary school, but dating and intermarriage also increased.

After 1974 Kyrenia and Famagusta existed for Armenians only as dreams, and Armenians seem to have been less hopeful than their Greek neighbors about their return. "They say, 'We'll go back! We'll get our lands back!' I tell them, 'That's what we used to say, too.' We know the Turks. We'll never get our lands back. And neither will they. It's finished."[8] There had not been many Armenian residents in those towns, and most emigrated after 1974, having lost all their property and most, if not all, their possessions. A few were later able to sell their property at greatly reduced prices. Those living in Larnaca and Limassol had also seen fighting this time but had lost little. Instead, the biggest change for these towns was a great increase in population, first as Greek refugees were rehoused and later as tourism, also displaced from Kyrenia and Famagusta, quickly developed in these areas. The airport was transferred from Nicosia, where it was by then a no-man's land occupied by the United Nations, to Larnaca, and these quiet port towns became crowded and very different, seemingly overnight.

A man in his forties, born in Larnaca, explained, "I loved Larnaca before, when it was a small, sleepy town. You knew everybody, you could go downtown and see your friends, you'd walk down the street and see all your friends. Now you can go along, stay downtown for a while, and not see two people you know. This morning I went there for half an hour and came back. There was nobody there. Everyone has left, anyway."

Not everyone had left, of course. But so many had by the late 1970s that every Armenian family had close relatives—brothers, sisters, children—living in other parts of the world. While immediate neighbors, both Armenians and Greeks, influenced their lives, so too did these far-flung relations, even though contact was limited by the distance. By then letter-writing was becoming replaced by the telephone and by more-frequent visits. There was more to the communication than a mutual exchange of information about family activities and growth. Knowledge of options and opportunities outside Cyprus could be gathered into a plan of how to stay in Cyprus while making some small investment abroad, or it could become part of a long-term scheme to gradually move the family. Those remaining wanted to stay, if it was at all possible. And at the same time some who had left used this communication as a means of keeping the option of return open "when things calm down."

Young people going abroad to study were often met and cared for by aunts, uncles, or close friends of their parents living in that country. Visits between Cyprus and other countries, especially Britain, kept Cypriots abreast of the latest worldwide styles in fashion, food, home decor, and other trends but also kept relatives overseas in touch with Cyprus. Cyprus, and especially memories of how things had been before 1963, served as a background against which the émigrés could compare life in other places. And though visits and calls revealed major changes, Cyprus also meant continuity and connection with one's past. This was important to most, but not all, who left.

Armenians in Cyprus still had a deep trust in Britain and appreciated the peaceful interlude they had enjoyed between World War I and 1950. The fact of living in diaspora, being vulnerable to neighboring groups, was never far from their minds, however, and they were aware that the balance could someday change. After 1963 there was also increased fear of assimilation. Fluency in vernacular Cypriot Greek became standard among the new generation, and many studied it seriously. The use of Turkish began to diminish. Insecurity and concern over the future had become a way of life, and with good reason. Many older people who had arrived as refugees in 1915 or 1922 were again homeless in 1963—and some again in 1974. "Moving, changing places, starting over—this is the real Armenian story," I was told by a woman who had lost her business twice in Cyprus—and had begun again each time.

Kai Erikson recognizes this increased feeling of vulnerability among those exposed to "extreme trauma." Analyzing the psychological aftermath of the 1972 Buffalo Creek flood, he notes that although people tend to overlook or come to terms with danger in the world "in order to maintain their sanity," victims of disaster react differently, "if only to compensate for the fact that they underestimated those perils once before; but what is worse, far worse, is that they sometimes live in a state of almost constant apprehension because they have lost the human capacity to screen the signs of danger out of their line of vision" (Erikson 1976, 234).

On the surface, Armenians who stayed in Cyprus after the traumatic events of 1960, 1963, and 1974 picked up what pieces were left and created a new kind of family and community life. But worry and fear continue to be constant, aggravated continually by developments in the rest of the eastern Mediterranean and the Near East.

Many chose to emigrate rather than continue to live with such uncertainty. The population of the Armenian community dropped from nearly five thousand in 1955 to just over two thousand in 1975. By the late 1970s, Armenians Cypriots had spread to Britain, America, Hayastan, Australia, and various countries in Africa, South America, and Europe. Connections with Britain were most frequent and evident, but as it became increasingly difficult to obtain long-term visas, as economic opportunities there appeared to wane, and as the cost of higher education rose, more and more students and emigrants looked elsewhere. Britain remained prominent in people's minds, though, through the networks that already had been established.

Chapter 8

London Life
Diaspora of a Diaspora

One day Stepan was given a new picture book, and his father sat down with him to take a look.

"What's this one?"

"A dog!"

"And this one, Stepan?"

"A mouse!" the little boy replied. And so on through cats, elephants, lions, tigers, until finally Stepan was stumped.

"What's this one?" the father said, pointing to a particular animal.

"Dunno."

"Yes, you do. Think a little."

"Dunno!"

"*Aman!*" his father cried. "This is not possible! My own son, and the only animal he doesn't know is a donkey?"

As Stepan's father mournfully recounted this story, he added, "How far have we come from Cyprus in one generation?"

Other events and symbols evoke similar questions from London Armenians of various backgrounds, and there often follows a discussion: "How far have we come?" "Who are we?" "Where are we going?" "What is important to us as Armenians and as individual people?" In this chapter the focus will be on Armenian Cypriots in London, their arrival and the building of community there, the continuity that the Cyprus connection gives to many, and the shared symbols and experiences that they feel separate them from other Armenians and from other British peoples.

Initially Armenians who emigrated were trading physical insecurity for the unknown or, in some cases, a mistaken conception of life in Britain. Armenians were acquainted with the English, having lived under colonial rule, but the picture some of the older generation had built up of life in Britain was probably closer to heaven than anything possible on earth. This had come from selected reading (clearly not Dickens), listening to the BBC, limited contacts with the colonial government representatives, and the accepted version of history at the time. Britain was a great colonial power. Nobody really expected the streets to be paved with gold, but certainly the new neighbors would be well educated, highly cultured, civilized people, life would be secure, and the children could take advantage of the more varied and advanced educational and job opportunities there.

One man remembered how his mother had pushed and helped him to study so that he would earn a place in an English boarding school. "We were coming from a colony where Anglophilia was the ultimate. It was everything. Everybody wanted to come to England, where education was the best. That was what we believed." His wife, a Palestinian Armenian, added that this was the same all over the Near East at the time, and she had come to England for the same reasons.

Between 1930 and 1950 a number of young Armenian men and a few women came from Cyprus to study in England: law, accounting, engineering, music. Several of these decided to stay, but all provided their families and friends with impressions of life in England through their letters and infrequent visits home. Life in England in the 1930s was a series of major adjustments for these student adventurers. They began to miss the comforts of home and certain foods they had once taken for granted.

"Ah, how we would wish for some figs or a piece of sweet watermelon in the summer! But did you hear what happened to Dikran? One day he came back to his boarding house, very excited. 'Look, boys! I've found a watermelon!' It was terribly expensive, but he'd bought it anyway, just so they could have a taste of home, a special treat. He handed it over proudly to the landlady with instructions to serve it after the evening meal. They sat down that night—it didn't matter what the main course was, boiled cabbage, gray meat, who cared? They were thinking only of what was to follow. So, as they finished, Dikran called to the landlady, 'Yes, we're ready now, you can bring the watermelon!' And she came in and placed it on the table, still steaming from the oven!"

Britain then had a very small Armenian population, based in Manchester (through the textile trade) and in London (through finance, banking, and education). Prominent among these was Calouste Gulbenkian, who provided the major financing for the construction of a jewel-like chapel in Kensington. Consecrated in 1922, Surp Sarkis was also used by the Armenian community for regular weekly services. Manchester's Armenian church had been built by 1870.[1] Approximately five hundred Armenians were in Britain by 1950, and the two major Armenian political parties and their associated cultural organizations had established local branches, though meetings were infrequent.

In the 1950s this gradual growth accelerated.[2] Some Palestinian and Egyptian Armenian families came to London (others had gone around the same time to Cyprus). These were joined in the later years of the decade by families from Cyprus. Surp Sarkis served as a hub of information and contact as people went to find out who had come, who could help, where to look for housing or jobs. Families who found housing then had a stream of others camping in their living room while they searched. Some were able to buy a house or apartment and then rent rooms to boarders to augment or supply their income. Traditionally, Armenian newcomers settle near their church and school, but in London there was no school, and property near Surp Sarkis was prohibitively expensive. Instead, homes were found to the west and north, in Chiswick, Ealing, Muswell Hill, Dollis Hill, Cricklewood, and elsewhere, all easily accessible by bus or underground.

"What were your first impressions of England when you came?" I asked Mr. Avedis. He had emigrated with his wife and two children, having taken early retirement in Cyprus.

"Well, after Cyprus, of course, where we were in a close-knit community, we used to write letters back home and say that we miss this, we miss that," he replied. "For instance, as I explained the social life. It was altogether different, like the North and South Poles. At least in the beginning. For several years it went on like that, until one gets, first of all, acclimatized—to the weather, maybe, and then to the social thing. And by and by, people started leaving Cyprus. You know, so-and-so has gone to England; why don't we?

"So, humans being what they are, they get used to the most difficult conditions and sorrows and things like that. We miss, of course, Cyprus. Again, for the sunshine and for the friends and for the community thing, which, compared to what we have here, in spite of the fact that we are active, both of us, in Armenian affairs [will never be the same]."

Though the households were spread out, men and women both made an effort to visit family and friends, to maintain somehow the ties they had once taken for granted in Cyprus. Those with cars had to overcome the formidable English driving test and then venture out into the maze of London's streets. The many without cars learned the workings of London Transport. Women who had never traveled across Nicosia alone found themselves sitting beside total strangers, changing trains and buses to spend an afternoon with a friend.

This was a far-reaching change for both men and women, and for their perceptions of each other and themselves, but equally important to both was the knowledge that their social life generally could never resemble what they had left in Cyprus. Distance and time spent traveling meant that most encounters had to be planned and thus were more formal. This changed the nature as well as the number of friendships and even family relationships. As in Cyprus, after 1963 the telephone became increasingly important.

The urban setting and size of London radically altered cultural patterns and hastened many other changes that might have come eventually in the old neighborhood and which, to some degree, did come with the displacements of 1963 and 1974.[3] The attention of all, but in particular perhaps that of the very oldest and most dependent émigrés, was focused on the act of settlement, rebuilding, and coping with London itself. Armenians in Cyprus had been living in a city, but the difference in population alone (in 1960 Nicosia's population was around 95,000; in 1961 the population of London was 7,992,443) made the change one of substance rather than just degree. There was much to learn from fellow émigrés, neighbors, and coworkers, and also from the children as they made their way through the system, bringing home English friends and new ideas.

The first priority was to pay the rent or mortgage and buy food and other immediate necessities. This meant a change in career for many middle-aged and older men and an introduction to work outside the home for a number of women. Former civil servants turned to working for others in bookkeeping, accounting, or insurance, as did others who felt it was too late in their lives to begin a new business of their own in a new country. Others did open their own shops, selling food or dry goods; some began (or continued) import-export businesses. Some young women with good English skills found secretarial work, while others, young and old, worked from home or nearby as hairdressers or seamstresses. Brentford Nylons, while under the ownership of Khatchig Metrebian, hired a large number of Armenians throughout the 1960s and early 1970s. Many remember him with gratitude, as he helped them to earn the important first paychecks and get started in London.

Some young people, male and female, aimed for academic or professional careers, beginning studies in art history, literature, architecture, journalism, music, law, pharmacy, accounting, engineering, and other fields. It had been "for the children" and young people that families said they came, and with this generation, Armenians from Cyprus pursued a variety of jobs that had not been possible before. But many found the transition more difficult than expected. Children under thirteen had had only one or two years of English lessons at the Melikian before arrival, unless they had attended one of the English-language schools, and those between ten and thirteen found it especially hard to catch up with their English schoolmates. A few of the wealthier families sent their children to private school, and a small number attended such schools on scholarship, but most attended their local primary or secondary state school.

One mother, a former teacher herself, remembered, "Education had become a political game in England. Our boys suffered in that time, and discipline had gotten worse as well. All the Cypriot Armenian children suffered—a new country, all the worries of the family, and a new language at school. The boys cried so much at night . . . and I suffered for them as well. The boys adjusted and learned the language very quickly. But until then, that point, they really suffered, psychologically and everything. There were those exams that the children had to take to get into the grammar schools—and the Armenians couldn't do it because of the language, and they lost confidence in themselves. They became shy and introverted."

Many found themselves facing prejudice for the first time on the school playgrounds. Mushegh, for example, arrived at age twelve and understood just enough English to follow the teacher. "But I couldn't understand the boys' accent at all, and aside from me, there were no other foreigners in the school at that time. Since they hadn't seen foreigners before, they bullied me.

"There was one hard year, but then gradually I found some boys I got along with and we became friends. But there wasn't any socializing because we were always with Armenian friends and relatives. My parents didn't really enter the local community much. There was this split between school and home life, friends."

Younger children and those who had attended either primary or secondary schools in English in Cyprus adjusted more easily to the change, but even the smallest ones had their problems. Rita, for example, went on to be an elementary school teacher, but she said, "I remember nursery. I learned enough English quickly. Mum helped me at home, and I started to understand what was going on. But there was one thing that always terrified me. In the afternoon, the class would sit in a circle and the teacher would ask each of us to sing or recite a nursery rhyme. Of course I didn't know any! How could I? So each time she would ask me, I couldn't do it, and each time she smacked me! And I was so humiliated—it was awful! I would go home and cry and cry."

Family, extended family, and old friends were relied upon by new arrivals of all ages to provide some comfort and relief as well as pleasure during the time of transition. In the early 1960s a house was acquired in Cheniston Gardens near Surp Sarkis. Hay Doon (Armenian House) became the social center on Sundays as families, single students, and working people walked over after church, had lunch together, and spent the afternoon chatting and catching up on news, playing backgammon or cards, or getting involved in budding community projects. These included a choir of Armenian sacred and folk song led by an Egyptian Armenian student and later by a Melkonian graduate, drama productions, picnics, lectures, and so on. As evening came families went home, some taking newcomers with them to continue sharing food and conversation there. Young people often stayed on to dance or went out to explore London together.

Tamar was a teenager at the time. "I suppose the social life was very much taken up by the Armenians, youth society. There were dances, very informal dances, not like they are nowadays. We were very few, and so we kind of stuck together and we went to church and then after church, it was Sunday, and everybody said, 'God, isn't London an enormous place and it's such an effort to get together!' And so then we would either sing in the choir or whatever and then we would go to the Armenian House and have lunch and sort of hang around all Sunday. Or organize, you know. There was a choir and a drama group."

The international Armenian organizations, which had lain dormant until the new wave of immigration, were rejuvenated, and other clubs were established. The key change was the increase in organization itself. This was a change both for London's small Armenian community and for the Armenians from Cyprus, for whom organization and planned activity would eventually become the core of their visible culture rather than a side product. The informal social life that Nicosia, Larnaca, and Limassol had allowed and fostered was fundamentally changed. Even with the displacement of 1963, Armenians in Cyprus had not been as physically separate as they found themselves in London. Extended families who had once shared homes or at least been only a few doors away were split by the move, with some members staying in Cyprus and others moving elsewhere, or, if all were in London, limited by the scarcity of affordable and available housing to separate homes in different neighborhoods.

Among those arriving in 1974 were Sona and her husband. They had just returned to Cyprus from their university studies in Hayastan, and though jobs were difficult to find in their own fields, they had settled in and found work in the textile trade with a relative. Not long afterward their first child was born, and then, four months later, the war started. Having lost their homes and work, they decided to try to join their sisters in England. I asked why they hadn't gone back to Hayastan, as they had been educated there.

"It's hard to explain," was Sona's answer. "It's our country. I love it. But being brought up in the West . . . and it's very different when you're there. There are so many things that I love, but there's a lot of Russian influence. And it's the system, both good and bad. The people are friendly, hospitable, they have time for you, spread the table, everything. But the freedom to travel is the most important. If that changed, then lots of Armenians would go there to live. But we don't want to go if we can't go out again.

"This [England] was the only country where I really wanted to go. It was difficult, we had no money, but we were allowed to stay on a yearly basis. Then, after four or five years, we were given British passports. I couldn't do my own work. I would have had to retrain. So I found a job as a secretary in an export-import business. And I did a quick course.

"When we arrived, the only one who helped us, outside our family, was the man from Brentford Nylons [Metrebian]. He really wanted to help, offered jobs, hired us in his factory, hired solicitors to help us. One day he even had his driver take me all the way to Croydon [where the passport office was located] in his Rolls-Royce!"

Mr. Metrebian was the most visible, and seems to have helped the largest number of people, but several other Armenians who had established businesses in London also helped the newcomers in the 1960s and 1970s by finding temporary jobs for them.[4] For the most part, family and close friends provided the network of aid and information. Those who arrived after the main group provided fresh ties with Cyprus and with the Armenian language.

ARMENIAN SCHOOLS

At work, at school, and in the neighborhoods, Armenian men and women came into more contact with non-Armenians than before. Because of this and the lack of an Armenian school, many teenagers did not develop their Armenian-language skills, younger children began to forget theirs, and new British-born children often did not learn more than a few phrases. Some parents made heroic efforts to continue language use at home and to teach the new generation. In the early 1960s this was done with the confidence of those whose first tongue was Armenian and who had not really thought of the possibility of speaking anything else at home with their spouse and children. By the mid-1970s, however, young parents no longer had this confidence.

For a time in the early 1960s Armenian classes were organized, but it was not until 1978, almost twenty years after the arrival of the first large group of families from Cyprus, that the first Armenian school was begun. By then a second church was open, and a church council had been elected by the community. Classes were held on Sunday mornings next to the new church, but student numbers grew from around 60 to 170, and soon they moved to a secondary school in Ealing. Today there are some twenty classes, separate ones at each level for eastern and western dialects, for ages ranging from five to adult. Though initially money was provided from a trust donated by Kevork Tahta, the parents and teachers of the school now raise the £25,000 needed annually.

Later two other weekend schools opened, one on Saturdays and the other also on Sundays as part of a Hnchak club. By the 1980s, then, a form of Armenian schooling was again available in London, though limited to one morning a week.[5] But the long break without schools and the distances involved meant that many Cypriot Armenian families found it easier to continue without schools than to rearrange their schedules around it.

An important change is that after the beginning of the first Armenian school, the other such schools in London have not been located next to the churches because of size limitations, convenience, and finances. This has meant a further break from the involvement and appearance of the church in daily life. Whereas children in Cyprus and most communities in the Near East saw the Apostolic Church and its priests as a matter of course in their daily lives, in London it became another matter for organization and planning. Priests and the bishop do visit the schools when invited, to explain some of the ritual and doctrine of the Armenian church, and teachers give lessons in Armenian church history as well as guide classes through some Bible stories. The children are taught to sing several of the hymns and prayers.

CHURCH

In the early 1960s there were a number of boys and young men who had had experience as altar boys and deacons in Cyprus, and these were available to help at Surp Sarkis. As this crop of altar boys grew older, however, there were fewer and fewer with the education and experience to replace them. The fact that so few were being trained in London was masked by the continuing arrival of new immigrants from Cyprus and later Beirut and Iran, but gradually the use of altar boys was phased out at Surp Sarkis except on special holy days. This was not only because of the lack of schools connected to the church but also the result of a general decrease in church attendance. Many children growing up in London were not regularly exposed to the church except on special occasions such as weddings, christenings, or Easter.

However, decreasing attendance on an individual basis did not mean that the church was less full each week. As the Armenian population grew, Surp Sarkis became too small. Its capacity of around a hundred was not enough for major holidays, large weddings, or big funerals. The need for a larger building coincided with the belief of many that it was time to have a church governed by elected laymen, as is usual in the Armenian church, rather than by an appointed board. The Gulbenkian Trust administered Surp Sarkis, and thus its congregation had to worry neither about its functioning nor about funding. The church council is also the only elected body to govern or oversee general Armenian affairs outside the more particular programs of the political clubs.

However, the transition from one church to two was clouded by conflicts of personality and politics, and the need for physical expansion and self-government was not the prime interest of all at the time. Rather, the beginning of the new church, named Surp Bedros, took the form of another split in the community.

FORMAL STRUCTURES TODAY

Today both churches are located in Kensington and are affiliated with the Catholicosate of Etchmiadzin. Armenian Cypriots and their families attend both and participate as choir members and directors, deacons, and wardens. Unlike Surp Sarkis, Surp Bedros does occasionally use altar boys, relying on a core group of committed families. Surp Bedros seats many times more people and, though uncomfortable and difficult to heat, attracts a very large crowd on holidays.

Vered Amit Talai discusses the debates over control of the Church Council (LACCC, or London Armenian Community Church Council, now called the Armenian Community Church Council of Great Britain) in detail, as her fieldwork coincided with a time when the relatively newly arrived Iranian Armenians and Lebanese Armenians were anxious to have a greater role in the official side of the community (Talai 1989, 20–21). By the mid-1980s an Iranian Armenian was the head of the church council, and many others from the two groups had been elected members. Just as earlier Cypriot control reflected the composition of the Armenian population in the 1960s and early 1970s, this also is an indication of the current composition of the population, in which there are many more Armenians from Iran and Lebanon than from Cyprus.

Hay Doon underwent many years of neglect as the community outgrew its small rooms and layout. In the 1980s young people complained that they felt unwelcome there and were discouraged even from using the small library. However, in December 1988 it suddenly became the hub of Armenian earthquake relief work in London and since then has undergone a transformation. In 1992 the trustees of Hay Doon invited the embassy of the new Republic of Armenia to establish itself on one floor. Meanwhile other places and organizations became more popular. Some are political; others, which call themselves cultural organizations, are only indirectly so. For example, during the 1980s the Tekeyan, a cultural association popularly associated with the Ramgavar side, published a newspaper (*Erebouni*) and organized programs of music, poetry, dance, and lectures as well as table-tennis tournaments and discos for the young. There are also more general meeting places combined with activities such as Armenian classes. The Tahtaian School, for example, also serves as an informal social center for parents while children attend classes.

Associated with the Hnchakian Party, the Homenmen Club was the first to provide a casual, large-scale meeting place for Armenians of all ages. This club, which used a large state secondary school in Notting Hill every Sunday afternoon, offered Armenian classes, another Scout troop, and individual and team sports. Its most popular feature was a large room where Armenian food was sold and people could gather casually for conversation and backgammon. The major donors and primary organizers of the Homenmen Club were Lebanese Armenians, but some Cypriot Armenians were active at its opening in London in 1985. The Homenmen Club originally enjoyed much popularity but by 1991 had lost most of its membership as a result of infighting and competition from a larger club.

In 1988 a building was purchased for the Armenian Community Centre (ACC), and the center opened on a daily basis in outer northwest London. Again, the financing and main organization came from Lebanese and Iranian Armenians, but many Cypriot Armenians were active members. Like the Homenmen Club, the ACC provided sports facilities (which attracted young people) and a large room for eating and talking, but it had the added advantage of being a permanent Armenian fixture where dances, theater productions, meetings, lectures, parties, and receptions could take place. The ACC was oriented toward the Dashnak side, but, like the Homenmen, membership (or even interest) in the party was not required of the club members. However, this club has since closed down as well.

The Dashnak and Ramgavar political parties continue to be active in London (though the Dashnaks have a much higher profile), as are the prominent social and benevolent organizations of the diaspora, such as the AGBU, Hamazkaine, Blue Cross, and Anahid Mioutiune (*mioutiune* means "association"). Those who are committed to any of these groups find themselves with a very active social life, attending rounds of meetings, benefit dances and dinners, concerts, dance performances, poetry readings, and lectures. Each has its own particular outlook or purpose, though many believe there is considerable overlap and would prefer that there be fewer.

In 1986 an independent organization was begun by a group of young people, led by a Cypriot Armenian and his wife, an Iranian Armenian. The Centre for Armenian Information and Advice (CAIA) depends primarily on local London government for its finances, rather than on the Armenian network, and its aims are to provide needed social services, especially for elderly and unemployed Armenians. The CAIA coordinates translation services, placement for housing and employment, a play group, Armenian and English lessons, and a quarterly community newsletter, among its other services. In the early 1990s the CAIA purchased a large building in west London for its permanent home.

INFORMAL SOCIAL LIFE

Accidental meetings still take place in London in areas where many Armenians live, such as Muswell Hill, Chiswick, and Ealing, in or outside the Armenian-owned shops or at the bus or tube stop. But these chance meetings are relatively infrequent. A small minority have regular business contacts with other Armenians, and a smaller number work as partners with or employees of Armenians. Most of these also work with non-Armenians, and all have non-Armenian customers as well as Armenians. Even some of those who do work with other Armenians in their shop or business sometimes feel they are isolated. A young professional mused one

day, "Sometimes I step out the door of my shop and look down the street
and I fantasize about it being Victoria Street and being back at my father's
old shop. You'd step outside and someone would walk by immediately,
and you'd say, 'Hey, what's up today?' and he'd stop to chat. You'd need
something and you could go to Bedros, a few doors away, and he'd have
it, or you'd send a boy off to fetch it from someone else a bit farther down.
All up and down the street, friends, characters—lots of characters. You
knew all of them, they all knew you. Remember Sapritch Mgrditch [a bar-
ber]? Everyone went there to hear the gossip! And one time they got so
carried away in a argument that he cut off a bit of someone's ear!

"Here, certainly I know some of the people. We've been here five
years on the street. But people keep to themselves. Maybe it's the weather;
maybe they have their own network and do help each other, I don't know.
But I miss Victoria Street even though it never was really my place. I wish
sometimes we could re-create it. Most of the time I think London is great,
though. I know it's different there [in Cyprus] now, too."

In Cyprus informal visits during office hours do continue during quiet
times, but in London one usually meets other Armenians during leisure
time, mostly by prior arrangement, whether through club activities or
one's own visits to family and friends. The primary and most common
connection is the informal circle of family and friends who get together in
the evenings and on weekends, often over a meal.

BEING ARMENIAN IN LONDON

Those who arrived in Cyprus in middle age eventually made new friends
among their British neighbors and coworkers, but most kept their core of
close contacts among Armenians. Students and other young people initially relied on old friends and relations from Cyprus to get started, but
many gradually found that shared interests in work or study became a
more important factor in friendships. Armenian contacts were retained,
but they were alongside (and for some increasingly in deference to) these
new interest-based friendships.

Most of those who came to Britain as children or were born there
have grown up in a world in which their personal daily interests—school,
playmates, work—nearly always involve non-Armenians. Their awareness of Armenianness is derived entirely from the home and from special
events or activities. During the mid-1980s the young Armenians of London had at least two regular monthly discos to choose from, in addition

to special-event dances organized by the youth branches of the different organizations primarily as a way for young, single Armenians to meet each other. Some amount of complaining by older people was heard at their inception: "Can't they do something serious?" Others countered that "serious" activities, such as language lessons, dance troupes, and theater, were already available.

Between the feeling generated by being part of a large group of young Armenians, the informal discussions in those groups, and the occasional formal articulations of the sponsoring organizations, the young people are developing their own views of being Armenian. This, of course, evolves in conjunction with parental views and the general atmosphere of the home. Within the family another factor that influences children's perceptions of being Armenian is the existence of cousins who are still in Cyprus or who arrived later than themselves from Cyprus. Here are examples among their own peers who differ considerably in their language skills, education, knowledge of Armenian affairs, and expectations within family relationships. Similarly, teenagers in Cyprus, through visits, letters, phone calls, and general gossip, are aware that their cousins' lives in London are quite different from their own. That is not to say that one side sees the other with complete envy or disdain, but rather that the awareness of various possibilities encourages a self-questioning attitude, even an uncertainty, for many. This is part of what makes it clear to them, they say, that they are part of a nation obviously in flux, and it makes them acutely aware of the ambiguity of their position.

DATING AND MARRIAGE CHOICE

One of the more ambiguous aspects of Armenian life in London and in Cyprus is that of young male-female relations (covered in more detail in chapters 9 and 10). Because of the small size of the Armenian community in Cyprus, young people there often feel more like brothers and sisters than potential mates. This is also true to a degree in London among Cypriot Armenians, for those who are active in community life form a relatively small core and see each other over and over. The many others who are not active in these groups mainly see other Armenians who are extended family and thus truly cousins.

Often Cypriot Armenians look to non-Cypriot Armenians in London or to non-Armenians. Many have married Iranian, Lebanese, Palestinian, or Egyptian Armenians; relatively few in the younger generation have married others whose family is from Cyprus. While the language is shared (sometimes with major dialect differences or variations in fluency), there are numerous other differences of tradition, attitude, and ideas that continue to crop up during the marriage and become the subject of teasing, complaining, and accommodation.

Armenians say that many of the non-Armenian spouses are Irish (especially wives) and account for this by adding that the Irish share similar feelings about the closeness of family and that they are a friendly and hospitable people.[6] Far more young men and women find English spouses, however.

The question of whether or not to marry an Armenian is one that crosses everyone's mind, but there is great variation in the importance attached to the issue—or the guilt associated with it. Young people find it difficult to coordinate their own values, interests, and background with those of a prospective Armenian mate. What should the most important feature be? An intellectual companion, someone who understands and shares work and leisure interests? If so, this narrows the possibilities considerably. Armenians who have branched off into fields newer to the community, such as journalism, architecture, literature, the arts, and law, meet very few other Armenians in their fields. A number of people remarked that they feel very much misfits in Armenian society because they seem alone in their interests. They find it difficult to meet other Armenians who want to talk about "serious" subjects, "something other than the next gala ball or where to go shopping!"

Men complain that women are not allowed or don't push themselves to achieve in intellectual fields. Women who have done just that complain that men don't like it, are too old-fashioned, and prefer to marry women who don't have a serious career interest.

One mother remembered how her two daughters had been pushed to go to Hay Doon in the 1960s, when young people used to meet there for informal parties and dances. The idea was to keep them in Armenian circles so they would meet Armenian young men, as there were no Armenians among their fellow students in college. "Well, finally they went one time, and they found all the Armenian boys had brought their English girlfriends and were showing off how English they were, each one more than the next," the mother said. Both girls later married non-Armenians.

But even those most immersed in their field or most compelled to fit in with the dominant culture feel a strong pull toward the Armenian tradition of the central importance of family. "Can a non-Armenian understand this?" many wonder. "Will he or she tolerate the constant demands of the extended family? Wouldn't it be better to marry someone who might understand and even enjoy it?"

The generation of Armenian Cypriots who came to London as children but are now parents themselves feel very much in between the old and the new, trying to find some way to accommodate both. Just as their own parents did for them, this generation pushes their children to do well in the British educational system, perhaps recognizing more than their parents did just how different these children will be from themselves as a result.

Some parents also take their children regularly to Armenian school one morning a week, but even these find it a struggle to keep Armenian spoken in the home. There are other aspects of Armenian life that the children can't possibly avoid, though. Certainly this includes the family as center, but it also includes a different view of the world. One mother explained, "Most of the Armenian children in the West, if you compare them with English children, they are not more intelligent but they have lots of stimulation from all over the world. There are so many people and contacts around. They are always watching the news on TV, hearing about politics. They hear us making a phone call to someone where something is going on, like Beirut, you're concerned about how they are, and they have also heard about it on TV. These kids are learning about the world. Somehow it's more real to them, I think, because of these personal contacts."

VIEWS OF OTHERS

Viewing oneself against the background of other groups is one important way of building a self-image. For Armenians in London, though they come in contact with a variety of British people, it is the English who are most often referred to in such conversations. The English are much admired for their academic and literary achievements, the care and interest taken in their monuments and parks, media productions of all kinds, and the arts and education generally, but they are criticized for their aloofness and reserve. This much, and the depressing weather, are more or less agreed upon across age and gender.

Those over fifty seem to have particular concerns that are not always shared by younger people. For example, some features of English life are to them neither good nor bad but just puzzling: How can a widow seem to recover from her husband's death so quickly? How is it that she is not crushed, and why doesn't she stay at home? Along the same lines, the English are generally admired as being quite tough—or possibly crazy— as they "cope" with their lives. Elderly people who walk to the shops in the cold rain, without complaining, are given as an example.

This same toughness is criticized in other spheres. How can they "throw their children out" at eighteen? Though everyone knows exceptions, most are convinced that English parents insist that their children move out of the family home at eighteen. The parents then take little interest and have no say in the child's choice of marriage partner, it is believed. Armenians contrast this with their own ideal. Children should live at home until married, unless at college or away at work, and the parents' advice should be sought on future spouses. Though a few Armenian children have gone to boarding school, most families do not approve and see this English custom as further evidence of parents putting their interests first, getting the children out of the way.

Most Armenians of all ages agree with the general stereotype of the English manner as being cold and formal. "We used to call the English 'cucumbers' [that is, cool]," said one man who has lived in London for over twenty years. "Now when I go back to visit [Cyprus], I find I've changed—or they [the friends] have changed. We are so different. . . . One time I asked an old friend, 'How do you find me now?' He said, 'You're a cucumber.'" This coolness is contrasted with the Armenians' preferred style, warmer and openly friendly, but many add that once an English person decides to become friends with you, it is a very close and loyal friendship.

In apparent contrast with Talai's assertion that "the social anonymity of London Armenians" allows for flexibility and "successful integration into the British socio-economic system" (Talai 1989, 95), nearly all Armenians over twenty-five whom I encountered felt that they would never be truly "accepted" by the English. This is believed to be especially true in the upper echelons of society. This last observation indicates that the opinions I encountered do not necessarily contradict Talai's assertion; rather, this sentiment has more to do with the renowned English sensitivity to fine gradations of *English* accent, nuances of educational background, style, and name, let alone indicators of foreignness. As one person pointed out, "The English are just as harsh on themselves when it comes to judging each other's background and accent. Sometimes I feel I am more easily accepted *because* I am foreign and don't fit into the usual lines of class division."

Younger people seem not so concerned with subtle discrimination; their attention is focused on A-levels, work, college, soccer, and who is going to the disco. Whether their perceptions of English life will later be similar to their parents' is hard to say, as the general sociocultural makeup of Britain, especially in London, is also changing.

Since the mid-1970s the basis of self-comparison has spread beyond the London-Cyprus and Armenian-English axes for all ages in both places. Armenians from places other than Cyprus began arriving in great numbers as wars broke up life in Beirut and later Iran, and within a few years Armenian Cypriots were approximately fifteen percent of the total British Armenian population. In Cyprus the permanent population of Armenians did not increase significantly as a result of these disruptions elsewhere in the world, but many came from Beirut for extended visits with relatives or to enroll children at the Melkonian. Others came to wait, in transit to another destination. Armenian Cypriots in both London and Cyprus found themselves adjusting to new customs, attitudes, styles,[7] and, in the case of those from Iran, another way of speaking. Those from Beirut and Iran, on the other hand, find the Armenians in and from Cyprus to be rather anglicized, in spite of their fluency in Armenian. Worse, from the point of view of Cypriot Armenians, those from Iran often call them *Turkahayer* ("Turkish Armenians"), implying that they are assimilated to Turkish ways (and then anglicized also). This is a sensitive subject for some. And there are many among the Armenians from Iran who also resent their common name, *Barskahayer* ("Persian Armenians").[8]

Those coming from Beirut and Iran often arrive expecting the London Armenian community to resemble something they are familiar with and are surprised to find it so different. One Cypriot Armenian, living in London for thirty years, mentioned that Armenians from Beirut and Iran wonder aloud to her why the Cypriots are so cool to them. "'Why don't they like us?' they ask me. Of course, they also don't approve of the Cypriots! But I like them very much. They're very warm-blooded. The Cypriots are indifferent [to Armenian affairs], but the Beirutsi and Barskahays care, and they work a lot. The only problem is they have no manners when they come—no English manners, that is. They love to shout and yell and have parties. But after a while that changes. It's already changing. And their children are quite different, more like the English already."

A woman in her early forties explained that in some of the associations she is part of, there has been a problem with prejudice between the different Armenians. "Especially, there is a problem because the Barskahays look down on those whom they call the Turkahays, people from Cyprus and Turkey. They criticize our language and customs. Others say that the Kibrahays [Armenians from Cyprus] are too easily assimilated with the English. I've met Barskahays who actually won't speak, unless it is absolutely necessary, to English people. Or, more realistically, they have no desire to make friends with them. They won't, for example, speak to anyone at the [Armenian] school who looks English."[9]

Language is a particularly delicate area. Those living in Hayastan are admired by many for their "pure" Armenian—their pronunciation is considered to be more closely aligned with the alphabet.[10] Though part of that eastern family of dialects, the distinctive Iranian Armenian accent is a source of puzzlement and often merriment among western Armenians. Cypriot Armenians note that they often have a hard time understanding Iranian Armenians unless the person is careful not to include the usual loan words from Farsi. "But we do the same with English," they often add. "It's just that everyone knows the English word."[11]

The much greater size of Armenian communities in Iran, Beirut, Istanbul, and elsewhere in the Near East encouraged the development of more elementary and secondary schools, theaters, and various periodicals, and generally made it possible for many Armenians there to live their lives and pursue their interests almost entirely with other Armenians. Armenians in Cyprus often give this as a reason why they feel their own Armenian language skills, even among those who attended the Melkonian, are not as highly developed.

The quest for learning is also part of the stereotype of different Armenian centers and remains an important part of the identity of Cypriot Armenians in England. But the fact that their education and jobs have been in English, mostly alongside English students and coworkers, means that their Armenian education, both formal and informal, has suffered. Their interests and outlook have become more generally British.

Cypriot Armenians in London are careful about their complaints about England. Too many have been asked, both by other Armenians and by English people, "Why don't you go back, then?" Or, before, "Why don't you move to Soviet Armenia?"[12] They value the education they and now their children receive, and many say they are too used to the lifestyle in London to go anywhere else. They would miss the excitement of such a large city, with its variety and many attractions. Others have not forgotten that in other places where they have lived, other kinds of problems exist.

"We still have friends and family in Cyprus," said one woman in her sixties. "But I couldn't go back to live. Somehow now I feel more at home in England, even though it was hard at first. Here there's always something to learn. The people are more critical in Cyprus. You aren't as free as you are here. It's not just that they know or see you more. They judge more."

For Cypriot Armenians living in London, Cyprus represents continuity with their past, a shared experience. Frequent visits back are important to many, for the visits renew feelings. As the years of relative peace continue in Cyprus, a number of people have begun to consider retirement there or the purchase of a vacation home. And a few younger people have sold homes in London and begun new jobs and lives in Cyprus. The tie is still a strong one.

As noted in chapter 4, the ties among people from each of the local communities are powerful ones. Though Armenians increasingly have been taught to see themselves as a nation and not to identify primarily with their local community, they complain that such divisions still exist. When the Armenian Cypriots arrived in London, they found that London *deghatsi* were helpful but aloof, as the *deghatsi* in Cyprus had been when the refugees arrived. Today Armenian Cypriots and those from Iran, the Near East, Hayastan, and elsewhere find much about each other to complain about. But the very high rate of intermarriage is a fair indication that these fissures are not too deep.

Aside from these adjustments of one group to another, there is a deeper, more disturbing aspect to the arrival of the "newcomers" in both London and Cyprus. The disintegration of Beirut and the disruption of the flourishing Armenian communities there and in Iran have underlined the fragile nature of the Armenian diaspora and serve as acute reminders of the past troubles of Armenian Cypriots. In the same way, the differences themselves are disturbing as indicators of how varied the Armenian world has become in diaspora. While some older people may remember how different the Zelifkiatsi seemed from the Adanatsi or the *deghatsi* in Cyprus around 1925, these memories are faded and pale, for attention is now focused on the immediate situation. Most younger people, particularly in London, seem to believe that prior to 1914 all Armenians shared the same language, customs, and beliefs. Thus the many dissimilarities they see between themselves and Armenians from other countries are especially troubling.

The question "How far have we come?" becomes all the more difficult to answer when one is not sure where one has come from. And while the necessary adjustments to diaspora life in Westernized, modern society preempt a continuation of the varieties of traditional Armenian life, a narrowed and more self-conscious concept of what it means to be Armenian emerges. Language, church, and history become the points of concentration as national survival becomes the major concern. While this is the message of countless sermons, articles, lectures, and books, the most important aspect of Armenian life as observed in practice, and the one upon which the others ultimately depend, is the family.

Chapter 9

The Web of Family

In her 1993 book *Armenian-Americans: From Being to Feeling Armenian,* Anny Bakalian contrasts "being" with "feeling" Armenian in the United States, noting that the latter enables American-born Armenians to avoid demanding or time-consuming behavior, such as linguistic skills or church attendance, while remaining emotionally tied to their ethnic ancestry. However, in formal lectures and discussions there, as in Cyprus or London, the family is the unit that reproduces new Armenians, educates them, and persuades them to "be" Armenian and continue the nation. "Being" Armenian, in this sense, means speaking Armenian, supporting the Apostolic Church, being acquainted with Armenian history and literature, and having an active concern for the larger Armenian community or nation. But what does it mean away from the rhetoric and repeated formulas, inside the everyday workings of the home?

The reproduction of Armenianness is generally not the everyday objective of even the most patriotic parents, and in those occasional cases where it is, it seems to backfire. The family's real importance as a social unit lies in its more general preparation of the individuals within it, their relations with each other, and the values and attitudes developed there. The individual's perspective on the world and how to deal with it grows as a combination of that process of early acculturation, his or her own personality and talents, and the circumstances of the surrounding community and environment.

As community for Armenians in Cyprus and in London has gone

through major changes over the last three generations, so too have families and the notion of "family." Survival and rebuilding in the face of insecurity in Cyprus, and emigration and rebuilding in an unknown environment in England, have had an effect on the way family members see their obligations to each other and toward the community or nation. Concerns over transience, assimilation, and even physical insecurity are put to the back of the mind but remain potent as people face the more immediate problems of getting along in the host country, developing appropriate language skills, obtaining work-related training, ensuring education for children, and providing a home and food.

The desire to achieve and the notion of sacrifice are inculcated in the individual by the family and community, but the ideal of success in one's chosen work, recently a more individual choice, is often at odds with the desire of extended families to live near each other. The mobility of people in diaspora fits well with the mobility of work in industrialized society in that Armenians are almost guaranteed that they will find a "home" in any country with an Armenian community. But one's own family ties are stretched and changed substantially over long distances.

The current state of the family in Cyprus as well as London is a complex one. I suspect that it has been so for many decades, probably well preceding the turn of the century. Certainly before 1914 customs, family structures, and relations varied between villages and most especially between villages and towns or cities.[1] Then and now, however, some patterns can be seen; most important, there is considerable mutual understanding even despite the differences. This understanding is the reason both parents and young people give for the desirability of endogamy, today interpreted as marriage with other Armenians and no longer restricted to fellow villagers and townspeople.

FAMILY RELATIONS

Once married, young people in Cyprus and London most often move to their own accommodations. They may live with either set of parents temporarily, depending on which home is more convenient. If one parent is widowed with dependent or single children at home, households are often combined, depending on which home is most spacious and convenient.

In both Cyprus and London, many older people have begun to remain in their own home upon being widowed. Likewise, single men and women who have shared a home with a sister, brother, or parent will stay in that house alone when their companion dies; previously they would have moved in with nephews or nieces. This seems to be a combination of changed attitudes of both generations and, especially in Cyprus, the effects of depopulation. In 1986 the first Armenian old people's home was opened in Nicosia. Most of the rooms were filled immediately, many by people whose closest relatives had emigrated years ago. Others came for the constant medical care available there. The companionship of other Armenians seemed to be an equally important factor for people (mostly women) who, as a result of age and/or infirmity, were unable to travel to visit friends and family.

Today there are fewer children and a greater number of modern household conveniences, leaving less work to be spread among the members of an extended family at home and more opportunity to either get in each other's way or to leave one feeling unnecessary. This is partially but not completely allayed by the increasing number of young women, including mothers, who work and who rely on their mothers or mothers-in-law to take care of the children or household. It is mostly a problem between women, as men within the home are often used to being waited upon and do not feel their identity is threatened if it continues.

The authority of the oldest generation has mellowed gradually. In extended families, households operate separately, and in these families or in businesses linking extended families, decisions are usually made by consensus among the adults. Some say they also consult the children on issues that concern them, but more often children will follow adult decisions until they are working or are studying away from home. Sons and daughters usually live in the parental home until marriage unless studies or work take them to another city or country. This does not necessarily imply a childish role for them; especially in London, the children may be relied on for help in understanding and getting along in the changing society (cf. Markowitz 1993, 212–30).

While better Greek- or English-language skills or specialized technical knowledge gives the younger generation added weight in family affairs, parents and grandparents can wield their own influence in other practical ways. The power of the gift (of money or of land) is considerable and is used by some parents to persuade young couples to follow their advice— for example, to marry sooner than planned, live in a certain place, or take up a certain job.

Where aunts and uncles in a more compact community were extra sources of love, discipline, and practical help, nowadays this resource is often too dispersed to be of daily importance for most families. They and other extended kin, however, can still be relied on for the help they are able to give, and this can include important entrées into other communities, room and board for a student attending school in Britain or America, arranging medical help, or looking out for an appropriate spouse for their niece or nephew.

As Paul Stirling (1966, 170) also shows for rural Turkey, the mother's brother was mentioned most often as an important person to rely on for advice and practical help and with whom a child could enjoy a most relaxed relationship in the past. One woman, now in her forties, remarked that in addition to this, her mother's brother frequently consulted her mother (his older sister) on matters of importance. "I think that was typical, probably an old tradition. The man doesn't ask his wife for advice. What would she know, coming from the outside? But his older sister— yes. I used to feel badly for my aunt, actually, because it was so obvious."

The godfather (*gunkahayr*) also was consulted on important occasions, such as the naming of a baby. Both these roles have changed in Cyprus and in London, however, with most people relying on those relatives and friends living closest to them.

Armenian contains particular names for different relatives on each side of the family, but in Cyprus and London there is much variety in the actual use of kinship terms. (See Appendix C for kinship terms and variations used in Cyprus.) Some Armenian terms are heard rarely or not at all, and there are more than a few instances of Turkish or Greek terms still being used for favorite relatives. Some examples are *dayı* or *dayday* (Turkish) for mother's brother (and sometimes father's brother and fictive male kin), *yaya* (Greek) for grandmother, and (rarely now) *doudou*[2] (Turkish) for aunt and female fictive kin. *Tantig* (derived from the French) is a popular term for aunt as well as female fictive kin. One reason suggested for the popularity and longevity of such terms was that small children can pronounce them easily, though childish versions of other long Armenian terms are also popular, such as *mokoor* for *morakuyr*.[3] The word *dayı* has warm connotations for many, and is linked with a particularly special relationship with a much-loved uncle. Possibly for this reason, the term has continued to be used in some families who otherwise use very few Turkish words in their everyday Armenian (or English) speech. In Cyprus, though, there is an increasing effort to teach children the Armenian terms for kin rather than continue old family traditions.

The Armenian family today, around the diaspora, is loosely bilateral in structure, in that ascent and descent are reckoned through both the male and female lines. All kindred (*azkagan*) are counted within the possible sphere of working family relations, and geography and personality determine the closeness of actual relationships. This is very similar to the kinship structure in other groups that are both flexible and mobile.

Most older people, when speaking of marriage choices, mentioned that the Apostolic Church had a rule that the bride and groom must be at least "seven steps apart." In other words, first and second cousins could not marry each other. But now, they say, this rule has been relaxed, and all knew of examples where second or even first cousins had married. This seems to have followed the splitting of extended families between different countries, where the children did not grow up in the same community; marriage of close kin from different countries is not an ideal, but the couple is accepted.[4]

Like English, Armenian reverses the order of "bride and groom" to "man and wife" after marriage ("*hars ou pesa*" to "*ayr yev giin*"),[5] but in Armenian a couple remain *hars ou pesa* even after they are also called *ayr yev giin,* not as a couple but denoting the relation of each to the spouse's family. For example, the husband is *pesa* to his wife's extended family.[6] "He is our *pesa*" might be an introduction given by a man's wife's aunt. It is significant to the older generation's understanding of marriage that this mutual relationship is expressed in the use of these terms. Today young people continue to be called "our *hars*" or "our *pesa*," but the expectations of those roles are quite different. It does, however, continue to reflect a close and affectionate tie with the extended families as the newcomer is absorbed into the respective networks.

Khnamie, loosely translated into English as "in-law," is an important word in the social vocabulary and one that is often left untranslated in an English sentence because so many Armenian-speakers are not satisfied that *in-law* really means the same thing. *Khnamie* is the extended family of the bride for the groom and his family, and vice versa. The understanding, even among those of the generation now getting married, is that this implies a relationship of families with each other, not just the relationship of the bridal couple with the two sets of parents. This also is said to have involved more formal expectations in the past but now implies a more generalized special status. *Khnamie* will make an effort to overlook political differences and include each other in their social circles if they are in the same community. For those spread in other countries, *khnamie* can also be expected to provide help or at least an evening's entertainment when visiting. The fact that personality problems or differences sometimes make this difficult or impossible does not diminish the importance of the idea.

How does someone learn and remember who all the relatives and *khnamie* are? Everyday conversation is full of that information. "So-and-so is getting married." "Who is that?" "Oh, you know, your father's sister's husband's cousin!" Or "I saw Hovsep at the store today." "Oh, yes, Aram's son." "No, not that one. I mean the son of Alice's mother's sister's daughter." One hears this most often in the oldest generation alive today as they retell old stories or hear news from abroad and try to place the vaguely familiar names.

The connections are also reviewed or ferreted out when meeting a new person. The first question is always "*Oor deghatsi ek?*" ("Where are you from?" or "Where are you native?"). Two generations ago, this referred to one's native village or town. Today it usually implies country (Cyprus, England, and so on) but sometimes refers to the last generation in the old village. The second question is either "Who are your parents?" or, if the other person is familiar with the family name, "Are you related to the so-and-sos?" In this way a connection can often be found, at least among mutual acquaintances if not relatives or *khnamie*. Young people, when meeting someone from another community, are more apt to ask "Do you know so-and-so?" and then to follow the inquiry through mutual acquaintances and relatives at the same time. When all else fails and no connection is found, it is still a special connection to be a fellow Armenian.

CHILDREN

One afternoon I was invited to a *hadig* party that Mrs. Shakeh was giving for her granddaughter. The purpose of a *hadig* party is to celebrate the emergence of the baby's first tooth, Mrs. Shakeh said, and as she was the one who had first spotted it, she was responsible for making the *hadig* (boiled wheat) and organizing the gathering. When I arrived at her daughter's apartment, there were eighteen or twenty others already there: all women, all ages. And all family, said Mrs. Shakeh. "These are the same ones whom we invited to come after the christening."

When everyone had arrived, including the father, who was laden with camera and film, Mrs. Shakeh announced that we would begin the party. A low coffee table was cleared of its crocheted runner and marble ashtrays. On it were placed various items, including books, some toys, a bottle of pills, car keys, a pen, and a comb, each representing possible directions or careers for the child's future. Baby Sossi was brought in, looking bewil-

dered, and was set on the table among the objects, her head covered with
a blue net veil. Mrs. Shakeh and her daughter sprinkled dry *hadig* and
silver almonds over Sossi's head and then removed her veil. The women
gathered closer to the table. The baby chose a book, which everyone
agreed meant she would be a good student and probably want a job that
involved studying or somehow working with books. They also agreed that
this was all in good fun and not to be taken seriously.

Sossi settled down with her book, and we turned to the other important part of the party, the *hadig* itself. Mrs. Shakeh had cooked a large
bowl of the wheat kernels and arranged it, buffet style, on a table at the
other end of the living room. Beside the *hadig* were small bowls containing
sugar, cinnamon, ground walnuts, ground toasted sesame, and raisins, to
be mixed together in each person's own bowl with the *hadig* as they
pleased. As I was enjoying my own combination, another woman told me
that the *hadig* is supposed to represent the bread of life.

Though Mrs. Shakeh thought everyone still performed the *hadig*
ceremony and party, I met a number of young women in Cyprus and London who had never heard of it. Many others said they had heard of it but
never seen one. When I mentioned it to older women, they all remembered
it but also remembered that cooking the *hadig* was a long process. Other
customs surrounding the baby's birth are also passing away in both places,
though the one that is considered most important, the christening in the
church, is carried out by nearly all parents, even if only one is Armenian.
One man who is married to an Englishwoman and spends nearly all his
time outside of Armenian activities had his children christened. "We need
all the Armenians we can get," he explained. "You know, a million or
so were massacred." To be christened in the Armenian church is to be
counted as Armenian.

The christening is the baptism and confirmation into the church as
well as the formal naming of the baby. The induction as a member of the
church has the most significance for the community or nation, while the
naming, until recently, was a clear indication of the continuity and con-
nectedness of families. The custom of naming the first son for the paternal
grandfather and the second for the mother's father was very popular into
the generation now becoming parents.[7] Girls were also named either for
grandmothers or for aunts, maternal or paternal, though this does not
seem to have been as imperative. Two other fashions coexisted alongside
the carrying on of family names. One was to give the child a "true" Armenian name, especially one that belonged to a mythical, revolutionary,
or literary hero or heroine. The other was usually more European-

oriented, as people selected the names of saints or simply names that sounded pretty to them. Today all three of these possibilities continue, though in the latter English names are replacing French ones, which were popular earlier. The choice of Armenian names has become restricted to those that are easier to pronounce, shorter, and less likely to cause the child problems with non-Armenian-speakers.

The birth rate in Cyprus has gone down considerably, even when viewed against the decline in population generally. In both London and Cyprus the size of families has decreased with each generation. Currently the most popular number of children is two, and rarely will a couple have more than three, though there are many families with only one, whether the mother is working outside the home or not.[8] Again, some attribute this to economic pressure. It costs more to raise children today, they say. This overlooks the far worse financial situation of the refugees in the 1920s and 1930s. A few women said they would have had more, but the insecurity of the political situation in Cyprus was already too much for their nerves. One said she had an abortion just after the intercommunal troubles began in 1963 and knew of others who had done the same. This does not directly explain why Armenians in London also have one or two children per family, though it is safe to say that a feeling of insecurity has not been erased from the minds of those now parents.

While the importance of insecurity should not be played down, there are other possible explanations. The trend toward fewer children did not begin in the 1950s; it had already been an ideal among some wealthier or more educated families. Mrs. Araxi, now in her seventies, was speaking to me one day about birth control.

"Now I know much more about all of these things than I did when I was young," she told me. "There are so many very good programs on the television about everything medical, and sometimes you see one about the reproductive system, the way a woman's body works, and so on. It's too bad we didn't know these things then! Then we thought that you could get pregnant anytime and every time that you had intercourse! So we tried to be very careful, and we were always tremendously relieved when our periods did come. My mother-in-law used to always ask me, "Has your period come?" And she said that it was a girl's biggest *achkt luys* ["congratulations" or "bravo"][9] when her period came, because it meant she wasn't pregnant."[10]

Methods of birth control during that time included the sheath for men, abstinence, coitus interruptus, and/or wearing a special medallion during intercourse. But the concern over not having too many children came after a couple was certain they could have children. Reproduction of the family, the presence of children, had (and for most, still has) the highest value.

There are other values that coexist with this, though, and an exploration of these may help in understanding the place and number of children in family life. Achievement (including education, business, or professional accomplishment), hospitality, acquisition, and display are also emphasized alongside reproduction. Success in these areas is much more difficult if there are too many children to divert one's time, attention, and resources. The physical appearance of women and men beyond the age of marriage has become increasingly important. Also, the home should be beautiful and sparkling clean, and fashionably furnished if possible. The evidence of children is usually restricted to their own rooms, with the exception of some family photographs.

LOVE AND MARRIAGE CHOICE

"What do *you* think, Shushan? Is there such a thing as love?" Khatchig and Mr. Vaheh had made their way through the crowded living room to where I was sitting with friends. Some people near us gave theatrical sighs and moved away. "Not this discussion again!" someone said. "Do you have to bring it up at every party?" another laughed.

But I was curious. "Of course," I said. "All different kinds."

"Well," Mr. Vaheh said, "it doesn't exist. It's always and only duty [*bardaganoutiune*]." Nodding and beaming, Mr. Vaheh seemed to enjoy the chorus of tongue-clucking and murmuring about his crazy ideas. His wife, sitting nearby, rolled her eyes and smiled at me before turning back to her own conversation with a friend.

"What is this male-female attraction?" Mr. Vaheh continued. "Simply sex! That is all men and women are interested in at first. Then what happens? After three years that sex appeal wears off, and what is left? Duty!"

"Oh, come on!" Azniv called out. "You aren't serious!"

"Oh, yes, I am very serious."

"What about parents and children?" asked Khatchig. "I'm a father. I know what I feel for my children. It's a combination of tenderness, caring about them, worry . . . and, okay, duty, of course, too, but—"

"Of course duty. That's what it is! That's all."

"Maybe for your generation that was true. But things have changed a lot!" Azniv laughed.

Mr. Vaheh was older than the rest of us in the discussion, and this was a good way to tease him.

"Really"—Azniv turned to me—"marriage is a combination of duty and love. I call it love. Of course sex is part of it, and why not?"

Meanwhile Mr. Vaheh was demonstrating the effect of a beautiful young lady's attractions on vulnerable men. Everyone was laughing but Mrs. Berjoug, beside me. A woman in her seventies, she took my elbow and said, "Look, for him it's all sex. He says, anyway. But that's not it. After you've been married awhile you forget about sex. It's finished. For us, for my husband and me, it's all over. We live together like brother and sister and we have for some time. But brothers and sisters love each other, too. It's a different kind of love."

As Azniv pointed out, attitudes toward love and marriage have changed over the generations, but within each generation there appears to be, and to have been, considerable variation in both practice and ideas. Kinship and gender are intertwined as people talk of ideals of love and duty in what Loizos and Papataxiarchis (1991, 25) call "a mixed idiom of domesticity and personhood." Today this continues to change as personhood or identity is increasingly being pried away from domesticity, both for women and for men.

One revealing aspect of family dynamics and personal identity is the ways in which a marriage partner is chosen. This shows much about the relations between children and their parents as well as those between men and women, both between the prospective bride and groom and between the sets of parents involved. A variety of attitudes toward and expectations of marriage also are revealed in the making of this choice.

SELECTION AND CHOICE BEFORE 1960

In London one morning Mr. Levon and Mrs. Yeran talked about how they had met and decided to marry. Both were then just over eighty years old. Before their marriage Mrs. Yeran had been living in Beirut and had come to Cyprus for a short visit. They met at a mutual friend's house and realized that they were attracted to each other. But there were serious problems, including their being "very young" and the existence of older, unmarried sisters.

"In those days you were not supposed to get married before your older brothers or sisters, especially sisters," Mrs. Yeran explained. "So I had to go back to Beirut. What could I do there in Cyprus? I had no one to stay with there for such a long time. And I certainly couldn't stay by myself!"

"Yes, she had to," her husband said. "And I had to stay in Cyprus and find work and earn money, as young men were supposed to do before starting a family. But we didn't realize then that it would take ten years to overcome all our difficulties."

Meanwhile they wrote letters to each other daily, though the post arrived only once a week. "That sounds very romantic," I said.

"Yes, romantic, yes, it was. They are beautiful letters," Mr. Levon began.

"Romantic—but it was a very long time! A waste of time." Mrs. Yeran started collecting our empty teacups. "But things have changed very much since then. We were quite modern."

"Yes, by the standards of our time, we were. We met, we made our own decision, and we persisted when there was opposition. Today things have changed, but it's still more strict in Cyprus. For example, if we had stayed in Cyprus, there might have been more objections when our children married *odars*. Here it is more accepted."

"But it is still not really accepted," added Mrs. Yeran.

"No. Do you know when things really started to change? In the late 1800s, early 1900s. Our teachers then, they were educated abroad and they brought back many changes with them. New ideas. Some of them we weren't ready for. I wonder about nationalism, for example. Anyway, things changed very radically with the foreign ideas introduced by the European-influenced teachers, including ideas about marriage and men and women."

Others placed the credit or blame for introducing major social changes on the movies and their romantic portrayal of Western lifestyles. Changes also accompanied each war: World Wars I and II, independence in Cyprus, the troubles of the 1960s there, and the division of the island in 1974. This included adjustments made to the new exigencies as well as the new decisions that were made as the distractions of resettlement allowed a shifting of priorities. The children of wealthier families (which in the early twentieth century were more oriented toward Europe than the Middle East) would have been more impressed with the new ideas of the teachers and would have been in school long enough to hear them at the right age. This was true in Cyprus among the *deghatsi* and in Cilicia in the large towns. At the same time, other families were aware that these changes were taking place but continued with variations on older customs, including choosing or suggesting their children's spouses.

Though parents with little money had more cause for concern for their child's material welfare being provided for, or for their own loss of help at home or the shop, the primary concern of such parents as well as of wealthy, educated families was usually that the match be suitable (*harmar*). This had a number of interpretations, with different factors receiving emphasis in each case. One should not marry an *odar* in any case. Apostolics should marry Apostolics, but marrying a Protestant was not so terrible as marrying a Catholic.[11] Similar economic status or work was important but often difficult to distinguish among the refugees. Fellow townspeople or acquaintances of fellow townspeople were thought to be ideal among the refugees, as Hirschon found among the Asia Minor refugees of Piraeus,[12] but some of the wealthier refugees made choices based more on shared interests or romantic attractions than the keeping of old traditions. Many say that the *kahanas* had a major role in matchmaking, as they had inside information on nearly every family in the community and thus could be relied on for advice and suggestions.

In the mid-1930s unmarried men and women were not to go out alone together before they were engaged. Some, perhaps many, managed to anyway and even made their own decisions to be engaged, asking their parents' consent. Most, however, met as part of groups at the club, church, choir practice, weddings, family parties, and other social gatherings. Mrs. Shoghig remembered her teenage years and early twenties, before she was engaged: "People used to meet at tea dances—at the Armenian Club, at the Armenian Football Players Club. After games there was great excitement. The club was near the church, and ladies on the committee used to prepare snacks for everyone. It was a big hall, and I used to think it was really very nice. We used to go and sit in chairs all around the room and wait for somebody to come and dance with you. We didn't have separate tables to sit around.

"You used to sit like this." She demonstrated, sitting demurely with head down, chin nearly resting on her chest, ankles crossed and to the side of her chair, hands folded in her lap. "First you saw a pair of shoes coming and you would try to think who that could be! '*Oriort, ge barek?*' 'Would you like to dance, miss?' You had to say yes, no matter who it was. Then after the dance he would take you to another room for drinks and snacks. The snacks were for sale, and the committee ladies used to tell us that we had to say yes and yes and eat so that they could sell the things! Even if you weren't hungry or you didn't want to spend time with that boy! But it was very friendly. The people in the community liked each other.

"There was modern dancing with a record player. No Armenian dances. They would sometimes bring in groups from outside who did the folk dances. Instead we did the tango, waltz. Now they hold all their dances at the Hilton or other hotels. You could bring your friends, whatever nationality they were, friends from school or work. But it was mostly Armenians, though.

"We used to go still after we were married. But after a while the dances became bigger, and they starting doing it in a big hotel, and it became a different sort of function. Before, they were small dances. We stopped going, and people like us started having parties at home, cocktails and so on."

Some young women, anxious to take part in community functions that were more closed or limited to single people, agreed to or even chose to marry men whom they were uncertain about. Mrs. Araxi explained a friend's situation in the 1930s: "She did it for the freedom, you have to understand. Life was so limited if you were not married, and she especially couldn't stand to sit at home. She wanted to go out, and you really could do that most easily with your husband. Maybe your brother doesn't want to go. You don't always want to go with your parents. So she said yes when he asked her to marry. But it was a mistake. She was too young and too headstrong to realize it then."

"Well, many young women still do something like that," I said. "It's a quick way to become accepted as an adult."

"What, in Cyprus?"

"Anywhere, I guess. I meant even in the States."

"Oh, no. It's not the same. I mean, when I say you couldn't do very much on your own as an unmarried woman, that means really you couldn't go out of the house by yourself—to do the shopping, to go to a lecture or a meeting, to go visiting in the evening, nothing. It's not like that in America, is it?"

Some young unmarried women did find ways to leave home alone. "People talked, but I didn't care," said one woman who used to meet her boyfriend in tea shops so that they could talk before they were engaged. By the 1940s and especially the 1950s, more and more young men and women did not just have veto power over their parents' choice but increasingly took an active role in making the decision and even finding a mate.

An arrangement was still made in that usually introductions were helped along by a middleman or -woman and both sets of parents were consulted before the decision was made. Many families continued to exert much pressure on sons and especially daughters to make the "right match at the right time," according to parental ideals. As men, or the man's family, were always the initiators, at least ostensibly, young women were not always convinced it was their time to get engaged, and some would have preferred to work for a while or to continue with their studies. The idea that one could both get married and work outside the home was accepted by very few until the end of the 1950s, when it began to increase somewhat.

"I feel real bitterness toward my parents even though I love them very much," said a woman in her early fifties who had spent some years away from Cyprus but returned to live in Nicosia. "Not just toward them but their generation. They really pushed me into marriage. When we were teenagers [in the 1950s] our parents thought that our only option was to get married and have kids. I remember my cousin crying for days and nights, with her red eyes bulging, because her parents wouldn't let her go on to university. And she had done so well at school."

In many other cases the suggested arrangement was happily accepted by both the man and the woman. One day as we were looking through family photo albums, Mrs. Sirarpie told me how she and her husband had met in the early 1950s. "From the time I was fifteen, people had been asking for me to get married. But fortunately my father said no when I was too young. Then Eugenie [her future husband's sister]—she knew us—and she arranged with [some mutual friends] that one day when I would be visiting them, Eugenie and Boghos would also come and see me there. They did that, and he must have liked me, because after that he sent someone to ask my family for my hand. They said, 'Sirarpie doesn't know him, so let's meet some more.' And then we went out several times with Eugenie and those friends. We went to restaurants, to the cinema, to Makedonitissa, and we decided to get engaged.

"We had a party at the Armenian Club—with nothing to eat; they just came and congratulated us, and we gave them small bags of sugared almonds. Now, of course, it's different. But I was very happy. And it has been a good marriage."

There is no reason to think that such matches arranged in the Armenian community were or are very different from those observed by Loizos in Argaki, insofar as the new couple's feelings toward each other are concerned:

> There was one feature of the matchmaking system which at first seemed extraordinary, and this was the speed with which a newly engaged couple appeared to fall in love before my eyes. Couples were being

"matched" by their families, on the basis of a handful of qualities, and were comparative strangers to each other. . . . People were emphatically *not* getting married because of grand passions, or of a meeting of true minds, or at the end of a quest for spiritual harmony. Yet, within a few days of the engagement, sometimes within an hour or two, the young people would give all the signs of having fallen in love. (Loizos 1981, 33)

At the same time, quite a few young men had gone abroad, mostly to Britain, to continue their studies. Some returned to Cyprus to be married; not all came back, though, and a number of these married non-Armenians. A gap of experience and outlook had grown between these young men and the young women who stayed in Cyprus, and this was a source of confusion and frustration. This is still considered a major problem today, especially in Cyprus, because of the greatly decreased population. It is further complicated by the different rules and expectations for single men and women, beginning in their teenage years. This is a continuation of old habits, when many men who are now parents and grandparents used to meet at coffee shops, *tavernas,* and cabarets, where they enjoyed the show, played cards, and gambled. Some also had affairs with *odar* women before eventually deciding, or being persuaded, that it was time for a stable home life of their own.

In earlier years this pattern took place in the context of greater pressure against marrying out and in a similar environment for both men and women. This, with the greater number of Armenian possible mates, meant that young men would most likely marry an Armenian. In many marriages, especially those that were arranged to any degree, the man was five to ten years or more older than the woman, which gave him considerable leeway to enjoy bachelor life and at the same time become established enough in his work to offer a steady income to his prospective bride. Some men seem to have needed extra persuasion to leave their relatively carefree pursuits. Others were devoted to their mothers, and a relationship of mutual care and dependence developed that could prove hard or impossible to break.

A woman now in her seventies talked about men in her generation and their relationships with their mothers. "Antranig's father died when the boy was very young, and Antranig was all the mother had. She devoted herself to him. She used to tell me that she went in to look at him every night after he'd gone to bed and make sure that he was covered up. Poor boy—he couldn't sleep with all the blankets tossed off! And so she would gently pull up the covers and tuck him in."

"Oh. Well, how old was he then?" I asked.

"About thirty or thirty-five. And another thing. No woman was good enough for him, as far as she was concerned. I would make suggestions to her, and so would everyone else. Not to Antranig, of course! And she would say, 'Oh, no, Armig, *yavrum*,[13] she is an Arab or something. They say they are Armenian, but nobody knows!' Of course, some families were of unknown origin—nobody really knew—but that girl, the one I was suggesting, I liked her very much, and it was a good family, honest and hardworking. What does it matter? But no, the mother insisted that she had to be pure Armenian and from the right family.

"In the meantime Antranig was too busy gambling and enjoying himself to really worry about getting married. He was always playing, betting, winning, losing. Actually, he lost a lot. After his mother died, he did get married—the *kahana* suggested someone to him—and he changed his habits completely and worked very hard the rest of his life."

UNMARRIED PEOPLE

In light of the central importance of marriage and reproduction, I was struck by the large number of single men and women in the generations over sixty. A number of other people had married relatively late, in their forties. While I do not wish to suggest that all people must marry, it seems important to understand why two out of four or even three out of five children in one family might remain single (more commonly, one out of four).

For those who came to marrying age between 1909 and 1922 and shortly thereafter, it is easy to project possible reasons, most notably the disruptions themselves (moving, temporarily different priorities) and the drastic reduction in the number of men. Others who would have married in the late 1920s or 1930s could also have been affected by the aftermath of the changes, by the problems inherent in resettling, and by population imbalance. By the 1940s, however, it is difficult to continue to stretch this point, and it is probable that some factors active then were also important in earlier years. In exploring these it is possible to learn more about attitudes toward family, marriage, and relations within the community.

As mentioned earlier, one older person living alone is a recent phenomenon in Cyprus and in London, but it is steadily becoming more common. Today these are not only widows or widowers but single people who have shared their life and home with another member of their family for many years (only rarely was this a nonrelative). These combinations are most often pairs: two sisters, a brother and sister, mother and daughter, mother and son. These pairs would have evolved from a home that originally contained both parents (one or both of whom died) and other brothers and sisters (who married out).

Mr. Mardiros, now in his nineties, had lived alone for many years when I met him. He and another unmarried brother had stayed in his parents' home until first their father, and much later their mother, died. In the living room of his apartment a few mementos of those days remain: framed photographs from the 1950s arranged on a low table, showing their mother, the brothers, the old home in the Turkish quarter. Between the photos there were some greeting cards from the same era, including a Christmas card sent to their mother from the United States.

My husband, Levon, had come this time to meet Mr. Mardiros, an old acquaintance of his father's, and he was first quizzed about whether I am Armenian or not. I was close enough, Mr. Mardiros decided.

"*Abris, deghas!* ["Well done, my son!"] The most important thing is for Armenians to marry Armenians. It is a shame when these parents allow their children to marry *odars,* just for their own pleasure. They must put our nation first."

Neither he nor a second brother had married. A third had married but had no children. "So we have decided to give our money to our nation to help keep the Armenian spirit," Mr. Mardiros told me. And they had indeed embarked on a plan of regular giving to a variety of organizations. But why had he—a man whose first comment was about marriage, who was in a male minority when it was his time to wed—and his brother chosen not to marry? There are many personal reasons possible, but also more general ones, for this apparent paradox.

For some families, including that of Mr. Mardiros, the shame of the radical change in status from landholders or skilled tradesmen to refugee was turned to bitterness by the cold reception given them by the people in Cyprus they considered to be their social equals, the *deghatsi.* The *deghatsi,* for their part, had no sure way of knowing who the newcomers were. Even their Turkish seemed cruder. Refugees themselves, unless they had known each other before coming to Cyprus, were unwilling to make such an important decision as whom to marry without at least a mutual acquaintance vouching for the other. In these cases the most conservative families, in the sense of those who wanted to cling to past images and traditions as long as possible, seem to have encouraged their children to wait as long as necessary for someone worthy of their own status. The children may have taken on this attitude as well, and for some this wait became permanent.

For Mr. Mardiros and others of his generation, another factor had a profound effect on their attitude toward family. The disruption he saw and heard of during his own early years helped to give him an urge to protect his parents, especially his mother. This is not to say that his mother or parents were necessarily in more danger than anyone else's or that he and others like him were more sensitive as children, but rather that the combination of external circumstances, the way children were reared in that family, and his own personality encouraged this outcome. The parent-child bond could become uninterruptible through mutual need, duty, and comfort, the years passing by without one's really noticing.

The direct trauma of the deportation years gave way to the more generalized feelings of a need for survival and of gratitude for sacrifices made by the older generation, and so continued to affect young women and men in the 1930s and 1940s. By then the question of status had changed also, but it retained many of the same characteristics. Old animosities between certain Cilician villages were not yet forgotten; different trades and educational standards carried with them connotations of status and thus marriageability. Mutual distrust between those building new wealth and security through trade and those putting their faith in education (and sometimes a more open affiliation with England and European culture) continued.

A related problem began to emerge among those pushing their children to be better-educated than themselves and their peers. As mentioned earlier, some men preferred to marry a woman who, in addition to her romantic attraction, could complete the more Europeanized vision of himself that he had developed. This could rarely be an Armenian; more often it meant a European woman who shared his intellectual interests and brought with her an implicit acceptance into her own society. The female counterparts of these men (sisters or women in similar families), some of whom must have had a personal interest in these same men, were encouraged to get as good an education as possible in Cyprus, to develop artistic or musical talents—and to wait. Again, a combination of luck, conservatism, concern over marrying below one's status, and sense of duty toward parents and community at the expense of one's self resulted in a number of such women staying single.

As old poems and literature and some of the above stories vividly show, the idea of romantic love and sexual attraction is not unique to Armenians in the last part of this century. Even during the time when a majority of marriages were arranged, stories, gossip, and rumors abounded of couples who "fell in love" but whose parents disapproved and insisted that they part. If the situation became public knowledge, the young woman, like one whose engagement was broken, could find it extremely difficult to make another match.

The suggestions above leave ample room for a modern criticism: Why should everyone want to get married? Perhaps many of these people had no desire to and simply didn't. Having spoken with so many, I think this would have been a very small percentage. No one mentioned such an idea, even with an air of bravado. Nearly all were very interested in other people's marriages and in encouraging young people in their family to marry (even insisting on it), and, like Mr. Mardiros, most were insistent that Armenians should marry Armenians. I take this latter feeling to especially show a concern for some kind of continuity—if not of their own family, then of their nation.

Life without marriage, of course, is not all bleak, and it would be a mistake to leave that impression of single people in Cyprus. Unmarried people still had other active family roles to play, as they do today where possible: sister or brother, cousin, aunt or uncle, daughter or son. Most single women, like men, continued working, but in addition to circles built up of friends and workmates, family networks occupied much of a single person's time and interest (as they also did for a married person). Both men and women spent time and attention in some way on the next generation, whether through family or through club or political ties.

As long as she was alive and able, the mother cooked and either supervised or did most other work in the home. As the sons and daughters began to work, the money they earned was mostly combined with that earned by other members of the family under the same roof. Both sons and daughters would help with the shopping and other errands. The longer this continued, the more settled the routine, leaving not only an emotional loss but a practical one when the mother died. Single men and women of fifty or sixty were suddenly faced with learning to cook and run the many aspects of the household they had taken for granted.

Where two sisters (or a brother and sister) have shared a home for many years, a pattern tends to develop. One will grow into the work inside the home, while the other produces a craft to sell, teaches music, or takes a job outside the home to bring in the money needed. In all these cases, the roles are complementary, with each helping rather than overlapping with the other in her or his work. In visits with these pairs, I was left with the same impression of pride in each other's work that I found in many of the married couples of their generation. Unmarried women and men take part in the same outside activities and clubs that married ones do, though they are most likely to take part in occasions that include all women or all men, family, or the whole community, rather than couples.

The presence of many single people is not so surprising if one remembers that the emphasis is on family and that marriage is but one part of family, albeit an important one. Not a few older people, when asked about this, answered that it seemed quite normal to them that one child in each family should stay single and remain at home to take care of the parents. "It's their fate," many said. No one knows whose "fate" it will be except in retrospect, as there is no conscious effort to prepare a specific child in the family to do this. Nor does it happen in all families. Again, this is a weak argument, because married children also care for their parents, though with many more distractions. It does, however, demonstrate that the concern is for the family as a whole, including both older and younger generations. The individual is seen in this perspective.

Chapter 10

Family Life in Diaspora

By the early 1960s an increasing number of young men and women were discussing marriage plans with each other before doing so with their parents. Today in Cyprus and in London, the decision of when and whom to marry is made by the couple themselves. There is, however, much variation within this, and during the 1980s some marriages were still spoken of as "arranged" (*garkatrvadz*). Most often this means that the idea comes from one side, usually the boy's, and has been delicately discussed within the parental generation before it is suggested to the possible bride and groom.

At the point of suggestion, either the man or the woman has the option of stopping the process. If both agree, they may make their own inquiries among mutual acquaintances and then arrange to meet. Once they have met, a decision will be reached fairly quickly because it is understood from the start that marriage is the objective. In addition, some young women in Cyprus generally have a difficult time persuading their parents to allow them to go out with a boy alone until they are engaged, and the families that try this method of matchmaking are usually among the more conservative.

Young women who have found their husbands in this way have stressed to me that *they* do not see it as very much different from the English tradition of blind dates. In fact, it is better, they say, because it is not completely blind: "People who care about you have found out important things about him ahead of time, and you know quite a bit when you actually meet." For others it is an awkward time, and they feel pushed, even if they like the man. If the answer is no, it is usually passed through the original channel so as to save face for everyone. The difficulty comes in facing parental disappointment and, if the person doing the refusing is a young woman, their worries that she has passed up "her only chance."

At the other end of the spectrum are students at universities abroad, who follow what they call "English-style dating" (going out alone) and make their decision to marry without consulting their parents. This interest-based, romance-filled, two-way alliance is most antithetical to the grandparental generation's understanding of marriage as a union of two extended families (cf. Bhachu 1985, 164). Though the majority of young people still consider their parents' feelings and sometimes advice in choosing a spouse, they are unlikely to worry excessively about the prospective in-laws' background, such as being of a certain village, status, or trade.

Young people are most often introduced to future mates by mutual friends or interested relatives at social events such as dinners, parties, and weddings. Because of the small number of Armenians in these diaspora communities, if one has decided that only an Armenian spouse will do, it is nearly impossible to meet at college, work, or any non-Armenian function. For young Armenians in both Cyprus and London, the question of whether or not to marry an *odar* is not an easy one, though some say that they would simply never consider it. Most recognize that this is always a possibility and spend much time discussing the pros and cons with their friends.

DATING, MEETING

Young people find fewer outward differences between themselves and non-Armenians (Greeks in Cyprus, or the British in England) than their parents and especially grandparents saw in their time. In Cyprus, while chatting with Alice and Vartan, both in their late teens, I asked what differences they saw between themselves and their Greek friends. Vartan had just finished telling me that he really saw very little difference at all when we were joined by another friend of theirs, a Palestinian and fellow graduate of the American Academy. He disagreed completely. "Of course there are differences!" he said. "For example, the Greeks are most European-oriented, trying to be more European, changing their traditions, letting their girls go out more. Armenian families are more bound by tradition; they watch their girls very closely and restrict them more."

Vartan and Alice agreed with him on that point, and Vartan added, "On Saturday nights I go out with Greek girls, never with Armenians. Because there are too many complications with Armenian girls—from the parents, the community. I can have more freedom with the Greek girls. Nobody expects anything to come out of a date with them, but if you take an Armenian girl out, everyone thinks you want to get married.

"On weekday nights I go out with my Armenian friends—boys—and we hang out together, maybe play pool, get a hamburger. But on Saturday nights I might have a serious date, and that can't be an Armenian. What if I took Alice out, for example? We could just go out for a meal and then I'd take her home and that would be it. What if I brought her home in . . ."

"Not so good condition?" offered Alice with a grin.

"Yeah, what would her father say? He'd get mad and come and see my father and they'd fight."

"That's crazy," Alice objected. "You're making it sound like Armenians fight all the time. My father wouldn't do that."

Variations on this conversation came up many times, most often with teenagers, young women, and parents of young women. Most young men said they saw nothing wrong with going out with Greek or British women, as long as they eventually married an Armenian. Young women countered that they were tired of sitting at home, waiting for the day the boys decided it was time to get serious. Both they and their parents added that, whether the boys originally intended it so or not, dating does often lead to marriage.

Teenage girls from even the most conservative families do not really sit at home behind closed doors but go out in groups of school friends or cousins or as part of one of the clubs. These are often mixed groups, boys and girls together, and they may have a party at someone's house, go out for *meze* (mixed appetizers) at a restaurant, meet at a club, or go to the beach or the mountains in the summer. The irritating point for them is the contrast between this and the many other things the boys are allowed to do, which they are left out of and *odar* girls can enjoy.

To add to the problem, until very recently more male than female high-school graduates were encouraged to go abroad to study. This leads to the obvious problem of a lower ratio of boys to girls but also changes the social and intellectual expectations of many of the boys, who find they then have little in common with the girls back home. Girls who wish to study abroad must first allay their parents' fears that they will become so preoccupied with their career that they decide not to start a family, that they will lose their "chance" to get married by becoming overeducated, and that they will be led into shameful behavior in the "licentious" atmosphere of Europe or the United States, or marry an *odar*.

As strict or traditional as some of these parents are, their own confidence is badly shaken as they see that, while they are trying to raise their daughters in what they call the old ways, many of the sons of the community either are going abroad and not coming back or appear dissatisfied with these traditions. Parents of unmarried daughters in Cyprus and even in London confessed their deep worries, guilt feelings, or confusion that somehow their own policies had backfired and been responsible for their daughter's not being married as yet. One father in London said, "This is a big problem. We raised our girl in the old-fashioned way, in the way we thought was best, and now we find that everyone else is different and that it is the other, more loose girls who are finding boyfriends and getting married. So how have we helped her? What should we have done?"

Increasingly, many girls as well as boys are going abroad each year to study at foreign universities or training colleges. A professional woman in her mid-twenties, Anna went to college in England after graduation from the English School in Cyprus. She returned to Cyprus to begin her career, and it was there that we met.

"My parents wanted to give us the best," Anna told me. "But they, and we, had to decide what was the 'best.' That is not so easy. At first my parents were not too keen for my sisters and me to go to university. Actually, my mother never did agree, but my father eventually persuaded her that it was necessary. My father's main worry was that I not marry a foreigner, for example, an Englishman, and he used to lecture me on every holiday when I came home.

"You know the Hodja story[1] about the daughter who is beaten up by her father, the Hodja, every time she went to get water? He would beat her up and say, 'Don't break the jug!' before she had even left the house. Why? Because afterward it would be too late. My father was like that. He used to drill into us a fear of *odars*—don't talk with them, don't associate with them, don't go out with them. It was extreme, and it was difficult for me to overcome that fear."

I asked, "Were there many other Armenians where you went to university?"

"No, you see, I had to make friends. Anyway, I don't believe in the old mentality where you put on blinders and only speak with Armenians. In fact, I was very attracted to someone and he would have liked to have gotten serious. I mean, I know the attraction was mutual. But I decided, very cold-heartedly, that I was going to stop it. Because he was not Armenian and I could see that otherwise we were well suited for each other and maybe it would even have led to marriage. That was a real sacrifice for me at the time—it hurt to do that. And, of course, I wondered then, and I still wonder, if that will be my only chance to get married.

"But at the same time, that did lead to giving me more of a sense of purpose in my work. And it made me feel the need for my life and my work to mean something. I think that there is a moral responsibility to history that you owe. I love history. And if you have to play a certain role in a certain moment of history, you have do it. You don't really have a choice. At least I don't feel I do."

Another young woman who had come to London for college and professional studies spoke of similar concerns. In her fourth year of study, Verjin began our conversation by saying that she had been really disconcerted by her last visit to Cyprus. She felt she had grown apart from her old friends, especially those who had stayed there and not gone abroad to study or work, and they had to struggle to find things to talk about. "On the other hand, here in London I have friends who are students—English, foreigners, all kinds—and we can sit and talk for hours. But there is always something missing! They aren't Armenians. My first three years here were really lonely because of this problem, even though there were some Armenian families here I could visit. But most of the time you're on your own.

"I don't know, really, what it is in me that makes me feel this need for Armenian companionship," she went on. "But I do know now that when I am ready to get married, which I am *not* right now, I really want to marry an Armenian. I guess because I feel so strongly about being Armenian myself. Actually I do wonder why I feel such a fanatic. I know it's partly because my parents repeated it over and over while I was growing up, but it's also something I came to myself during those years when I was so lonely here. I think that being Armenian, my identity, was the only thing I had during that time.

"My mother always told me that it was *very* important to marry an Armenian. I wonder anyway if I could really be happy with an *odar* husband. So far I've resisted getting close to any of my friends because I'm afraid of what it might lead to. It's probably easier to stop something at the beginning."

Both Verjin and Anna had been trusted to go abroad to study and felt that responsibility deeply. They were well aware that other young women, both in their own generation and certainly many more before, would have liked to have gone but were not able. This bore heavily on Verjin's and

Anna's sense of duty to their parents and to the community. In comparison, a number of young women and men who had been pressured to play the game by the old rules and who had been disappointed or had a bitter experience within the community were more open to finding an *odar* mate (or even sought one out) and were more likely to slide away from the Armenian world.

Others, both men and women, are much more ambivalent about how to balance the expectations of the family and community with their own perceptions and needs. This has been true for some time, especially in England, as contacts become more diverse and the Armenian population more dispersed. The older emphasis on the couple as part of a larger household or as a unit within the community had changed by then to a more individual notion, one surrounded by variety and choice. The ideal mate became one who would make a good companion, lover, helper, and then mother or father to one's children. Much less important was the idea that a spouse should be a link to the community and other families within it. The idea of a companion has come to imply an intellectual as well as a physical and emotional attraction, and this is where differences in education and experience can sometimes be seen as a problem.

EXOGAMY

At the turn of the twentieth century and in the few decades following, endogamy was the rule, and Adanatsi parents were concerned if their child was attracted to someone in a Zelifkiatsi family, and vice versa. Since then, marrying out, exogamy, has taken on a general meaning throughout the diaspora: marriage to a non-Armenian. Exogamy in this sense has increased in Cyprus since the mid-1950s, and again after 1974. Whereas the biggest worry over exogamy previously was for young men studying abroad, since 1974 it has become a local problem on Cyprus: Greek men and women have become possible spouses as a result of their own system of marriage choice being upset by the conflict and invasion.[2]

Marriage to a non-Armenian is nearly always spoken of as a problem. Though everyone knows of happy, long-term marriages in which one spouse is an *odar,* this is not taken as either an ideal or a norm. Some argue instead that marital harmony is not really possible for a mixed couple. Priests and teachers seem most vocal on this subject. As one priest said, "We always say to our young people, 'Don't have mixed marriages! Yes, you are in love and in this year the love is something that kills your good thinking. Later on you will realize that. Because in each national life there is national spirit. A Greek cannot feel the same as you feel, and you cannot feel the same as your wife feels, and there starts the real trouble.'"

Those who have chosen a mixed marriage, whether pleased or unhappy at present, often see it as a natural development of their own growth. Some point to their education in foreign schools or a particular interest that has led them to feel they are as much a part of the wider world as of the Armenian community. This does not always indicate a weak link with Armenian activities, but rather often an equally strong interest in other ideas or occupational fields, accompanied by the feeling of being a slight misfit. This feeling increases as *being* Armenian becomes more and more a formulated idea of what Armenianness is, rather than something one is by accident of being born.

On the other hand, some may actively be seeking a way out of Armenian circles, as one woman said, speaking of her own marriage in the late 1950s. "When we were growing up, a woman was always a woman. She had to cook, clean, and so on. But we knew that European men didn't think like that. They weren't so narrow-minded. Another thing—I wanted to get *out* of Armenian customs. Even from my father I saw that. 'Annig! Get me a glass of water!' Demanding. Women are not equal.

"My father was very patriotic, and nobody would ever think that he could *let* his daughter marry an Englishman. It was a shock. But it was during the EOKA days. Later my husband did learn Armenian, and he could understand *everything*. He used to speak Armenian with [my grandmother] and she used to love him. They used to dance together. They were both happy-go-lucky and jolly. He mixed well with Armenians."

While the idea of *odar* spouses is still spoken of in very disparaging terms, specific cases rarely are. It is the unusual family, especially in England, that does not have an *odar* in their midst at the larger gatherings, and the reality of an *odar* brother-in-law or sister-in-law is quite different from people's general fears about it. When the couple has overcome the initial resistance and disappointment or been greeted with a welcome from the start, the *odar* spouse is brought into the circle of the family and treated very much as part of the family. Insofar as he or she is willing, the new spouse becomes absorbed into their world.

If he or she learns some Armenian, this is especially appreciated, and the few who learn to converse are brought up as examples of how well a mixed marriage can work. In Cyprus many children at the Nareg elementary school are half Armenian, an indication that (usually Greek) *odar* spouses are willing to help their children learn Armenian and be part of that community as well as their own.

On the other hand, if the couple begins to associate more frequently with non-Armenians and drops out of Armenian activities, it is blamed on the *odar* spouse. Only rarely will a relative admit that perhaps it was the Armenian person who really wanted to put some distance between himself or herself and Armenians, and that a mixed marriage may simply have been the first obvious step. In a few instances couples reported that parents never did approve and relations remained strained. In general, though, the mixed marriage goes against a community ideal, but, like the other rules, this is interpreted quite differently at the community and individual levels.

Armenians who, having married an *odar*, continue to be active within the community can find the frequent tirades against marriages such as their own very painful. The language used, especially in formal speeches and sermons, is usually blunt and rough and does not acknowledge any redeeming features of such unions. This style is reminiscent of the Hodja story mentioned earlier and is part of the same attitude, as the words are directed at those who have not yet married and at their parents. That intended target group are not the only ones who hear, however, and it is difficult to feel completely part of a community that is heard to reject such an important part of one's life.

Clearly the prohibition or rejection by others in the community of an *odar* as a marriage partner is as much or more a fear of communal fission than it is of personal friction between the couple. Instead of developing and strengthening ties among Armenian families, such a marriage cements relations with *odar khnamie*. Not only a non-Armenian *hars* or *pesa* is now part of the family activities but also, if they wish, all his or her extended family. This is only practicable insofar as the *odar khnamie* wish it to be, of course. In any case, the family does not gain Armenian *khnamie*. The social net is not widened, or if it is, it is drastically changed in order to accommodate the newcomers. A few welcome this as a sign of progress, a broadening of horizons, or an escape from the restrictions of Armenian circles.

This is most obvious in London, where not only language but British family relations and expectations differ greatly from Armenian custom. The first and most obvious change in family gatherings is confusion over when it is proper to use Armenian. Even if the youngest generation of the extended Armenian family understands little Armenian and speaks less, they are used to being surrounded by the language, and no one feels guilty about using it while they are in the same room. But the presence of an *odar* spouse at such gatherings is much different, as he or she will at best be bored and at worst resentful if very much Armenian is used. This results in a paradoxical situation in which relatives desire to see as much of the young couple as possible but must deal with an accompanying decrease in the amount of time during which it is acceptable to speak Armenian.

Not everyone worries over this, though some parents find it deeply upsetting. The lack of reciprocal hospitality by many (English) *khnamie* is perplexing but stirs rather more ambivalent feelings. Hospitality is missed as a sign of goodwill and friendship, but in the case of *odar khnamie*, less-frequent contact means more time in Armenian circles and less in English or other ones. Such experience with English families often serves to rein-force the stereotype of cold northerners, but, as Michael Herzfeld (1987, 21) points out, hospitality also only lightly conceals control and social obligations, which some people may wish to avoid. By marrying an *odar,* a man or woman makes a break with this world and reenters on different ground.

The strength of each individual mixed marriage is not the concern of the community so much as is its own fate. The family's greatest concern, by contrast, is for the future success of each couple's marriage—that is, for stability, fertility, and prosperity. As ideas change about who or what qualities make an ideal mate, so too will the fit between couples and the larger family and between families and community.

HUSBAND-AND-WIFE RELATIONS

"You have seen, during the wedding ceremony, when the bride and groom put their heads together, haven't you? Well, we used to hear that there was a custom that during that time, the bride should step on the groom's foot so that she would always have the upper hand in their marriage [*khoskt g'antsni*]! We used to hear old stories about a bride and groom stepping on each other's feet, one after the other, until the *kahana* had to interfere! I never saw any of this, but our parents used to tell us."[3]

Mrs. Anahid, in her seventies, was telling me how wedding customs and ceremonies had changed over her lifetime. At the same time, we also spoke of how major decisions within families were reached, work distrib-uted, and daily life organized. As the above anecdote illustrates, the divi-sion of power and labor within each household was not to be taken for granted. Instead, decision-making seems to have rested on strength of per-sonality as well as particular circumstances, alongside communal expec-tations of male and female roles. Martine Segalen analyzes similar cus-toms in rural France, showing how they also indicate a loose and changing power structure within the home (Segalen 1983, 155–72). In the stories told by this generation about themselves and their parents, one frequently hears of both men and women taking part in major decisions—whether to move and where, whom the children should marry. In some cases the mother is clearly in charge, at least in several important areas.

One of the most widely believed stereotypes of Armenian life is that until the mid-twentieth century Armenian family life was patriarchal and the father's rule authoritarian, both within and outside the home. This, I think, is not so much a reflection of the everyday workings of family life as of the outward face of protocol and the organized side of community and national affairs. In those generations, men represented the family outside the home; the public realm was their undisputed domain. With the exception of some teachers, all figures of institutional authority were also male. This outside activity and structure, however, rested on the strength of the many households making up the community, and thus on the women as well as the men. The emphasis on the importance of the home and the work within the home gave a sense of worth to those most involved in the running of it. In a critique of ethnographies of Greece, Jill Dubisch points out that the usual focus on the public realm of power relations means that women are not taken seriously

as centers and organizers of social systems. . . . Since domestic life tends to be devalued in Western society and since there is a tendency both to separate the domestic from the "real" social world and to perceive the domestic world as in some sense "natural" and unproblematic, the significance of women's "domestic" roles for the society as a whole may be overlooked. (Dubisch 1991, 40)

With the disruptions of the deportations, war, and emigration, many Armenian families were broken apart and regrouped. The physical survival of the family became the only important issue and in numerous cases this was left to the women, as many men had been killed or transported away. The children of these women speak vividly of the physical and emotional strength of their mothers, aunts, grandmothers, and sisters. Joan Bamberger writes in a similar vein about Boston Armenians: "Today a younger generation of American-born Armenian women proudly speak of the family 'matriarch' in recalling the authority of their own mothers and grandmothers" (Bamberger 1986–87, 84).

This picture of the Armenian woman as possessing strong inner will and character while showing a modest face to the outside world is combined with the notion of sacrifice for the family. The husband is to present an appearance of control to the outside, including a display to guests visiting the household. Hirschon portrays marriage among the Asia Minor refugees of Piraeus as based on complementary gender roles, "a cooperative effort, essentially a working partnership founded on the separate qualities of men and women" (Hirschon 1989, 143). This was also an ideal among Armenian Cypriots, but in practice, it seems, things were not so clear-cut. With each other and the rest of their own household, the harmony of relations between men and women was built on respect for these roles but flexibility behind the outer facade. This we can only gather from the impressions left on their children, who have tried to combine what they learned at home with the changing social and political circumstances around them.

Many people under sixty, women and men, spoke of marriage as a "partnership," as did quite a few above that age. For some this was an ideal that had not been realized, but for many it was an accounting of their own experience. One morning in Cyprus I was sitting with Mrs. Rita in her living room, enjoying tea and her homemade cakes. A married woman in her mid-fifties, Mrs. Rita spoke of her ideas about marriage.

"Before—many years ago, maybe one hundred years ago—Armenian women did do whatever the men said. Whatever they wanted. But it's changed. Now it's more or less fifty-fifty. Before, the bride had to wait until the mother-in-law and the father-in-law went to sleep before she could go to bed." It was Mrs. Rita who told me the story of the sleepy bride who dozed off and fell on top of her father-in-law's bed.

"They showed a film on [Turkish] TV the other night that showed these old-fashioned ways. And they are still doing it in some of the Turkish villages. [In the older generation] if a man had a grocery shop, his wife used to make tomato sauce to sell or other things to help. They also made *bekmez* [carob or grape molasses] to sell. Wives tried to help their husbands and families in whatever way they could. But my mother, I never remember her working. She was much younger than my father, by eighteen years. A very sweet girl. At that time, that happened often. But they loved each other very much."

While at a party, Mr. Vasken, also in his fifties, spun around from a groaning buffet table, having just seen his wife bring in one of his favorite foods. "Look, Shushan!" He waved his arm with a flourish. "You see what it is. Armenian women care for their husbands, and we care for them. We don't have to tell them what we want—they know and they do it. And we do the same for them. We try. No, we really do—that is why we are happy together."

The sense of duty about which Mr. Vaheh was so adamant (see chapter 9) is indeed a potent motivator for married couples. An active sense of duty and respect for each other seem to be the crucial ingredients in long-term marriages, and certainly some carry on with only these two as their base. But as Azniv and others pointed out, love is another factor. It grows from the initial physical attraction to include a sense of joy at being with the other person, sharing important phases of life with him or her, and enjoying the mutual support that is given. It is difficult to say where one attitude ends and the other begins, except in cases at either end of the spectrum.

Today it is more likely that a young couple will marry, as they say, "purely for love"—in the sense of a romantic physical attraction combined with a shared intellectual or political commitment or other common interest. This may take place without a sense of duty toward extended family or community, or even without more than just a vague idea of what one's duty toward the marriage partner might be. In earlier generations, if one was fortunate, love grew from duty and respect. Today it is hoped that duty and respect will grow from love. As before, this does not always evolve as hoped, but it is perhaps more difficult to maintain a long-term relationship on the basis of love only, especially when that love is rarely as unconditional as that of the parent for the child.

A confused sense of priorities in marriage is currently resulting in an increase in separations and divorce, but there are still few enough of these for the couple that is going through one to feel isolated and unable to find others who understand what they are experiencing. One evening in the summer of 1986 I was talking with a woman in her thirties about my work. She told me of changes she had noticed since coming to London and then added, "Have you heard about the divorce now in Cyprus? It is the first one there!" When I told her (without mentioning names) that I had heard of several divorces from the 1920s and others since then, she was amazed. "That's not what we hear!"[4]

The biggest changes in the relations between men and women and between the different generations reflect concurrent changes in attitudes toward work, both inside and outside the home. Some call these changes mere "fashion" and others say it is the result of education, but whatever the cause, the attention previously given to home crafts, whether for sale or for posterity, has dwindled drastically over the last three generations. Girls, like their male classmates, take up an interest in secondary school, which they dream of following into a career. In secondary school both girls and boys are encouraged, even pushed, to achieve high marks. Parents who don't wish their daughter, or sometimes sons, to go on to college want them to get the best secondary education possible. This career orientation in education is reinforced by roles seen on television and in the movies, so girls as well as boys come to see all valuable work as taking place in offices, shops, or laboratories. And it is done in exchange for money.

This relatively new ideal—for both the husband and the wife to work outside the home—is not shared by all, but it is at least part of the realm of possibilities for everyone. Those who do agree, at least in principle, that both will work can find it difficult to work out all the details, as is also the case with couples elsewhere. If a grandmother lives at home or nearby, children can be taken care of, but numerous other household tasks remain, some highly symbolic of the male or female role.

Over and over I was told that men do not or cannot cook, and of course they would not do the laundry, make beds, or clean the house. At first when I noticed a man in the kitchen I made special notes. Also the second time and the third. After some time I realized that many men, especially those married to women working outside the home, had developed culinary skills. They seemed to be a mixture of those who cooked only for entertainment and those who also joined in the day-to-day cooking.[5] Another, larger group helped with serving and cleaning up after company dinners. This is still unusual enough to bring out a chorus of astonishment, admiration, complaints, or insults, depending on who is present, but it indicates clearly that male roles are also expanding.

Some claim that more women are working now because each household needs more money to operate. This is part of the older attitude that women would work for money only if the family was so desperately poor that she could not afford to stay home. Certainly the losses that many suffered in 1963 and 1974 served as an opportunity for women to persuade their otherwise reluctant husbands or parents that outside work was a good and necessary idea. However, many of these say they had wanted to work before that time, out of interest.

FAMILY DYNAMICS

Between parents and children, in London and in Cyprus, there is much demonstration of love—kisses, hugs, hand-holding, touching, caresses—throughout their lives together. At the same time, the speech and tone of voice used by parents, especially after the child is in school, are frequently very stern. For some, especially the older generations, outright praise may be rarely used apart from the occasional, very spontaneous *"Abris!"* or "Bravo!" given a child for a special accomplishment. Until recently, teaching in the home and at school was not by positive reinforcement but by criticism of failure or possible failure, or by teasing. Corporal punishment, especially a ruler across the knuckles, was common at home and school.[6]

During visits, conversations between adults do not usually include children who may be in the same room. They listen and can take part, if asked, in the adult conversation, but it is unusual to gear a conversation toward a child. When young, children are encouraged to perform for guests by reciting poetry, singing, or playing an instrument, but otherwise young people are not supposed to require adult attention.

In the past, most entertainment involved the whole family, either with other families or with other adults only. Children in Cyprus, especially in the old neighborhoods before 1963, could play with each other outside, in the streets, yards, and moat of the old city, without worrying the parents; they would almost always be within sight of someone who knew them. Recently, one mother found similarities with the old style of entertainment when she brought her two children back to Cyprus after a few years away among British and American families.

"In [the other country]," she said, "life revolved around the children, and they had their own social worlds. There mothers would drive the children from one house to the next, host parties for them, invite them back again. Children would always ask friends over for lunch, dinner, overnight, and they were used to a lot of socializing. Here it is totally different. At first I tried to invite a couple of their schoolmates to come here for lunch with the children. They came. And then a week, two weeks went by, and they weren't invited back to the others' homes. So we tried again with others, and it was the same thing. Again and again, no reciprocation.

"[The other parents] don't want to bother, I think. Because they think it is a lot of work. Why go to a lot of trouble to prepare a special meal for children? Because, at the same time, they think it is *amot* [shameful] if they invite them and just give them something ordinary. The children don't care what they eat. They just enjoy the company. But the mothers say, '*Amot bidi ullah!*' ['It will be a shame!']"

"But you are invited out quite a bit, aren't you?" I inquired.

"Oh, yes, all the time. And the children are expected to come along and sit quietly. That's what I mean. They don't have their own social life. They are supposed to be a quiet part of the adult social life."

But in fact children are not quite quiet, or at least not quiet all the time. The other side of adults and children visiting together is that children spend evenings out, have flexible bedtimes, and often go to parties and bigger gatherings with their parents. When with their relatives, children spend time with their cousins while the adults chat. And the adults themselves are not terribly quiet. Children enjoy the jokes and stories, too. The problem, from a child's point of view, is the diminishing birth rate. There are fewer children at family gatherings than there were even a generation ago, and often there may be no other children present at all.

In London, children do have their own circle of school friends with whom they spend time, in each other's homes and at other activities for children only. But there, like in Cyprus, hospitality and keeping up ties with relatives and old friends is central to family life.

DISCIPLINE

Children are expected to show respect for their elders and conform to their wishes when expressed, but there is also considerable allowance made for small children doing as they please. In Armenian there is an expression that roughly translates as "The naughtiest boys turn out to be the nicest men." Mrs. Anoush, in her eighties, explained, "I can give you an example of this. Haig was the naughtiest of boys. You can't imagine. He was extreme. I remember one day his poor grandmother had just finished washing the clothes and was hanging the white sheets up on the line. He cut it down! While she was hanging the sheets, he took a knife and just cut the rope! The neighbors heard her shriek! Of course they had fallen in the dirt, poor woman! He was very young then, and now, you know him, he has turned out to be the sweetest of men."

This willingness to overlook "naughty" behavior extends to older boys, long after girls are supposed to have absorbed the rules of proper behavior. Paul Magnarella mentions a similar attitude in Turkey whereby abnormal behavior by adolescent boys is excused or explained by temporarily labeling the boy *delikanlı*, "mad-blooded" (Magnarella 1974, 105). When more Armenians were Turkish-speaking in Cyprus, they also used this expression for boys in their late teens or twenties, especially for someone who was "running after the ladies."

Girls, on the other hand, are trained to be quieter and more helpful in the home and to assimilate these qualities so that they do not need adults around to remind them of how to behave. This has changed, but not drastically, with each new generation. Adrineh, now in her early forties, remembers growing up in Nicosia in the 1950s. "Socially I was pretty well invisible. Truly invisible. I mean, up to the age of seven, for instance, my parents loved for me to perform for other grown-ups—one-act shows of other people and imitating them or anything. You know, jokes, or dance routines or piano, if you like.

"And then at the age of seven or eight, suddenly I was supposed to be very quiet. Because then I was becoming a woman or a girl. And the girl was supposed to be silent. And so just at the age when you want to start joining in and communicate about more interesting things, then you suddenly have to shut up. And then that continued, and it got worse and worse. And the older I got and the more ideas I got, the more I had to shut up, and I found it pretty well intolerable."

Adrineh noticed at the same time that her female cousins didn't seem to have the same conflicts as she felt and wondered if the problem might have been too many strong-willed people living in the same house. But, like a few other girls and boys in her generation, Adrineh had begun attending the English elementary school and was being exposed to new ideas of behavior, both from the formal learning and from her English friends there. Her parents, like the others who sent their young children to English schools, had perhaps not realized that the impact of the schooling would be as deep on a cultural level as it was educationally.

CONTINUITY WITHIN CHANGE

A desire for a better education for one's children, while fitting into one generation's general outlook, can work out quite differently in practice than expected. Accomplishment in the educational sphere is usually individual, but this then reflects on or includes the larger family. At the same time, it can take a person farther away from Armenian circles, and often away from Cyprus, where the variety of jobs is limited. Ingrid O'Grady, writing about Armenians in Washington, D.C., observed this as a conflict between the collective and the individual, where the aims of each are quite often at odds (O'Grady 1979, 128).

Within each generation, and probably within each person, there are conflicting ambitions and desires of which one is either more or less consciously aware. The striking feature is the continuity of central values passed on between generations, in spite of the many outward disturbances and changes. Making similar observations about the family generally, Segalen writes,

> There is a permanence about the family and it seems to offer many
> forms of resistance to social change. . . . It occupies a mediatory posi-

tion between the generations and ensures continuity at a point where
macrosocietal changes and changes within the family converge. (Segalen 1983, 293)

The concept and importance of family itself receives its different interpretation with each new generation but remains at the core of Armenian values. While young women may object to pressure to be submissive (and,
now, to pressure to work only within the home) and young men may object to the idea that they must become high earners or enter a certain career, they still think in terms of the strongly linked family, with its well-
maintained connections to relatives, *khnamie,* and other Armenians. The
security of these networks of warmth and support may also be the cushion
that allows flexibility and resilience in the face of major sociopolitical and
geographic changes.

   Close family and communal webs can also produce other effects, often at the same time. Volkan describes Turkish Cypriot family life as being
mother-centered and tightly knit while bearing vestiges of patriarchal
tradition.

> Each family member is to some extent the psychological extension of
> all the others and all feel dependence on the same interpersonal web
> for support and emotional nourishment, sharing emotional, social,
> and economic problems and presenting a unified front to the world.
> (Volkan 1979, 53)

Volkan describes the individual Turk as being in a "satellite state," fixated
in orbit around the central, powerful figure of the mother. This he sees
as "indicative of failure to complete entirely the process of separation-
individuation."

> In the family many moths orbit together around the candle, delicately
> keeping apart from one another. The small hit-and-run collisions that
> occur are, in human terms, psychological assertions of one's identity;
> the bickering, nagging, and sulking that take place within the family
> fold serve to reduce anxiety over the possibility of becoming genuinely
> symbiotic. (Volkan 1979, 55)

On the level of intracommunal, intrafamilial affairs, this assessment can
be extended to the Armenian family in Cyprus as well, though I differ with
Volkan's use of entirely negative adjectives and terms in this otherwise
very apt analysis. Certainly there is an active element of attraction and

repulsion in intrafamilial and intracommunal relations, as many of the quotes in this chapter should indicate, but to describe lack of total separation as a "failure" or to say that certain behaviors project anxiety over a "genuinely symbiotic" relationship seems heavily weighted in favor of Western ideals of the individual. Instead, for all its problems, the family is seen and used as an emotional and practical resource by the individuals within it in a way that is possible only through their own nurturing of the relationships within it.

Volkan suggests that Turkish Cypriots, like Greeks (and, I would add, Armenians), expand their view of family to include community and nation when crises with another group occur. The ethnic group becomes a superextended family, subject to the same unqualified support for their own group and unmitigated repudiation of the other.

THE CHANGING FAMILY

Insecurity, informed by memories of and reactions to the massacres and deportations as well as by more recent disturbances in Cyprus and the Near East, fuels an already potent concern for achievement or accomplishment. The desire for physical security that pulls many toward the West and toward the development of language skills, business skills, and education that will lead to success in Europe and the United States contrasts with the emotional security of the memories of Armenian community, with a sense of duty toward the past, and with the high value placed on relationships within the extended family. The tensions between these often conflicting directions are found within many other groups of refugees and immigrants, as shown, for example, by Hirschon (1989) for Greek refugees from Asia Minor or Boyarin (1991) for Polish Jews in Paris. Boyarin also highlights the intellectual conflict between generations, whether it is the result of differing levels and kinds of education or the result of historical context while growing up.[7]

In today's Western terms, achievement, whether in education or career, demands a more individualized view of work, one more inclined toward self-satisfaction or fulfillment for both men and women. Once viewed as a means toward an end—that is, the support of the family—work has become an end in itself for many. This increasing emphasis on individual achievement, male and female, creates new sources of friction as roles evolve. The old sense of the primary importance of work within the home and the nurturing of the extended family is gone, but at the same

time women must compete on unequal and difficult terms with men outside the home. Contemporary ideas of women as autonomous and in
charge of their own bodies compete with ideas of the traditional household as a network of interconnected, interdependent people. Young men
are also confused about their own roles and direction. Dubisch suggests
that in Greek households in the past, power (female) was traded for prestige (male), saying that "men's public performances, rather than being an
indication of their power, may be a manifestation of their lack of power in
a central institution of social life, that is, within the domestic realm" (Dubisch 1991, 44).

Today life in Cyprus and in London revolves around the needs and
demands of the job and around the individual rather than the family. The
most poignant reminders of how greatly this has changed are the older
women living alone. Raised in large, bustling households in which the
mother or grandmother was the fulcrum of power and activity, these
women have raised their families and watched them leave to set up independent households. For them there is no longer a question of power or
prestige; all that remains is bewilderment and loneliness, punctuated by
periodic visits from kin. For younger Armenians, as families become more
atomized, floating separately, both women's power within the home and
networking between homes become more limited and often more regu-
lated by the needs of the husband's job. As outside work for both men and
women increases in prestige, with certain jobs requiring increased mobility, extended families break apart and move to different continents.

In spite of these changes, studies of Armenians living in the United
States consistently emphasize the importance given to family affairs and
relationships (O'Grady 1979; Phillips 1978; Bamberger 1986–87; Bakalian 1993). What the family *is*, however, continues to change. Once part
of a large network of other families, institutions, and neighborhood, Cypriot Armenian families in London and even Cyprus are becoming more
isolated in their own affairs. Hovanessian writes of a shift in France from
the collective "we" to the individual "me" (Hovanessian 1992). The older
emphasis on the couple as part of a larger household or as a unit within
the community is changing to a more individual notion. As the mixed
idiom of personhood and domesticity begins to unravel, and as Armenians
in Cyprus, as in the rest of the diaspora, begin to define themselves differently, new variations of the strong family emerge: more restricted in size,
less restrictive in control of its members. In negotiating outside changes,
the family itself is changed, but the strong value its members place on it
remains.

Armenians in Cyprus and Cypriot Armenians in London have found that the process of surviving and rebuilding in a diaspora in the last half of the twentieth century includes the shedding of many shared customs and traits. Ironically, flexibility is crucial to continuity. But what is being continued? As the community in Cyprus grows smaller and contacts with the Greek community increase, and as in London distance continues to discourage immersion in Armenian activities, the responsibility for passing on particularly Armenian knowledge and language skills falls more and more on the family. Thus, at a time when they are least able or likely to do it, families are being relied on to reproduce what once whole communities worked together to create. What is important to pass on has been pared down to the Armenian language, the Apostolic Church, and knowledge of Armenian history. But each of these also undergoes its own transformations in diaspora.

Madagh ceremony outside Surp Astvadztsadzin. Following the blessing, the donated sheep will be slaughtered and cooked for a community meal.

Community meal following the *madagh* for Surp Magar held on the grounds of the Melkonian Institute, 1985.

Surp Astvadztsadzin main altar. The curtain on the right is drawn during the blessing of the sacrament but otherwise open except during Lent.

Two generations of choir masters in Nicosia and the parish priest.
left to right: Vahan Bedelian, Der Vasken Sandruni (holding Bible), Hayrabed Torossian. Mr. Bedelian is wearing a *shabig,* the vestment worn by deacons serving at the altar.

April 24, 1985, genocide commemoration ceremony, the 70th anniversary.
This year a short ceremony in the courtyard followed the church service. Young people had prepared symbols for survivors of the genocide to carry in a procession between the two ceremonies: candles to represent those who were lost; drawings of old churches; portraits of artists, writers, and poets.

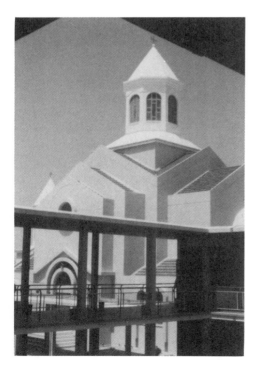

Nicosia Armenian Apostolic Church. Surp Astvadztsadzin from the courtyard of the Nareg School.

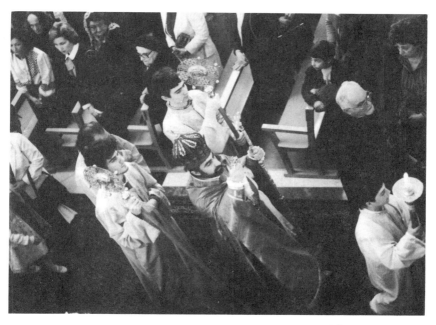

Recessional following mass
at Surp Astvadztsadzin,
Nicosia. Yeghishe Vartabed
Manjikian officiating.

Nicosia Community Church,
where Armenian Protestants
worship. Note contrast in style
between more ornate Apostolic
(and neighboring Orthodox)
and simpler Protestant
religious symbols and
decoration.

Nareg School sports day. Children dressed in costume, performing traditional line dance between sports events.

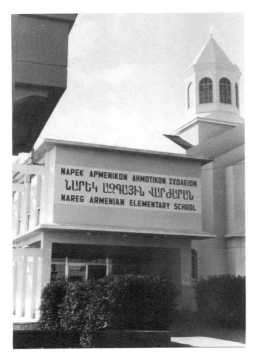

ΝΑΡΕΚ ΑΡΜΕΝΙΚΟΝ ΔΗΜΟΤΙΚΟΝ ΣΧΟΛΕΙΟΝ
ՆԱՐԵԿ ԱԶԳԱՅԻՆ ՎԱՐԺԱՐԱՆ
NAREG ARMENIAN ELEMENTARY SCHOOL

Entrance to Nareg Elementary School, next to the church in Nicosia. Name given in three languages.

Looking toward the north of
central Nicosia. Section of
the old Venetian wall in
foreground, Kyrenia range
in background.

Nicosia street within the walls
of the old city. This section is
being renovated.

Chapter 11

Learning the Mother Tongue

"When children used to come into our shop, I would hold them and cuddle them, and I called them *hokis* ["dear"; literally, "my soul"] or I would say *anoushig* ["sweetie"] to them. And they would look at me and say, 'Mrs. K., what does that mean?' And I would say, 'It's my language. I can only express such special things in my mother tongue!'"

Mrs. Annig smiled broadly as she spoke, nodding toward the front of the house, where the fruit-and-vegetable store she and her husband used to run now stood empty. He still managed to buy the best fruits available, however, and we were enjoying slices of watermelon with macaroons, both special treats in London. Mrs. Annig looked over at me.

"It will be the same for you when you have children. You can only tell them these things in the language of your heart, in your mother language."

I smiled, and she smiled even more. I continued with my watermelon, thinking, *That's interesting. She usually insists that I use and learn more Armenian, but here's a minor concession. It's okay if I use English with my children.* I decided to ask to be sure.

"You mean, in English?"

"Oh, no!" She seemed shocked. "In Armenian, of course! It's your mother language!"

"Well, no . . . ," I admit. "Actually, English is."

"But your mother is Armenian, isn't she?"

"Well, yes . . . " I was starting to catch on.

"Then your mother language is Armenian, of course, and you will use it, too." Having made her point, Mrs. Annig was smiling very happily at this thought.

What *does* "mother tongue" mean?[1] While many Armenians in Cyprus or London may not make the leap of faith that Mrs. Annig did, most would agree with the general beliefs that Armenian is the mother tongue of Armenians, many things can be expressed only in Armenian, and Armenians must speak Armenian.[2] The "mother" tongue links all Armenian "children" not just in an obvious, external way but also with an internal, mental code. Even if an Armenian person's family had not known the language for a number of generations, Armenian was still that person's mother tongue.

At the turn of the century, relatively few Armenians in Cyprus spoke Armenian as their first language. Turkish was the vernacular, and important second languages included Armenian, French, English, and Greek. Thanks to the peace and relative prosperity of the island, the *deghatsi* had nearly a generation's head start on learning Armenian, and by the time the refugees began arriving, the *deghatsi* could look down on their Turkish speech. Learning Armenian at that time, for both *deghatsi* and refugee, was a direct result of a national awakening, of the wider spread of elementary education, and of the circumstances of the time in the Near East and Europe.

As Benedict Anderson outlines in his 1983 book *Imagined Communities,* the nineteenth century brought the rise of philologists and others who traced linguistic origins and built lexographies. At the same time, nascent print capitalism demanded mass markets, made possible by publishing in one rather than many dialects of a particular language (Anderson 1983, 69). This happened alongside the decline and rearrangement of empires, resulting in a decrease in the pervasive use of the language of power and the increased identification of particular vernaculars with emerging nation-states. Armenians in diaspora were also affected by this conjunction of ideas and events, even without a state. Language became synonymous with nation, as it did for many others. The spread of printed matter in vernacular Armenian also increased its importance in the popular mind and, as Anderson points out, "Print capitalism gave a new fixity to language, which in the long run helped to build that image of antiquity so central to the subjective idea of the nation" (Anderson 1983, 47).

While the idea of Armenian is one of an ancestral tongue, existing for several thousand years, the reality in the early twentieth century in Cyprus was that it had to be learned. A primary school next to the church in Nicosia in the late 1800s was staffed by teachers who were from Istanbul or who had been trained in the Jerusalem seminary. This close connection—physical, administrative, and idealistic—between church and school gave a moral imperative to the learning that went on in the classroom. The shift in language took place over one generation not only because the teachers and clergy wanted it so but because parents themselves were anxious that their children learn. The idea had been born, and was being fostered, that true Armenians speak Armenian. And without their familiar old surroundings, connections, and livelihoods, the refugees, at least, were forced to build not just new homes but new personas in Cyprus. Everything was in flux and could possibly change. The idea of changing one's language must have seemed no more daunting, and indeed more positive, than many other adjustments being made.[3]

The few parents who knew Armenian well taught their own families and often helped or taught at the school. Most Turkish-speaking parents encouraged their children to learn Armenian and learned as they did. Mothers were particularly important, judging from stories people remember. Some even insisted that their own children, and any others within earshot, speak only Armenian, not Turkish, in the home. This decision was a certain way to speed the learning process for all generations, but it also posed an obvious problem for the parents. Mothers whose Armenian was limited to their own children's standard must have struggled greatly to communicate ideas and orders to them, and one can imagine that this must have somehow altered parent-child relationships in those families. Whether mothers actually kept this resolution on a daily and hourly basis seems unlikely, but the ideal of the rule made a deep impression and brought the desired results. Those who remember their parents' efforts to learn Armenian describe it as a sacrifice they made for their children's and the nation's sake. The teachers, clergy, and media of the time portrayed the Armenian people as emerging from a long dark period, their new life beginning with the learning of Armenian or the improvement of their existing language skills.

Deghatsi and refugees spoke other languages as well, and the language used in conversation shifted as the subject and context changed. For example, Mrs. Siranoush, who married into a *deghatsi* family in 1925, described the languages she heard around her. It began when I asked how she had learned French, the language of our interview. She explained that she had gone to the French convent school after the Shushanian primary school. She said that afterward, when she married, "We had a cook who was from Turkey and who didn't know Armenian, and so in the house with her we spoke Turkish," which Mrs. Siranoush then learned. In the house, mostly Armenian was spoken between family members. "But unfortunately, Shushan, the Armenians, even the educated ones, mix Turkish with the Armenian language. At my home, like at every Armenian's house—*bakkal, patates, tomates.*"[4] There were also Armenian visitors from Turkey who sometimes spoke Turkish or French more comfortably than Armenian, and so French continued to be used. She continued, "I don't speak Greek well because for twenty-nine years I lived with my mother-in-law and we always had relations with Armenians."

Mr. Haig was born into a refugee family just after their arrival in Cyprus. His parents did not know Armenian, and "though they heard it every day [in Cyprus], they couldn't learn. So we spoke Turkish with them, and among us, the brothers and sisters, we spoke Armenian. My father used to write Turkish words with Armenian letters—and he used to read the Bible the same way."[5]

During the same period, Miss Alice and her family were refugees who had come to settle in Larnaca, where Armenian homes straddled both Greek and Turkish neighborhoods. She recalled, "From childhood we learned five languages. Armenian first, though our parents were originally Turkish-speaking and they found that easiest. But they insisted on speaking Armenian at home. Father was so much *hayaser* [patriotic] that they decided not to speak Turkish at home, and so we children learned quickly by paying attention and absorbing what we heard.

"Our second language was Turkish. We did use it at home and with the rest of the [extended] family. After that was Greek. We learned it with friends, playing in the neighborhood. Greek was learned in the natural environment, playing games, shopping, buying and selling. Our Greek was good enough for that. Unfortunately we didn't learn reading or writing [of Greek] at school then.

"At Armenian school we started French and English lessons in the fourth class."

The transition from Turkish to Armenian took place in stages, however strongly held the ideal. The youngest daughter of a refugee family outside Nicosia, Mrs. Azadouhie represents the end of this period. She talked about her first days at school in the 1940s, the importance placed on education, and the need to learn different languages quickly. "It was hard to learn Armenian," she said, "because they only spoke Turkish at home. My mother only spoke Turkish, and so did the grandparents."

Mrs. Azadouhie's first school was Armenian, but World War II forced the evacuation of the children to the mountains, where she attended a Catholic school and learned French. "After that I went to the American Academy, to the boarding school. My oldest sister did the translating between my parents and the headmistress as they arranged which class I would enter. Or they bargained for it. My parents insisted that I skip the first year, which the foreigners spent mainly learning English, so that they would only pay for the four years, which they could barely afford.

"Finally the headmistress agreed to try it until Thanksgiving. But if I didn't succeed, I would be sent down to the first class. When September came, my mother took me to the bus to Nicosia and saw me off, wagging her finger at me. 'You must do well or you won't come back at Thanksgiving!'"

Mrs. Azadouhie laughed. "Other mothers would have been waving and crying that their daughter was going! But I remembered that and tried very hard to do well." By the end of the year she had earned the top prize in English.

As in other aspects of communal life, different degrees of status were attached to varying levels of knowledge and use of Armenian, Turkish, and other languages, depending on one's outlook. For those most closely associated with the church and school, the more refined one's Armenian was, the more highly regarded the person. Knowledge of European languages was an additional asset. French had been an emblem of the elite, useful for some of the largest traders but also as a means of participation in the "more advanced cultures" of Europe. In Cyprus, though, English quickly became the most important European language.

Turkish continued to be used and learned. A few families reported that Turkish became completely taboo, but most used it in the home with the oldest generation, in the neighborhood, and in the shops. For many born in Turkey, Turkish remained the language of joking, storytelling, proverbs, and curses. As long as all the good laughs and interesting gossip came in this way, the next generation would learn the language. There is evidence, too, that Turkish came to be more a "men's language," with women abandoning it more quickly or at least restricting its usage.[6] Its use also reflected education and ideas of class, Turkish being most accepted among tradesmen and craftsmen and least accepted among educated women. While the language had taken on a negative and highly charged association with those who perpetrated the massacres, it remained an important and comfortable vehicle for the most relaxed communication. Even women who tried hard to speak only "pure" Armenian continued to use Turkish proverbs or sayings. In the 1980s such informal conversations were still freely sprinkled with Turkish aphorisms. As one woman explained, "We admire their language, even if they are terrible people" (cf. Boyarin 1991, 111). In contrast with Mahadev Apte's observation that "a negative view of language is often just one aspect of the overall deprecating way in which a society or culture are evaluated" (Apte 1985, 196–97), the Turkish language is held in great esteem by many Armenians who are fluent in it. Turkish, many pointed out, is easy to rhyme and renders important insights with compact, singsong, often comic phrases. "*Yaşa, yaşa gör tamaşa*" ("Live and learn") and "*Tencire yuvalanmış gapağını bulmuş*" ("Two similar people have found each other") are but two of many possible examples. Other frequently used phrases represent ideas resonant in people's lives. "*Köprüden gecerken göt göte değidi* ("Two people brush against each other as they pass on a bridge") is said jokingly to indicate a kinship connection so far removed as to be barely traceable.

Curses and insults were and are considered more colorful in Turkish but also thus removed from the intimate status of Armenian. (English and Greek serve a similar purpose for the younger speakers.) Armenian can remain the language of church and home while Turkish adds the spice. Though today's Armenian Cypriots declare a real nostalgia for the donkey, the animal bears the brunt of the old Turkish insults: *eşek*; *eşek oğlu eşek* (pronounced *eşol eşek*); *eşek oğlu* ("ass," "son of an ass"). A schoolteacher in his late seventies gave me an example of his old teaching style: "*Zo eşek!* You know who Khorenatsi is? He's even better than Herodotus. . . .*" Pezevenk* ("pimp") is also general but stronger abuse. *Siktir* ("fuck off") is considered very crude but not a mortal insult. It can be a joke between friends, meaning roughly "Get out of here," but is also used in anger.[7]

Few Armenians in Nicosia were fluent in Greek, nor did many try to learn until the generation coming of age in the 1950s. One *deghatsi* who did study *demotiki* at school tried to explain why most people his age (he was born in approximately 1910) did not learn very much, saying that Armenians were aware of the lower status of Greek as spoken in Cyprus: "We knew that the Greek they spoke on the street then was not good. They don't even call it Greek. They call it 'Gibriayka,' you know, what they speak in Cyprus. If we were going to learn, we should learn real Greek [*demotiki*] or speak like people from Athens. But first we had to learn Armenian and English."

Lines between these languages were not firmly drawn. Meetings of the charitable organization Parekordzagan in the 1930s, for example, were polyglot, and in the early 1940s its local president did not understand Armenian. But however intertwined the lines drawn, certain speech did and continues to have connotations that are more positive or more negative. When the refugees arrived, those who spoke Armenian often used a dialect, which their descendants describe as "very rough" and "half Turkish." Then, as now, eastern Armenian, as spoken in Hayastan, had a higher status than western Armenian. Among western dialects or even accents, that of the Bolsetsi (from Istanbul) was considered the best, in the sense of being cleanest, clearest, and most refined (cf. Anderson 1983, Gellner 1983). As one woman who came as a young refugee said, "No wonder the *deghatsi* looked down on the refugees! Even the Turkish the Adanatsi spoke was crude and rough. I asked someone much later if it was just the Armenians, and not the Turks, from Adana who talked like that—if it was their own accent—and he said, 'Oh, no! The Turkish the Turks spoke then in Adana was like cockney English! Not at all like what was spoken in Istanbul!'"

When a person's family background was unknown, accent or dialect, plus the particular languages known, could say much about that person very quickly. Especially as other indicators of wealth, status, or profession had been lost or greatly altered, linguistic codes were helpful in sizing up new acquaintances.

Gumperz suggests two concepts with which to measure the "verbal repertoire" or dialectic and linguistic variety of a community: "linguistic range . . . distinguishing among multilingual, multidialectal, and homogeneous communities," and compartmentalization, which "refers to the sharpness with which varieties are set off from each other, either along the superposed or the dialectal dimension" (Gumperz 1972, 230). Clearly the Armenian community then was both multilingual (Armenian, Turkish, Greek, English, French) and multidialectal (Armenian and Turkish variations). Compartmentalization was not clearly defined, and probably only the liturgy of the church was distinctly monolingual. Government work or secondary school was conducted in English, but even there, with fellow students or workmates, casual conversation might be in Armenian, Turkish, or Greek. Few situations were entirely restricted to one language all the time for every person.

Verbal play, a favorite and honored pastime, was built on the knowledge of several languages. Punning between languages continues and, as Apte suggests, is often obscene (Apte 1985, 181). Double entendre makes vulgarity, though still recognized as such, more acceptable: "*Vets kir dur,*" Armenian for "Give six letters," is understood to mean *siktir,* but the retranslation makes it more comic and less insulting.[8]

By the 1940s, with the new generation educated in Cyprus, Armenian was becoming standardized as well as widespread. In addition to the home, school, and church, a variety of public events, meetings, and *hantessner* provided opportunities to practice and expand the use of the language while reinforcing the idea of being part of the community and the message that being Armenian is speaking Armenian.

Men and women who believed this very firmly took an evangelical approach and influenced many people in Cyprus. More gradually Armenian became not only widespread but natural to use, something to pass between parents and children without the motivation of ideology or guilt. By the mid-1940s some parents had begun to feel it natural enough to take for granted and rethink the educational priorities of their own children. Armenian was something the children now heard all around them, at home, in the neighborhood, in the club. They would certainly learn it. But English at that time was thought of as the language of education for those wishing to compete in the workforce outside the world of trade—for example, the civil service—and also, for some, as the highest standard of education for girls within Cyprus.

Many boys had been attending the English secondary school, but now a few began at the Junior School (and later other English-language primary schools), followed by a small but steady stream of boys and girls in the 1950s. In Larnaca, for similar reasons, a small number of boys and girls were attending the elementary section of the American Academy. The great majority of children continued to go to the Melikian-Ouzunian or the Armenian schools in Larnaca or Limassol, but for linguistic as well as political reasons most of the girls and boys who continued their education did so at English-speaking secondary schools rather than the Melkonian, even after it had lost the taint of being an orphanage.[9]

As the parents knew, the children attending the English primary schools did consider Armenian "their language" and had a firm rooting in conversational use of the language. Further knowledge in reading, writing, and grammar was gained with special tutors after school or by joining the students at the Melikian-Ouzunian on Saturday mornings. Inevitably, while the world these children occupied broadened considerably beyond that of their Armenian cousins and playmates, some of them also developed a feeling of being on the fringe of the community, though very strongly tied to it through their own family network—and their language. A teacher in her forties living in London, Maryam, told me that when she was a student at an English school, she was a Brownie, and one day they were told they were going to go camping outside Nicosia. They piled into the bus with all their gear, very excited, and drove for what seemed like miles until finally they arrived at the Melkonian, a place Maryam had never known existed until that day. Even so, she did not understand the significance of the place until it began to rain and the children were shepherded into the buildings in the front of the property, where they would sleep instead of camping out. Maryam recalled that she had been struck by the huge, drafty, ancient-looking buildings. The children were given beds in one of the dormitories, with the girls who boarded at the school, and Maryam was wonderstruck by the doves flying overhead under the lofty ceiling. In such different surroundings, she and the other children were comforted by all the big teenagers around them, who were telling them not to be afraid. Suddenly she recognized the language they were speaking to each other. "That's my language!" she kept telling the other children and the scoutmasters. "That's my language!"

"That's my language" was Maryam's cry of recognition. Armenian is still Maryam's language in a very real way, even though today she has a degree from a British university, teaches in English, and has relatively little contact with Armenians. Most Armenians over twenty in Cyprus and London are bilingual, if not multilingual, and each language serves a certain purpose and/or context—becomes compartmentalized, in Gumperz's scheme. At different ages, too, people make transitions between languages, changing the emphasis from one to another.

In the 1930s, for example, Miss Emma had managed to learn English quickly in order to succeed at the American Academy after finishing the Armenian-language school in Larnaca. But upon graduation, a priest persuaded her father to send her on to the newly opened Melkonian teacher training college. Miss Emma worried that though she spoke Armenian at home, she had been introduced to abstract words and ideas in English at the American school, and her Armenian was considerably limited in that respect. She did go and stayed on to teach for several years before going back to the American Academy again to teach. Like many others then and since, Miss Emma found herself shifting between at least two languages (which entailed different approaches to learning and teaching), translating and accommodating very different perspectives as well as words.

Mr. Serop, a teacher at the Melikian-Ouzunian during the 1940s and 1950s, gave a few examples of the complex linguistic and educational world students occupied during that time. "When I began there [in the late 1940s] it was very interesting. The girls were better-educated than the boys, on average. The girls would go on to the American Academy, but very few boys went on to secondary education because they were encouraged to go into business. But soon that also changed because many boys decided to go on to more education. And the conditions in Cyprus were conducive for the young men to become professionals rather than shop owners.

"At that time those boys who graduated from elementary school and went on to the English School had to leave the school a year early to sit an [entrance] exam in Turkish. They had to prepare the exam in Greek or in Turkish. They preferred Turkish because it was easier for them. What an ironic thing to have Armenian boys taking an exam in Turkish for an English school."

Mr. Serop met with the headmaster of the English School and arranged to prepare the boys in English and math in their last year at the Melikian-Ouzunian so they could take the entrance exam for the English School in English. "So that is what we did, and the boys succeeded very well and even were jumped into the second form instead of the first, where the Greek and Turkish boys were learning English. After that I encouraged them to go on to university, especially here in England."

By the 1950s Greek was also spoken among Armenians in Nicosia. Mr. Serop recalled, "One day a term we would organize a picnic with buses. And on the bus it is a natural thing to sing! But what did they sing? Greek songs! They were all the rage then. I am still angry when I think about it. I asked the young man who was helping with the music lessons to do more work with the students. I told him that the reason he was there was because I wanted to hear those children singing *Armenian* songs on the bus next time! And he succeeded very well. The next time we were on the bus, they were singing beautiful, lovely patriotic songs."

Very likely the Greek songs continued to be sung elsewhere after they were barred from the bus, but Mr. Serop's aim, like that of other educators in Cyprus, was to make a wide range of Armenian speech possible for the students, in the hope of making them fully fluent and thus creating a community firmly anchored in that language. Though the Melikian-Ouzunian went very far toward accomplishing this, and the Melkonian certainly refined the language skills of those who went on to study there, the reality of being a small minority within a colony ensured that different languages would continue to compete with or complement each other in Armenian Cypriot speech. Likewise, the different educational styles and content of the various schools, the aims of the families regarding their children's futures, the changing political scene, and relations with neighboring ethnic groups all interacted to create a complex array of speech styles. On the surface the people called Armenian spoke Armenian, and certainly few non-Armenians did or do.[10] Even in a relatively small community such as Cyprus, however, the variation beneath that surface was rich and considerable.

LANGUAGE TODAY

The headmaster looked around the assembly room, gave a significant tilt to his head, raised his eyebrows, and began with a great swing of his arm. The children fell silent. "Today, dear students, we are celebrating the birth of one of our great poets, Taniel Varoujan." The Nareg students were gathered for their Saturday morning assembly. A number of parents, mostly mothers, had also come that day and were sitting in the back of the large room. We all listened as Mr. Vartan gave an introduction to the morning's program. Behind him was a portrait of Varoujan on a red curtain, with red flowers and a sign, "1884–1915."

Poems were read by small groups of boys in white shirts and bow ties and girls in their gingham uniforms. Representatives from the Melkonian, including that year's guest teacher from Hayastan, were in the front row. Behind them, children sitting next to their teachers told them about ones farther away who were giggling. Others began interesting experiments with different ways to clap after each work. Mostly they paid attention, especially as the readings changed to recitation. A group went into silent hysterics as one classmate tried bravely to add dramatic gestures to his recital.

While reciting or giving a reading, most of the children pitched their voices a few notes higher than their normal speaking voices and spoke distinctly and loudly. Midway through, a new student, who had known little Armenian two months earlier, recited a poem. Eleven years old, her style contrasted with that of her classmates, perhaps showing traces of her former English education. She too spoke clearly, though not as loudly, and her voice was pitched more at the level of conversational speech.

Next three girls clustered closely together. A smaller boy stood off to the side. They alternated verses of another poem and then shouted the last one together. I was bewildered by the shouting. How much of it was due to the general style of recitation? How much was called for by the content of the poem? As another girl took the stage, someone leaned over to me and said, "This is our best student." With hands behind her back, she looked out at the audience and aimed her voice and gaze directly at us. Pleading, demanding, she alternated between the high-pitched shout and an intense, distinct whisper.

Finally the whole class stood in an arc on the stage. My neighbor whispered again that this poem was always done as a group.

The Lamp [11]

Night of triumph, night of joy.
    —Daughter, fill the lamp—
Victorious from war comes my boy.
    —Daughter, wick the lamp—

A cart is grinding by the well.
    —Daughter, light the lamp—
My boy returns with wreath and bell.
    —Daughter, raise the lamp—

The cart bears a young body spread.
    —Daughter, draw the lamp—
My boy lies gored, my boy lies dead.
    —Girl, snuff out the lamp—

The headmaster was not a pessimistic man. The choice of this poem was part of the community and family telling and retelling of the national trauma with a directed sense of sacrifice and purpose, keeping the fragile nature of the Armenian situation in the foreground. The message of the assembly was clear: Those who have survived are responsible for carrying on. The light was extinguished only temporarily, and the survivors and the newer generations must work hard to keep the flicker of its flame alive.

Currently there is a real sense that the language is in danger again. *Again* is not exactly the right word, however, because, though most in the older generations know it, few people stop to think that when Varoujan was writing, very few of the ancestors of these children could have read or understood his poetry. The great push to make not only speaking Armenian but reading and writing it universal among Armenians was successful to the point where it became taken for granted. Today's concern often overlooks the very large number of Armenians in the early part of this century who had never spoken Armenian. When this is remembered, it is spoken of as a situation that was forced on them by the Ottoman Turks and had nothing to do with sharing the lingua franca of the empire and their neighbors.

As the language is in danger, many believe that so too are the people and their literary past. Who will appreciate and understand the works of these poets? What will it mean to be Armenian as language skills fade? Older people complain that even they are daily using more Greek or English, even in Cyprus. Loan words and expressions increase within Armenian usage, but so too does time spent speaking Greek or English only. Television is a prime mover behind this, but films, the printed media, and books, as well as the work environment and the smallness of the community, add to the popular immersion in these two languages. Use of Turkish is maintained, and the youngest generation is acquainted with it through television now that there is no personal contact. In families where one spouse is Greek or English, those languages are often spoken at home, leaving the learning of Armenian to school or visits by extended family.

One reaction to this is to try to instill fear and guilt in the next generation: fear of the assimilation of language and people, fear of the disappearance of Armenian, and guilt at the neglect of the mother tongue. Another simultaneous response is to try to make not only the children but all of the community proud of their language and their heritage. Teachers, clergy, and active club members promote this aspect of the language and encourage people to admire its special qualities.

When Professor Feydit of Paris took part in the annual Armenian week sponsored by the Melkonian, he gave two evening talks. The one people seemed to most look forward to was entitled "The Advantages of the Armenian Language." Already it was exciting that an *odar* should have learned Armenian for his studies, and many had heard that he spoke it "extremely well," even "perfectly." But the word *advantages* struck a particularly popular chord, and people spent the week speculating about what those advantages might be or which of the many he might choose to talk about.[12]

After the speech was given, I had to admit that I had understood very little of it.

"Don't worry! We also understood only the main points," people consoled me with polite exaggeration. "His Armenian is excellent, much better than ours. *Shad partser* [very high]."

"What were the advantages, then?" I asked.

"You can explain yourself more efficiently and fully in Armenian. Any idea can be expressed in Armenian. You can build words from root words. So we should not be borrowing words from other languages. Other languages, such as Greek, English, German, and French, are not pure. For example, English is full of Greek, Latin, et cetera. But Armenian is pure."

"Of course he means classical Armenian," others hastened to add.

"And the Armenian alphabet was invented by an Armenian, not an outsider." These were the important points people had gathered and were talking about the next day.

St. Mesrob Mashdots, the inventor of the alphabet (or discoverer, as some call him), is commemorated every year at the schools and churches. A decorative plaque showing the alphabet, and often St. Mesrob, is displayed in most Armenian homes in Cyprus and London, and he is often found on calendars and Christmas cards. A well-meaning English journalist, writing in an English-language paper in Cyprus, touched a raw nerve in the community when he used the Hodja (and also Santa Claus) as an analogy to the St. Mesrob story. The point of his article was lost in the commotion stirred up by his apparent trivialization of such an important figure and by his choice of a Turkish comparison. The man had heard enough Hodja stories, told with great enjoyment, to think that Armenians would not be offended by a figure they had virtually co-opted into their own discourse.[13] But the point about St. Mesrob is his role in providing the Armenians with a very different alphabet, thus aiding their continuation as a separate people at an early and important stage. For Armenians, his position is, by definition, unique and completely intertwined with their concept of their own uniqueness.

The question of myth or storytelling had come in the author's criticism of the popular version of St. Mesrob's invention as a sudden inspiration or "discovery" given by God. A teacher explained how she felt the journalist had misunderstood the Armenian view on this. "We believe that Mesrob Mashdots had help from God, yes. But he worked very hard for many years. He studied all the languages of the surrounding countries and, of course, he prayed for help to do his work well. He was a monk, after all! And we all pray for help with our work. I do, anyway, every day. So we think that one day or night, after he had been working so long, he had a dream, and God showed him the new alphabet, and he woke up and wrote it down. That could happen. You think and think and then lie in bed and ideas come in sort of a dream. Anyway, he [the journalist] was mocking the Armenians for how they think of Mesrob Mashdots, but he didn't understand it."

The "discovery" or invention of the alphabet is often presented in mythological—and, it is hoped, inspirational—terms. The alphabet is explicitly linked to the sacred in Armenian telling. It was inspired by God, penned by a monk, used first to transcribe the Bible. Its eventual position as an integral aspect of Armenian identity thus brings with it a residue of the sacred, and this is emphasized in the lectures, sermons, poems, and songs that seek to inspire pride and loyalty in Armenians.

Chapter 12

Language in Everyday Use

Pride in the language and fear of assimilation are in the minds of all who have attended an Armenian school or many lectures at church or clubs, but communication is not based on these concerns alone. There are, of course, everyday exigencies that impinge on and sometimes counteract the more directed efforts of school, church, and parents.

One day I was sitting inside a shop, drinking tea with the proprietor in between customers. The shop owner's father, Mr. Yervant, stood in the door, looking toward the street, his form outlined by the bright sunlight, bolts of colorful fabrics stacked on either side of him. His head turned slowly from right to left as he looked up and down the street, calling softly to passersby. "Hello . . . please . . . yes . . . ," he said as some UN peacekeepers in blue berets walked by. "*Kopiaste*" (Greek for "welcome") was his greeting to others. To still others he called, "*Hrametsek*" (Armenian for "welcome, come in"). All this occurred between chats with neighboring Armenian and Greek shop owners in their own doorways. "*Buyrun*" (Turkish for "welcome"), he said softly as someone else passed.

Armenians today generally speak Armenian together. Greek and English are frequently used, and Turkish is not yet forgotten. For many over fifty, Turkish may be very strong. For some, like Mr. Yervant, Turkish is firmly connected with shop conversation and his working life, and it comes out automatically, even if there is no one left to respond. Those who travel or deal with foreign companies for their work develop not only English but French, German, or Italian. The main linguistic range of Armenians in Cyprus continues to include Armenian, Greek, Turkish, and English, but the balance between them has shifted.

GREEK AND TURKISH

By the 1980s few people could operate in Cyprus without a reasonable knowledge of Greek. This varies from basic elements of the vernacular *demotiki,* needed to be able to shop, take a taxi, and exchange pleasantries with a neighbor, to being able to hold forth in a court of law. While older people are slow and sometimes reluctant to learn this "new" language, most of those under fifty have taken to Greek as their elders did to Turkish. It is the language of their environment, business contacts, government, and neighbors—and, in some cases, *khnamie.*

One Sunday afternoon after church, Bedo and Siran, a middle-aged couple, took me to someone's house. Bedo decided to take a slight detour, along a back road toward the border. He pointed out where his old warehouse used to be, just beyond where we finally stopped. We pulled into someone's driveway, beside a stack of timber where an older, plumpish man in a suit was walking in the sun, smoking a cigarette. Bedo leaped out of the car. "*Yassoo koumbare!*" he shouted in Greek (loosely, "Hello, friend!"), and the man hurried over. A woman appeared on the balcony above us. "Siran, *kori mou!*" ("Siran, my daughter, friend"). Former neighbors, they chatted happily for a few minutes. Siran and Bedo resisted offers of food and drink over and over again—we were due somewhere else soon.

"Look how these people live," said Bedo as we drove off. "Right next to them!" He pointed to the Turkish bunkers across the field. Bedo was around fifty, old enough to have learned fluent Turkish before the division of Nicosia, but he was young enough then to have since learned Cypriot Greek vernacular well. His English was also good, but he claimed Greek and Turkish were easier for him. He still used Turkish frequently with his mother, traded a few Turkish jokes, insults, or stories with friends, and occasionally watched Turkish television.

Siran, who was younger and grew up in Larnaca, said she knew very little Turkish. Her family spoke mostly Armenian at home, and though she could follow a film or someone's conversation in Turkish, she found Cypriot Greek vernacular much easier. In her work she used Armenian almost entirely, though her own secondary education was in English. For both Bedo and Siran, Armenian was their first and most comfortable language and the one they used with each other.

Their teenage children, like others their age, grew up speaking Armenian. They used it at home and with Armenian friends and relatives, though not always. Their secondary school was English, and they used that language with their schoolmates and also at home for television, videos, and leisure reading. They spoke the Cypriot Greek vernacular with Greek friends and neighbors and when shopping. *Demotiki* had been taught to them at the Nareg by a Greek teacher provided by the government, and it was continued in secondary school; it was also heard on television. They were acquainted with Turkish, from television and their grandmother, but never spoke it themselves.

Television plays an important role in learning both Greek and Turkish. I often noticed older people watching Turkish television, and they would explain that it was more relaxing, as they understand the language so much more easily than Greek. They were also interested in how the language has changed since they were children—for example, it now includes fewer loan words from Arabic. One middle-aged woman told me that her family enjoyed watching Turkish television "for the music especially, because it reminds us of our ancestors, the old days. They used to sing those songs, too." Her sister-in-law was English and lived in Cyprus for a long period. "She used to get mad at us. 'Why do you hate them but watch their TV?' She didn't understand."

Just as I was impressed with the knowledge of English that I found among so many people, both adults and children, Greek people with whom I spoke nearly always mentioned how well Armenians speak Greek. Armenians generally were far less confident of their own abilities, or perhaps they were sterner critics. Many conversations similar to the following started out, as did this one, with me tripping over my tongue in Armenian and a few good-natured jokes about that.

"But you mustn't worry about it! We all do the same thing when we speak Greek." Mrs. Anahid, a woman in her sixties, shrugged and made a face. "How can we help it? We didn't learn as children, and even now we don't use it *that* often. We mostly speak Armenian in our circle. We don't have that many Greek friends."

"Yes," her friend added, "but we do watch the television—that helps. And of course, we have improved very much since 1963." Both of them looked at Mrs. Anahid's thirty-year-old daughter. "Certainly your generation is much better than ours!"

"We're still not that good, even so," the younger woman said. "Any Greek can tell we are *odar* because we make so many mistakes. After all, we didn't go to Greek schools. And Tavit [her husband] speaks better Greek than me because he uses it at work all the time—but he is still not perfect."

"It is their complicated grammar," Mrs. Anahid concluded.

Though their Greek neighbors compliment them on their abilities in the shops and on the street, Armenians judge themselves by the standard of *demotiki*. The school classes provide a good base, but learning "perfect" Greek requires a special effort, which, many said, very few manage. When I heard some younger Armenians speaking English with their Greek official visitors at two different public gatherings, I asked why, as I had heard the same people speaking Greek in other situations. They explained that while they could understand well enough, they didn't feel their Greek was up to the standard of the occasion. Formal occasions demand language skills that are more formal as well.

Now, in the younger generations, jokes and insults are being passed around in Greek instead of Turkish, and a few words have made their way into everyday Armenian or English speech. The most popular include: *endaxi* ("okay"), *mana mou* ("my dear"), *yassoo* ("hi"), and *koumbare* (literally, "godparent," but often used to indicate close friendship). *Armeniki visita* is jokingly used, as apparently Greek Cypriots do, to indicate a very long visit, lasting hours.

ENGLISH

If *endaxi* is endemic, so too is *okay*. It is really not okay to say either in an Armenian sentence, according to the purists, who worry greatly over these invasions, but everyone does. Greek and English are attractive to the young people and are widely disseminated through TV and the newspapers. There is a creeping sense that Armenian is a luxury while these two languages are necessities. English is also a language of the past in Cyprus, and there is ample evidence of this in the large number of older people who speak the language very well. Before independence, many received their secondary education in English and it was also the language of government and banking. More Armenians were involved in these kinds of work before independence than afterward, and therefore the older generation often used English every day in their work.

Today English is still often used, even between young Armenian friends. One day Ani, a student at the English School, mentioned that though her family spoke Armenian in their home, when she wanted to talk about something "really important" with her mother, she used English. "I want to talk faster, not try to find the words—and she usually keeps talking in Armenian and we go on like that." Other teenagers told me that they frequently spoke English with their Armenian friends—"to show off different accents, American or English"—or to talk about certain subjects, especially sex, English films or TV shows, or rock and roll.

Secondary school for Armenians is in English, even at the Melkonian, with the exception of Armenian language, history, literature, and music classes. The orientation of these students is outward, at least for the time being, with hopes of college or even just travel in Britain or America, Hayastan or Europe. Cyprus becomes small, as home does for many Western teenagers as well, and even claustrophobic. English and Greek are seen as the languages of opportunity by many.

ARMENIAN

Armenian as spoken in Cyprus is the western variant of the vernacular language. There is a recognizable Cypriot accent, I was told, showing the influence of Turkish, though not so heavily as among those Armenians living in Turkey (Istanbul). When both parents are Armenian, that language is spoken in the home. Except for Greek and English classes at the Nareg, Armenian is used there for all studies, assemblies, and music. In the church, the Bible is now often read in vernacular Armenian, and the sermon is often given in vernacular rather than classical Armenian, but no other language is heard during the service.

The Melkonian Institute provides classes in Armenian language, literature, and music, including a popular choir, but officially all other classes are in English. The teachers may lecture in Armenian or English, and the students may ask questions or hold a discussion in Armenian, but the readings are in English. Leisure activities in Armenian are encouraged, and students attend the many evening events held at the Melkonian.

Most people listen to the Cyprus Broadcasting Corporation's Armenian hour, which includes music, information about the community as well as the larger diaspora and Hayastan, and occasional interviews. Radio Yerevan jokes are also a regular feature. There is no Armenian television. The various clubs also arrange regular lectures, concerts, and other events, always held in Armenian. If *odar* dignitaries have been invited, an introduction in English and/or Greek will also be given.

Armenian is also the core of casual conversation between Armenians but, depending on the generation, work, interests, and, again, context and subject of the conversation, a mixture of foreign words or sentences are included. A few foreign words, such as *merci*,[1] are so firmly entrenched that they are nearly thought of as part of the vernacular—but not quite. Other such firmly embedded foreign words include a large number of Turkish food terms and other Turkish idioms, especially in the speech of those over forty. These include *canım* ("my dear"), *yavrum* ("my child"), *çocuk* ("child"), *tamam* ("done" or "okay"), *maşallah* ("what wonders God has willed" or "if God wills . . . "; "wonderful"),[2] *eş* ("donkey"), *falan* ("and so on"), *kuruş* ("small change"), *ya* ("you see," "indeed"), and *ki* ("that," "in order that"). Also heard are insults such as *köpek* (dog) or *eşek* (ass).

Armenian Cypriots are sometimes teased by speakers of eastern Armenian for the use of *gor,* an insertion from the Turkish present continuous tense *yor,* which has become embedded in everyday speech. "*Gertam gor,*" for example (as in Turkish *gidiyorum*), is used to mean "I am going."

MULTILINGUAL SPEECH

Speech no longer includes multiple dialects of Armenian, but Armenians in Cyprus share a wide verbal repertoire in everyday conversation. If a phrase or word from Greek or English fits the thought best, that is inserted. If a Turkish word is comfortable, it slips in. A few Arabic phrases and some French also can be heard. When one hears pure Armenian speech, one can be sure that the speaker has made a mental note at some time, if not just then, to purify his or her speech and discover the Armenian equivalents of the more commonly used foreign phrases. *Television* (in Armenian, *heradesnel*), *telephone* (*heratsiyn*), and *record* (*tsiynabnag*) are examples of foreign words that go virtually unnoticed in an Armenian sentence, but use of the Armenian word serves notice that the speaker "cares" about the language. This desire to use only "pure" Armenian is also the source of fun and self-mockery, as when Armenian words are created for things such as macaroni (*yergaraglorakhomoratsag,* "long round dough hole").

Compartmentalization of the different languages has changed, but there is still considerable overlap both within contexts and within individual speech patterns. Generally, more Turkish is used by the older generations than by the younger ones, and men use it more than women, though women understand it. Fluency in Greek increases in the younger generations. Though there is a mixing of languages within common speech, the situation in Cyprus is still not what Gumperz calls "fluid repertoire," in which "one speech style merges into another" (Gumperz 1972, 230). Each language is distinct, and it is mostly vocabulary or whole phrases that are mixed.

The variety of multilingualism in Cyprus is in contrast to that of Armenians in London, where the host linguistic context is radically different. Between Cyprus and London there are differences not only in language shift, which is happening faster in London, but also in style within Armenian, influenced by the British social context. Some phrases meant quite hospitably in Cyprus are sometimes understood as aggressive or interfering in London.

Conversation in Cyprus is encouraged, for example, by the words "*batmeh nayenk*," which, loosely translated, mean "What have you been up to lately?" Literally translated, the words come closer to how they fall on young Londoners' ears: "Talk! Let's see. . . ." In English conversation in London, questions tend to be more subtle and more specific. Young people visiting Cyprus or speaking with older people in London feel they are suddenly under the spotlight. If they become tongue-tied, things get worse: "Why doesn't he talk?" "Why is she so shy?" "What's the matter?"

To a Cypriot, the phrase "*batmeh nayenk*" (or a variation, "*batmeh desnenk*") indicates verbal hospitality: "The floor is yours—tell us about whatever is important to you." Given the importance of conversation, this is a generous offer, indicating that the speaker is interested.

LONDON

Language shift in London is toward eventual monolingualism rather than other varieties of multilingualism. In Cyprus and the Near East, it is rare to find an Armenian who speaks only one language. Children and adults hear and use a variety of languages according to the place and situation. While Armenians are unusual in the number of languages they speak, they are surrounded in this region by many others who are bilingual or even multilingual. Many Greeks with whom Armenians come in contact in Cyprus are bilingual in Greek and English or have studied in Eastern or Western Europe and speak other languages. In Great Britain, by contrast, Armenians look to the overwhelmingly monolingual English as their models, rather than their fellow minorities. The media—television, radio, newspapers—are monolingual. In short, it does not seem natural in London to be multilingual. Speaking languages other than English, even on the simplest level, requires effort, determination, and a different attitude toward language than that of the host culture. This is not easy to instill in the younger generation.

A couple who had come to London with two boys under ten years old spoke about their experience on arrival. "We decided to speak Armenian with our children. It worked for a while, but gradually the boys became aware that other people were speaking English all the time and, for example, we'd be walking in the park and there would be a tug at the trouser leg. 'Baba, speak English!' They would look shyly around at the passersby. Now our boys say that English is their first language. They do understand most things [in Armenian], but they prefer to speak English, even with us—and certainly with each other."

A grandmother told a similar story, talking about how she had begun by speaking in Armenian with her grandson but how he eventually resisted. "One day I called out to Arto to come and get his tea. He was playing in the garden, watching some men [English] who had come to do work for us. When he came inside he was furious. 'Medzmama! Don't ever use that language in front of other people!' And he was very young then. It hurts me very much, but what can I do?"

Children want to blend in, to be the same as their friends (or would-be friends). François Grosjean suggests that "children will become bilingual when psychological factors create a need for communication in two languages . . . and . . . they will revert back to monolingualism just as quickly when such factors disappear or are no longer considered important" (Grosjean 1982, 179). It is usually the child who decides whether the factors are important or not. Looking different is bad enough, but it is crucial to sound like the others in the neighborhood in terms of accent, vocabulary, and style.

When the children are young, many parents begin with Armenian only or with both Armenian and English. Some continue to speak Armenian when the children begin to answer in English, or the parents even pretend they don't understand until the child speaks again in Armenian. As the children know from an early age that their parents do speak English, this can lead to troubled times, but these parents feel it is worth it. For some it has worked very well, as their children do grow up speaking Armenian as well as English. Many, however, gradually decrease their insistence on making the children learn and speak Armenian. Most continue using it around them, hoping that some of the sounds, if not the language structure, will sink in and eventually be resuscitated. "When he grows up, he will be sorry! He will want to speak Armenian, but it will be so much harder to learn then."

In addition to learning at home, Armenian classes are offered in London on Saturday or Sunday morning at one of three schools, and in the mid-1980s a play group for children under five was started. Periodically there have also been evening classes for adults (often non-Armenian wives) and more advanced prep courses to help students taking the former O-level or current GCSE Armenian-language exam.

The oldest of the schools is the Tahtaian, mentioned in chapter 8. Mr. Assadour, one of the founders, spoke to me about the reasons behind the creation of the school. "We started as a [church] council school. We went to the council and explained ourselves. 'What are you going to teach them?' they asked. 'Surp Kiirk [Holy Bible], religion, is what you must teach on a Sunday morning if they are going to miss church,' they said. But I said, 'They can't learn religion without learning our language. They are intertwined.' So it was approved."

After my own visit to the school, I gave a twelve-year-old boy named Vahakn a ride home and we chatted about the Tahtaian, where he had been going for six years. We began our conversation in Armenian and ended in English, like so many others.

"Today we were learning about history," the boy said. "It's really supposed to be about reading and writing, but my teacher is more interested in history, so that's what we mostly learn."

"Do any of your friends from the Tahtaian live near you or go to your school?" I asked.

"No, but there's a boy from our [Armenian] Scout troop at school."

"Do you speak any Armenian together there?"

"Yeah! On the playground! We like to call the other boys names so that they can't tell what we're saying!"

Vahakn told me that he read and wrote in Armenian only what was required for his homework but that he did understand and speak Armenian frequently with his parents and their circle of family and friends. For him and other children like him, contacts and visits with relatives in Cyprus are an important influence. Among the psychological factors Grosjean describes as creating motivation are when such a child wants to communicate with people who speak better Armenian than English or wants to feel as though he is part of a group that is speaking Armenian. The Tahtaian and the other Armenian schools and Scout troops in London also provide the children with other Armenians as friends and classmates, encouraging them to feel as though they are part of a larger community of Armenian-speakers. While doing so, Cypriot Armenian children also meet children from Lebanon and Iran and become aware of the variations in language knowledge and dialect that exist.

A minority of the children of the London Armenian community attend these schools regularly, though. And despite the best of intentions on everyone's part, some attend one or two years and then quit, having retained very little. It seems that only particularly fortuitous combinations of family encouragement (including use of Armenian at home, regular Armenian classes, and contact with other Armenian-speaking children) can persuade a child, especially a London-born one, to learn.

There are a number of parents who feel ambivalent as to whether their children should learn Armenian. Even among those who agree that Armenians must speak their own language, some worry that Armenian at an early age may slow down the development of the child's English-language skills. They have read, in newspapers or magazines, that bilingual children sometimes have smaller vocabularies than monolingual ones and take longer to get started at school. They see their own desire to pass on Armenian as more romantic than practical and thus an unfair burden.

Others have no desire to have their children learn Armenian. "What for? It is useless. Let them learn French or German—or Japanese, if they want!" These parents may or may not continue to speak Armenian themselves at home but dismiss the "duty" to pass it on, which all are aware of from their own schooling and childhood, as not only old-fashioned but also out of place in England. The development and refinement of English-language skills and assimilation into the mainstream of English life is their primary goal.

Learning Armenian, even for the most dedicated families, is but one goal among many when raising children. And teenagers in London are free to choose whether they will continue Armenian lessons, go to Armenian activities, and meet Armenian friends and cousins on their own. The family activities take up only one portion of their time. Other goals or leisure activities might have to be juggled or even cut off if one is to continue in Armenian activities enough to keep up with the language. As students reach university age, this dilemma becomes more pronounced, though while the Armenian Community Centre and the Nor Serount Club were in operation during the 1980s, these venues provided more regular, casual opportunities for people of all ages to meet other Armenians.

MULTILINGUAL SPEECH IN LONDON

By the late 1980s multilingual speech was still important in London, especially to all those over thirty. Armenian speech is peppered with more
and more English but still contains the occasional French, Turkish, or
(especially among the younger people) Greek word or phrase. Language-
switching indicates much more than simple proficiency or lack thereof.
Armenian is often used between old friends or cousins, even though both
might speak better English, because they are used to it, and because the
language is a private one and indicates intimacy. Along the same lines, I
met with resistance in a few cases in London when I tried out my Armenian but the other person felt there was no need for it: "She speaks English
better than Armenian, and so do I. We don't have a history of speaking it
together—so what is the point?"

But one cannot spend an informal evening with Cypriot Armenians
over forty and understand every word, let alone nuance, without a good
knowledge of Armenian, Turkish, and some Greek and French. The enjoyment of verbal play has been considerably diluted but is still there and is
very much part of communication.

The most obvious changes are the gradual decline in Armenian-
language skills among native speakers, the weak or nonexistent skills of
those born in England, and the concurrent turn, especially in the English-
born, toward effective monolingualism. Many students take foreign languages at school but rarely incorporate them into their normal speech, as
their parents did, nor do they speak them as fluently. "Pure" speech is
expressed as the ideal, whether English or Armenian, and no one com-
plains directly that speech is not mixed in the younger generation, though
older people do speak wistfully of enjoying the verbal skills of entertainers
in the past.

There have been several important interruptions in the process of language change, however. The first was the second arrival of Cypriots in
1974, injecting a new supply of native Armenian-speakers who were used
to speaking the language regularly. This was followed by successive waves
of immigrants from Beirut and Tehran. If Cypriot Armenians were confident in their Armenian, these people were more so and somewhat over-
shadowed the Cypriot Armenians in their knowledge and Armenianness
(see chapter 8). The Armenian language was given new life in the community, and Cypriot Armenians were encouraged to continue to speak
Armenian. While Cypriot Armenians are active in each of the political
groups and cultural clubs, so too are many Armenians from Lebanon,

Iran, Egypt, Iraq, Ethiopia, Istanbul, and Jerusalem. Cypriot Armenians may be disproportionately active in these groups, as some say, but sheer numbers add to the influence of the non-Cypriots (approximately two thousand Cypriot Armenians to between seven thousand and ten thousand others). The pervading impression one gets upon visiting one of the club meetings or lectures is that everyone speaks Armenian. This is partly due to the number of newcomers who are actively seeking out other Armenians at these places, but in part it is also a tautology: Those who speak Armenian come to the places where Armenian is spoken.

As in Cyprus, the lectures and introductions at meetings are usually given in Armenian. Newspapers, journals, and announcements are predominantly in Armenian. So while informal and home life for Cypriot Armenians in London is becoming increasingly dominated by the English language, the language used in Armenian public places, both formal and to a degree informal, is still Armenian.

One other major area remains most steadfastly Armenian-speaking: the church. While club leaders are willing to give the occasional welcome or lecture in English, the church is kept pure. Marriages and christenings involving non-Armenians are conducted entirely in Armenian, for example. Though one priest in London has said that he would like to include a few words of English in order to make the *odar* and his or her family feel welcome, there remains a strong opposition to this among the clergy and lay people, both because of the linguistic intrusion into the only remaining solely Armenian area and because it provides a symbolic stand against marriage to an *odar*.

The contrast between the linguistic styles of public and private life in London now is similar to that in Cyprus at the beginning of the century. However, without the small, compact community, Near Eastern/Cypriot environment, and nearby school for all children, it is less likely that the two spheres will eventually both be Armenian again, especially as so many are ambivalent about the need for it. The sense of urgency is not as widespread as it was in earlier times. Instead, as long as the public sphere is primarily Armenian-speaking and young people do not understand the language well, those young people are cut off from the community and know about being Armenian only through their own family and its informal network. Just as important, young Armenian-speakers also complain that the content and overall style of formal events and writing is too "heavy" and old-fashioned.

Still, among most young people there is a shared passive knowledge of the language, if nothing more. Often there is some limited conversational ability, which is displayed if the young person feels it is "necessary." "Necessary" can involve a show of respect for an older person who speaks better Armenian than English or the rare occasion when they meet someone who speaks little English—for example, a visitor from Hayastan. Like the shared multilingual style of their parents, the little that young Cypriot Armenians know serves to tie them together when they meet. Sapir notes that

> the extraordinary importance of minute linguistic differences for the symbolization of psychologically real as contrasted with politically or sociologically official groups is intuitively felt by most people. "He talks like us" is equivalent to saying "He is one of us." (Sapir 1970, 17)

Armenian Cypriot young people recognize each other in this way but at the same time are more likely to overlook differences between eastern and western dialects and are more concerned with the educational background, outlook, and interests of their peers. "He or she may not talk *just* like us—but close enough" is an example of the distinction between the communicative and symbolic functions of a language (Edwards 1985, 17).

Those who care about the Armenian language worry that if current trends continue and communication becomes predominantly English, a way of thinking will be lost along with the language. Certain things can be expressed only in Armenian, they say, and certainly poetry and literature should be read in the original to be fully appreciated and understood. This view is basically that reality is a reflection or creation of language. How we perceive reality depends on the language we speak, and many Armenians feel they will thus cease to be Armenian when Armenian is no longer spoken.

As the concept of what it means to be Armenian is constantly changing, I interpret this concern about language disappearance as meaning that Armenians will be farther away from the ideal of the literate, well-read, pure Armenian-speaker that the community leaders and nationalists of the past and present dream of. In my own observations, the presence and use of multilingualism is as much a key to the thinking of Armenian Cypriots, and probably Armenians everywhere in the Near East, as is the Armenian language by itself. The reduction of options for code-switching from a number of languages and language styles to one language, albeit with its own internal switchings, is itself a profound change. If particular languages *do* frame one's perceptions of the world (and nationalists seem unaware that there is a debate on this), then surely the variety of language styles used by Armenian Cypriots has as deep an effect on their thinking and the formation of their thoughts as does one of those languages by itself.

While the verbal play associated with knowing these languages is truly playful and enjoyable, the reasons for learning so many languages are quite similar to those responsible for the tendency toward reduction to one language that is now so prevalent in London. This reason is functional: the need to earn a living and generally get along in the surrounding society. Edwards discusses language shift as being dependent on sociopolitical factors:

> However, retention of an original language, in its communicative form at least, is often seen as detrimental, not so much because of external sanctions but because of internal desires. We should thus expect language shift in tolerant societies, but we should also expect retention of other group markers, markers which are not perceived to interfere with social mobility and advancement. (Edwards 1985, 92–93)

It is most striking that, in this sense, learning Armenian was not really essential in the early part of the century. One could conceivably have learned only Greek, or only English, or continued in Turkish (as some did), or a combination of these, and survived quite well. Instead, the "original" language, Armenian, not only was retained for those who did speak it but also was learned by the majority of nonspeakers. The difference seems to be in the outlook of the time—that of a people used to the rule of empire, aspiring at most to secure good jobs under the rulers but not to join or be them. At the same time, Armenians then had vivid hopes of establishing their own nation or national province, or of joining the nation in Hayastan. Today both of these hopes are still very active for some, but most see the diaspora as home, for better or for worse, at least for the foreseeable future. Meanwhile, the concept of being a citizen of a democratic state, in Cyprus or in Great Britain, is far removed from that of being a colonial subject. There is a reasonable hope that better language skills (Greek or English) will help one to fit into the majority society better and more quickly.

While those who actively support the learning of the Armenian language realize this on one level, they usually say that this is evidence of the selfishness of Armenians today, who are interested only in themselves, and that a sense of duty to the community, to the language, and to the historical nation is criminally lacking. Meanwhile, every effort is made to keep as much of formal community life in the Armenian language as possible, including lectures, recitals, announcements, most news, and especially the church.

Gaboudikian's poetic injunction "Though you may forget your mother, never forget your mother tongue" is clearly hyperbole meant to drive home the importance of knowing Armenian. But the relationships within the family remain more important and binding than that between a person and a particular language. Armenians in Cyprus and London consciously identify with Armenian as their mother tongue, but the communicative aspect of the language is dwindling in Cyprus, as that community grows smaller, and in London, under the dominant influence of English. Parents have other, more immediate concerns for their children, including the maintenance of family ties, and if a language seems to hinder rather than help a relationship, the language will suffer. On the other hand, in an informal, symbolic role, knowledge and use of Armenian can have the effect of making children feel that their own family is special and tied to the larger Armenian family.

Armenian, especially as it is formally presented in romantic-style poetry and song, historic literature, and patriotic lectures, is increasingly tied to the symbolic aspect of language and less to ordinary, working communication. Of all the spheres, only the church is left to verbally communicate solely in Armenian while fully incorporating the symbolic aspect of the language as well. Periodic suggestions of the inclusion of English or even increasing the amount of vernacular Armenian in the service are met with horror in London. One priest stated that by keeping the church purely Armenian, Armenian people will eventually realize they must learn the language to understand the service and their religion. This is an integral part of the church's place in the community and at the same time a great burden for it. Chapter 13 explores both these aspects of the church and the people who support it.

Chapter 13

Religion and the Church

L ike the family and language, religion and the church have two overlapping spheres. One involves the everyday, more private, and practical aspects, and the other is more public, rigidly defined, and symbolic. These two influence each other in a variety of ways. Throughout
this chapter I will use the word *religion* to mean a set of beliefs about
spiritual life and a person's or community's concerns about their relationship with God or the supernatural. *Church* is used to indicate the institution that is meant to mediate or facilitate religion, and includes the
physical building, ecclesiastical hierarchy, doctrine, and services. Unless
indicated otherwise, the church referred to in this chapter is the Armenian
Apostolic Church.

Generally, there has been a radical reduction in daily contact with the
church and in the amount of time spent daily on individual or communal
matters of religion or church. This was accelerated by the loss of the old
neighborhood in Nicosia and by the dispersion of households in London,
circumstances that not only affected then-current practices but also enabled change to happen more quickly. Despite these circumstances, the
changes were already in gestation—multiple strands were already developing within the old traditions and were accompanied by a simultaneous
building of secular nationalism. Among the influences working within this
process was an increasing emphasis on the individual, which resulted from
the Western tradition in secondary school, higher standards for and an
increased length of education, changing work prospects, the increased

specificity of work and training for work, and (through the Protestants) the idea of the importance of the individual's relationship with God. Radio and, later, television are also noteworthy for encouraging more time to be spent within the home and introducing new ideas about the world and how it works.

In his 1982 book *Person and Myth,* James Clifford describes the missionary and ethnographer Maurice Leenhardt as one who did not see religion as a separate, clearly definable category of experience. "Rather, he assumed that 'religion' referred to a basic and universal mode of knowledge, an access to transcendence permeating all realms of human experience" (Clifford 1982, 3). In the Melanesian world where Leenhardt worked, people conducted their lives on this premise, without the distinctions between realms of interest and activity that those in the modernized West now regularly make and live with. Armenians at the turn of the century were considerably closer to Leenhardt's view than are their descendants today. The cycle of the church not only took up more time during the week and year but penetrated daily life to the point where borders drawn around solely religious activities or words were blurred and indistinct.

Hirschon writes that in the 1970s this remained an apt description of the religious life of Asia Minor refugees in Piraeus (Hirschon 1989, 218), although she notes that the particular urban neighborhood in which she worked might have differed from others, both urban and rural. This could stem in part from the refugees' sense that the celebration of their religious life marked them as different and "superior" to the local Greeks and was an attempt to retain some of the remembered lifestyle of their Ottoman days. The construction of the neighborhood itself also encouraged this continuation. However, Hirschon does mention that the younger people did not participate as enthusiastically or as much, although she assumes this will change as they grow older (Hirschon 1989, 233). This prediction is not completely convincing, given factors such as the differences in secular education between generations and decreasing exposure to the church and family religious life.

For Armenian Cypriots today, especially those in London, the sphere of religion is becoming increasingly isolated and definable as a distinct category of experience. This is in contrast with the church as an institution, and especially as a symbol, that remains pervasive in community life and important as an umbrella for a variety of aspirations and beliefs, secular as well as religious. Overlap is continuous between church and politics and between church and nation. Believers, atheists, agnostics, and anticlericals alike participate regularly in the major life-cycle events held in the church, including baptisms, christenings, marriages, and funerals and subsequent memorial services. And unless one states and acts otherwise, all who are christened in the church are members for life.

As a national church, the Armenian Apostolic Church is an explicit and active medium for religion and for nation and thus fills both spiritual and functional roles. The following sections explore these two roles, the interplay between them, and the nature of faith in both these aspects.

CYPRUS TODAY

Surp Astvadztsadzin, in Nicosia, was built in 1981 on land donated by the government of Cyprus. Its shape is based on a traditional Armenian church form, with a cruciform plan and a conical roof. Though there is much nostalgia for the old church in the Turkish quarter, most Armenian Cypriots are very pleased that this new church appears so clearly Armenian.

Inside, the pale walls, high ceilings, and bright sun from the upper windows give a feeling of space and light. The simplicity of the building design and lack of architectural ornament contrasts with and sets off the many-tiered crystal chandeliers and the ornate altar display. Just inside the main body of the church, on either side of the main aisle, are two marble boxes filled with sand. This is where people light their candles and make their prayers as they enter. A red patterned carpet runs between the rows of light-colored wooden pews and stops at the half-circle apron of the altar, which is enclosed by an ironwork fence and gate.

The altar itself is white marble, about twelve feet high. It is reminiscent of a small Armenian church itself, with a central conical cupola. Two smaller altars stand on either side. Layers of lace and crochet work cover the midsection of the main altar, where a Bible, cross, flowers, and silver objects lie before a modern portrait of the Virgin and Child. Around the inner walls of the church are hung large paintings by the same artist depicting the life of Christ.

The central importance of the Crucifixion and Resurrection is clearly depicted in these pictures, the frequent crossing of oneself during the service and at prayer, the wearing of a gold cross (often given at one's christening), the use of the cross motif on vestments and ornaments, and in the number and importance of services during Easter week.[1] Easter-week services have been shortened and some cut out entirely over the last fifty years, but the week is still the fullest of the year, beginning with the psalm reading and Mass on Palm Sunday and a special service, *terenpatzek* (the opening of the door).

On the Wednesday morning before Easter in 1986, Nareg students attended the last of the weekly services, receiving a blessing and communion before school started for the day. The next day the children returned to participate as the choir for the morning Mass. In the late afternoon the *vodnlava* service began with young boys reading Bible verses from the altar and continued with the commemoration of Jesus's washing of the disciples' feet as the priest washed a foot of each boy and anointed it with holy oil.

After a short break, the evening service began at seven o'clock. The curtain was changed to a black velvet one with a large cross embroidered in gold sequins glittering in the center, and was drawn across the altar. A large Bible rested on a stand in the center aisle; a black cloth, also embroidered with a gold cross, covered the stand. On either side six unlit candles were poised, symbolizing the twelve apostles. One on the far right was black, symbolizing Judas, and the rest were white. Priests and deacons chanted the Bible readings and sang the hymns.

An hour later, all the candles except the black one were lit, and two small boys in long white robes entered, bearing candles. Another brought the *vartabed*'s staff, an incense burner, and a small cross wrapped in lace. One more, holding a gold-embroidered black cape, arranged it on the shoulders of the *vartabed*, who began a reading from the Bible in midaisle. "Amen, amen," he then sang slowly and with a strong voice, holding the staff in one hand and a cross wrapped in lace in the other. The congregation heard a portion of the story of the Last Supper.

The deacons and priests sang a counterpoint response, and most people sat down. Some of the women, middle-aged and older, remained standing and sang with the deacons from their places in the congregation. A deacon put the black and gold cape on the *kahana*, who, followed by the boys holding the candles, went to the Bible to read. He sang about Simon Peter asleep. He sounded a little tired himself, but his voice was always very expressive, light, and beautiful. As he finished and the cape was removed, more responses were sung, and then two candles were extinguished.

The oldest of the young boys hurried back and forth, his very serious, bright eyes darting, as he directed the smaller ones to do their jobs, asking the priests for instructions. The boys with the candles and staff came back. A deacon went to the Bible. The staff was sent back to the side room, and the incense was brought and placed beside the Bible.

By nine o'clock there were forty to fifty people present, men and women. The reading, chanting, and responses continued until all the candles had been put out. A small pulpit was moved to the left side of the altar, outside the curtain, while one of the boys swung and shook the censer in the central aisle by the Bible and then in every corner of the church. The little boys came out with their prayer books as the cape was placed on the *vartabed* again. The boys were sent back for candles and then joined the *vartabed* by the pulpit above. We were awash in a haze of incense, a steady hum of chanting and singing, and a feeling of general tiredness. Time went by; my mind wandered and came back. It was easy to imagine the disciples falling asleep that night in the garden of Gethsemane.

But at ten o'clock all lights were suddenly extinguished except for two thin candles flickering dimly in the very back of the church. The singing continued, and a few minutes later a candle was lit behind the closed curtain. In the open space between curtain and ceiling, the white cupola of the altar was lit with a pale glow, a fantastic effect. The congregation sang a loud, intense, and very long song. From behind the curtain, a haunting and beautiful solo followed.

The lights in the front came on, and the service seemed to begin again. When we finished, at about eleven o'clock, some friends gave me a ride home. "We've finished early tonight!" they said—partly because the service had begun early but also because every year something is taken out. That night one of the young men was teasing the priest who had said that he was hungry. (Priests traditionally fast during Lent, especially during Holy Week.) "How can you be hungry when you've 'eaten' so many of the hymns?"[2] They laughed but added that it was a serious problem. Some people said the services were too many and too long. Others were concerned that the traditional services were being butchered and soon would be whittled away to a bland nothingness.[3]

The next morning several women met at the church to arrange the flowers and the sepulcher for the Good Friday service. When I arrived, they had already made the base of the sepulcher, a long table with a box on top, layered with white lace and embroidered cloths. My job was to sew a long rope of white carnation heads.

A silver-covered Bible was set, open, on top of the lace and crochet work, an upright cross behind it. White flowers were arranged all around the top of the table, by the Bible, and on the sides. Mrs. Rita sewed more carnations into the shape of a cross and attached it to the front. As we stepped back to admire it, Araxi said that after the service everyone is supposed to pick one flower from the sepulcher, take it home, and put it under her or his pillow at night. Afterward, she told me, it must be burned or saved because it is holy. Alice added that her mother got furious when she saw people taking more than one flower: "'Are they trying to make a bouquet?'"

Araxi laughed. "It's like they've never seen a flower!"

"What does it mean, to take the flower and sleep on it?" I wanted to know more about this.

They shrugged. "I don't know. It's like that. We just do. It doesn't really mean anything," Alice said.

Araxi wondered aloud, "Maybe it was meant to bring you good luck. Or, I think, if you dream something good that night, it will come true during the following year. Something like that."[4]

"But," I was told, "whatever happens, all these flowers must be taken away on Saturday, and then we put out all red flowers for Easter." (Blue ones are used for Christmas.)

Alice said, "There will be red everywhere on Saturday. You know, we celebrate Easter on Saturday, really. For Armenians, Sunday begins when the sun goes down on Saturday. Sunday is from sundown to sundown."

As it later turned out, there were also blue flowers on the altar because someone had made a last-minute donation and apparently preferred blue. Like the taking of a flower from the sepulcher, the custom of using a certain color of flower—and others, such as deciding when to stand during the service or whether women should wear hats—were in a state of flux.

As the Good Friday service unfolded, it appeared very much like a play (a musical) about a funeral. The coffin was displayed, with the flowers arranged all around. The priests and deacons knelt in front and beside it, then stood again, singing the hymns of the service. The roots of Christianity seemed to be part of the display.

At the end of the service, the congregation formed a line in the middle aisle as each person went to the sepulcher, kissed the Bible, and took a flower. Araxi brought one to me, and we watched together as some did indeed gather bouquets. "Why do they do that?" she sighed.

As we stood on the church steps, the evening breeze was cool and the sky already a rich, dark blue. I had found the flower debate interesting, but something else concerned me: I had felt quite moved at points during the services but was still very much an observer. I really missed singing and participating. A few minutes later the choir director, Mr. Margos, came over to talk.

"Shushig, why don't you sing with us in the choir tomorrow?" he said at one point.

"You must be kidding!" I replied. "I don't know the service, the songs . . ."

"Don't worry, *mana mou*.⁵ You can read music, can't you? And . . . Armenian?"

"Yes . . ."

"Then it's no problem! Everything is very slow, and the others will help you. Only you must sing alto because we have too many sopranos."

If singing alto really is the only problem, I will be amazed, I thought. But Mr. Margos's suggestion seemed the obvious answer to my thoughts a few moments earlier, so I promised to join the choir. *How else can I learn the songs at this point?* I thought.

When I arrived on Saturday, just after four o'clock, Hayr Surp ("Reverend Father," referring to the *vartabed*) was reading from the portable pulpit on the altar edge. The pulpit was covered in red velvet with a gold embroidered cross. The large curtain had also been changed to red velvet but remained closed. A cross in gold sequins shimmered in the middle. Hayr Surp also shimmered that day. Over his black robe was a purple cloak with an overcape embroidered in red and gold.

He finished reading, and the small boys in white *shabig* took their turns to read in high chanting voices. As each boy finished, he kissed the priest's hand. The boys continued, and the church began to fill. In the background, doors slammed and money clinked in the plates by the door as people made donations for their candles. The choir began arriving for the main part of the Mass. In the choir loft, many people were chatting softly.

On the altar, the curtains were swept back (having been closed during all of Lent) and the liturgy began. Soon I was engrossed in the alto part, happy to find that most of the music was within my five-note range. A rich voice beside me and another behind me pushed me over the edge of interested observation and into immersion in the majestic flow of the music and, thus, the service.

Afterward I went home with Mrs. Ani and her family, as we had been invited to a name day party later at another house. Just after we arrived, there was a knock at the door: The *kahana* had come to bless the house. The family gathered in the living room, and we had a quick cup of tea together as Der Hayr ("Father") explained to me that he did a round of all the Armenian families twice a year, at Easter and at Christmas. While we were talking, one of Ani's children gathered a glass of water, a piece of bread, and a dish of salt and placed them together on the coffee table in front of us. Der Hayr added a wafer and then a piece of incense, which

Khatchig lit. We gathered around the table as Der Hayr sang, holding up a small, lace-wrapped cross. When he had finished, he brought the cross to each person to kiss. He then left quickly, as there were many more families to visit that evening. Ani accompanied him to the door and gave him some money.

On Sunday morning were the last services of Easter week. The church was very full. Someone said that this was partly because there were so many people "in transit." "We don't know many of these people—they are from Beirut or Iran." Indeed, one man whom no one seemed to know had gone to the front, and as people lined up to take communion he watched from behind the olivewood throne, tugging at the altar boy's elbow to get his attention. It seemed he wanted the boy to make the people return to their seats by the side aisles, not down the center (a few people walked backward to their seats, down the center aisle). The altar boy was busy and just nodded at the man. His job for the moment was to hand out scarves to hatless women waiting to take communion.

At the end of the service, standing at the edge of the loft, I could see several hands reach out to touch the cape of Hayr Surp as he passed, leading the procession down the aisle.

People greeted each other with *"Kristos haryav i merelots"* ("Christ has risen from the dead") and its response, *"Orhnial e haroutiun Kristosi"* ("Blessed was the resurrection of Christ") as they left the church. (I was told that in some years, when enough eggs have been prepared, people gather in the courtyard to knock eggs.)[6] The congregation then lined up to greet the *vartabed,* who was waiting in the large reception room of the vicarage. His secretary stood by the door with a large tray of sugared almonds. People took one as they went in, shook the priest's hand or kissed it, gave the traditional greeting, and received their blessing. The Easter services were over.

THE EXPERIENCE OF THE CHURCH

In Cyprus and London, the ritual of the Easter services is the richest of the year but, in essence, no different from those held every Sunday. The basic Mass itself is the same, ornamented by topical hymns and readings in the particular services. More important, the atmosphere and expression of the service are also the same. While content (theology and doctrine) cannot really be separated from form (liturgy and performance), most Armenians speak of being affected by the latter when in church. Relatively few debate or discuss the former, and when they do, this occurs more in conjunction with special incidents or while talking of their private spiritual life.

The spiritual life of the community is directed through all the senses. The rich and dazzling colors of the priestly vestments, the intricate embroidery, the profusion of delicate crochet and lace work, the fine silver and gold ornaments, and other decorative objects occupy the eyes while the ears are filled with the music of constant chants, responses, and hymns. The rattle of the metal *keshots* (a flat-faced rattle) punctuates the music, as does the percussive shaking of the incense burner, which at the same time fills one's nostrils and the entire sanctuary with its special perfumed haze.

This is not background but very much a part of the liturgy. Combined with the classical language, the effect is both ancient and timeless, an illusion of unchanging form, unencumbered by a specific message. At the core is the relationship with God, the mystery of entering a holy presence, the creation of a space, time, and atmosphere wholly different from the everyday. For Armenians, this is the traditional, accepted introduction to God.

At the same time, the feeling of being in a completely Armenian environment, entirely cut off from contemporary distractions, provides a link with past generations of Armenians, giving both a sense of comfort and a sense of duty. For most Apostolic Armenians, these two aspects are intertwined to the point of being indistinguishable. The idea of the church without its national elements, the classical language, the music, and the visual display seems a hollow shell, difficult to imagine.

In his book *Recognizing Islam*, Gilsenan writes that he (at first unconsciously) found the green neon of the Koran verses on a Cairo mosque wall disturbing to "all my efforts at perception and a feeling for the real meaning of the event." He wrote that after many months, "one day . . . I turned away . . . and saw, not neon, but simply greenness. Greenness, and letters that did not 'stand for' anything but simply were powerful icons in and of themselves. No gaps existed between color, shape, light, and form. From that unreflecting and unexpected moment I ceased to see neon at all" (Gilsenan 1983, 266).

This experiencing of all parts of the ritual as one, rather than as fractured though interesting or beautiful segments, is a given for most Armenians born and raised within the tradition but is difficult for the outsider to attain—and even harder to continue. For me, taking part in the music filled the gaps Gilsenan mentions. But to what degree is this sort of experience on the level of engagement in the ritual itself, in the litany and affirmation of belief? This question extends to those raised in the tradition, many of whom are moved by the experience of the service but who hesitate on the edge, engrossed in the aura of social solidarity, comfort, and timelessness.

An Armenian is born into his or her religion,[7] and until recently it was taken for granted that he or she would grow up in that religion, absorbing rather than actually learning the tenets and doctrine. Children are told Bible stories, but learning is reserved mainly for the liturgy and history of the church. Theology and intellectual points of faith are left to the clergy.

Tamar, an artist in her early forties now living in London, explained how she liked this very aspect of the church. "The music is very, very moving. I value the fact that it has been going on for centuries, and it seems to put me in touch with feelings and experiences that I otherwise have no contact with. I guess I like to pray there, and I find that it's conducive to prayer. And I find other people's ideas and thoughts a tremendous obstruction because very often I make judgments about them and I think, 'Oh, that could be expressed better.' You know, the intellect is always getting in the way, and I like it when it's not there.

"It leaves you free to think for yourself and just meditate, float about in your own mind. And I think a lot of it probably has to do with having gone to church as a child and identifying that with being Armenian and being safe and being in a community. I mean, the sense of being surrounded by other Armenians. Because the church in Cyprus, in Nicosia, was an old twelfth-century abbey. A lovely church. And there was a fabulous choir when I was young, with very good singers. It was probably one of the best musical experiences I [had] because I certainly didn't go to concerts or recitals. They didn't exist. But this was *great,* a very thrilling thing. When the Melkonian choir was there and the church choir was there, then they sang four parts and so on, it was super! I loved that.

"I suppose part of it was teaching, that the Armenian church is very important to the Armenians and is one of the sole surviving institutions, and I'm sure that seeped in."

While most women and men echoed Tamar's praise of the church services of their childhood, many were less content with the learning that accompanied it then and with the situation today, whether in Cyprus or London. One of Tamar's own contemporaries, Maryam, offers a very different perspective. Like Tamar, Maryam went to an English-language elementary school, but instead of receiving private Armenian tutoring, she joined the Melikian-Ouzunian students for their Saturday classes.

"Religion classes stick out in my mind because it was all so different. It was all about church history, liturgy, and especially about the church furniture and vestments—and it was all illustrated from a dusty old book with terrible photographs. Much later on I concluded that the Loosavor-chagans [Apostolic Armenians] don't have religious experience, they have ritual experience. There is no content, none that they either understand or want to understand. I heard that on Sunday mornings there was a more relaxed religious Sunday school where ladies from the community told Bible stories to the children. But my own experience at the school was that religion meant church history and ecclesiastical information. Church hierarchy. And very boring at the time. Now I am not a believer anyway."

While Maryam's thinking was clearly influenced by the teachings and expectations of her Protestant upbringing, there were many others in Apostolic families who were questioning the style of religious education in the church well before her time. Today satisfaction with and criticism of the church cuts across boundaries of gender, age, and profession, and even many of those who speak as enthusiastically as Tamar are infrequent visitors at church. Support for the church comes most often in speeches and conversation about its idealized form. Practical support and even attendance have been very much reduced, not only in London but also in Cyprus, where distance is not such a deterrent.

One of many aspects that have changed is the expectations people have of the priests and their role in the church and community. The role of leadership generally has changed as a bigger proportion of the people has become better educated. In earlier times the priests were clearly the best-educated, or among the best-educated, in the community, but this has not been true for some time. Criticisms are now aimed not only at personality differences or private indiscretions but also at the role of the priest and his ability to lead the spiritual life of the community.

Of course, private indiscretions can also affect the way people view the priesthood. Though older people remember other scandalous local tales from the past, the former Yeghishe Patriarch of Jerusalem did much to damage the general reputation of the priesthood in the minds of the younger generations. His alleged complicity in the attempted London sales of valuable manuscripts from the vaults of the Jerusalem convent is but one of the affairs that concern Armenians in both Cyprus and London and reflect poorly on the trust placed in the priesthood.

A young professional woman, raised in the Apostolic Church, was critical of the hypocrisy she and her schoolmates had seen in the church and among priests. "But," she added, "I am a believer. I believe in God, but not in the church. Older people say that the church has gotten Armenians through very difficult times—you can go all the way back to Vartan Mamigonian. The church preserved our identity as Armenians. But that was the past. Now it is a second-rate institution. Nobody cares much about it; it has no real influence. Look at any Sunday. Nobody is there. If it's a dinner dance, they're all there. But they have no time for church. Because it's nothing to them, really. Actually, I don't go myself very often. For special occasions."

When I first began my fieldwork, an artist in his thirties explained to me that one of the big differences between the Apostolic Church and Protestant ones was that "we accept our church as it is. We don't go around shopping for the best church in the neighborhood, the one with the priest who gives the best sermon or whatever. Because it's not the particular priest who is important, it's the church, and we have to support it no matter what the priest does or doesn't do." In the 1980s in Cyprus and London, I found that it was mostly true that people did not go from church to church if they were dissatisfied. They simply stopped going, except on special occasions. Others are not particularly dissatisfied but do not go, except on special occasions, because they say they are too busy, (in London) the church is too far, they are tired, they need one day to rest and be with their family, or they have to work.

This is not unique to the Armenian church. Michael Attalides briefly alludes to a similar situation among Greek Orthodox in Cyprus, where he notes declining church attendance and writes of the "picture of the church [as] being the venue of children, women, and the old, as against adult males" (Attalides 1981, 174). Also, a very small proportion of the British population as a whole attends church regularly.

The larger proportion of women present at church services that is mentioned by Attalides for the Greek Orthodox case also holds true among Armenians in Cyprus, though married couples frequently go as far as the church together. Men often then stay outside, chat, and smoke with each other, or take care of church business in an adjoining office or by the door. Mothers of small children frequently stay home with them, saying that the service is too long and there is no nursery or Sunday school organized to occupy the children while their mothers attend.

Of course, church attendance is not the only indicator or measurement of spiritual life. It is, however, the church itself that is spoken of as important to Armenians as a community or nation; thus attendance is an important factor insofar as it is a sign of support and continuation. As fewer people attend, fewer and shorter services are held, and the experience and understanding of the service changes as one attends less frequently or not at all. Noting that church attendance in Greece is estimated to be between 2 and 20 percent, Hirschon (1989, 194) argues that declining attendance should not be confused with a lessening of religious commitment. It would be equally false, however, to assume that the nature of commitment and understanding of a particular religion is not affected by less contact with the related church.

The physical proximity of the church in Cyprus to the Nareg school, and to the community centers not much farther away, keeps the church central on the visible landscape, if not in the actual activities of the people there. In London, one rarely passes the churches unless going there especially. This is perhaps not so important to the older people in the community, who grew up near a church, but it presents a very different picture to the children raised in London. Church becomes something that is heard about, talked about, and visited occasionally, rather than part of daily life; as a result, again the place of the church in the community changes.

RELIGION

In what way, then, does the changing relationship with the church affect the ways in which people think of their religion? How do people today think of God, and what place does a divine being have in their lives?

As mentioned, at the turn of the century and even in its early decades, the church was a major part of daily life. Beginning with being christened, following parents to Mass, and participating with schoolmates in the service, it was through the church that children were introduced to a God of history, community, mystery, and emotive feeling. At home, where families celebrated saints' name days, made palm leaf crosses, observed feasts and fasts, and used the language of belief (for example, "God willing,"[8] "God rest his soul"[9]), the idea of God and one's relation with the holy was also a familiar one.

Today, in both Cyprus and London, there is great variety in the ways in which people conceive of the nature of God and their relationship to such a being.[10] This includes outspoken atheists, some of whom are active in the church, supporting its national function. There is little explicit teaching about who or what God might be, nor is there much encouragement to read the Bible. Ideas are instead absorbed and developed in the atmosphere of the church—and also from outside learning, including secular schooling and the media.

The overwhelming national aspect of the church often obscures the spiritual or religious life of the community and its individual members. Many priests and other representatives of the church tend to speak first of the national aspect when talking of the importance of the Armenian church, and they do not seem to realize that in some ways this obscures the spiritual aspect. But there are many within the two communities who go to the church to worship and pray to a God who is important to them. For others, the nationalism of the church impedes this, and these people have often sought other religious or philosophical institutions or sects, including Rosicrucianism, Jehovah's Witnesses, Gurdjieff, and Zen Buddhism. Interestingly, while Protestant Armenian families attend their local Protestant churches, and some meet together to worship in their own homes in London, few disgruntled Apostolics today seem ready to convert to Protestantism. They are more likely to drop out, except on special occasions, or be attracted by a more unfamiliar form of religion. This is possibly due to the considerable antagonism expressed in earlier years against Armenian Protestants and Catholics for having broken away from the mother church.

Among Apostolic Church members, the concept of God, and of the Trinity, seems to be fairly undefined. As William Christian points out for Spain:

> In most cases belief, as such, is not the issue. A man or woman does not sit down and think, 'Do I or do I not believe today.' And, in fact, having little or no occasion to formulate beliefs verbally, the beliefs themselves lie suspended between poles of commitment and scepticism, fluctuating and ambiguous. More important than talk about belief, which is indeed a problem in a plural society but not in a fairly uniform rural Catholic culture, is attention to emotional commitment and act. (Christian 1972, 168)

Today the plural cultures of Cyprus and of London do affect the ways in which Armenians talk about belief, though not necessarily the basis of that belief. In Cyprus, Armenians are conscious of Greek attitudes toward the Apostolic Church, but this is mainly important in the context of the national aspect of the Orthodox and Apostolic Churches. Belief is, for the most part, taken for granted, but it is sometimes elaborated on or explored in the context of others' beliefs, or popular perceptions of them. This is done most explicitly by those who have graduated from the American Academy, where they learned of specific attitudes or beliefs against which they can judge or contrast or develop their own.

Otherwise, most comments concerning neighboring religions in Cyprus and in England center on emotional commitment and act, as mentioned in the quote from Christian. For example, when Armenians hear the call to prayer from the loudspeakers of the mosques across the Green Line in Nicosia, some complain that this is too bitter a reminder of the old days. But older people have commented that I should note how much more "religious" the Muslims are: They are called to prayer five times a day. By contrast, Armenians in London often mention the empty churches of Britain.

In Spain, Christian finds two main and overlapping attitudes toward the divine, one instrumental and the other more generally concerned with salvation and purification. This also seems appropriate to the Armenian case, as does his observation that some people or families fall more toward one or the other end of this continuum. The idea of salvation through Christ is explicit in Apostolic Church doctrine but is more popularly understood as a "right" attitude (humbleness, patience) and relationship with God.

The instrumental approach includes wishes and prayers for specific problems: healing, safety, good marriage. In times of stress, both men and women were known to make oaths or promises to God, to be fulfilled if their prayer was granted. In earlier times, and still today in Hayastan and Iran, this could involve the sacrifice of an animal or bird. These also show overlap with the surrounding cultures and religions and with pre-Christian times. The symbol of the eye of God, seen over many doors and within the church itself, is known throughout the Near East. Some families sew *gabouyd achk* ("blue eye"—a glass bead) onto infants' clothing as protection against the evil eye. Many women carry one in their handbags. Other people place them in their cars. The taking of flowers from the Good Friday sepulcher seems also to have connections with older Armenian customs as well as with their Greek neighbors.

Middle-aged and older people sometimes speak of the evil eye and remember many instances from their childhood in which this was an issue, but most say they are not sure how important it really is. Young people are still less convinced. Evil spirits are not altogether forgotten, just not invoked specifically. Instead, they are incorporated in a world view that includes a powerful presence of evil, contrasting with the presence of a righteous and more powerful God.

Many believe that faith in God's redemptive power should automatically serve as protection against misfortune in this world. Interestingly, this idea is also stated by atheists—particularly in newspapers and poetry—when disaster strikes the Armenian people: "Why should God forsake such a faithful people?"[11] God may not exist but somehow is blamed anyway for not having prevented tragedy.

Leonardo Alishan writes, for example, about Charents's poem "Lamentation," noting that though Charents was a committed Marxist, when he saw "his fellow Communist Armenian intellectuals perish one by one . . . how strange that he should now call, not his dream [Marxism], nor his Communist Party, but God, 'deceitful'!" Alishan continues,

> Charents was not unique in this. Tekeyan in "We Shall Say to God," Shahnur in "Kitipious," and a great many other Armenian writers and poets had, directly or indirectly, knowingly or unknowingly, accused God of allowing the holocaust or any other disaster which has since befallen the Armenians to take place. Why? Had the post-genocide Armenian intelligentsia forgotten that its predecessors or contemporaries had abandoned the Christian God as a "deaf Hebrew God" and had raised their arms in prayer to Anahit and Vahagn?[12] Why was not anyone cursing the mighty Vahagn now, or the protectoress, Anahit? Here a total confusion of beliefs and values becomes evident, born of the dire desperation and confusion resulting from the genocide. (Alishan 1985, 46–47)

In these poems and literature, God is discussed explicitly, in the vernacular, in the context of Armenian concerns—something which, within the church, is reserved for the priests to do. The confusion, produced not only by the genocide but also, for Charents and others, by the Stalinist years in Hayastan and other more personal tragedies, showed itself in changes in the literature among some of the writers. In 1917 Tekeyan, who previously had taken a secular view of the world, wrote the poem "We Will Refuse and Say," telling God,

> Send us to hell. Send us to hell again.
> You made us know it alas, but too well.
> Keep paradise for Turks. Send us to hell.
>
> (Papasian 1987, 49)

But his later poems included "Prayer on the Threshold of Tomorrow," with the following verse indicating a rather different attitude:

> Lord, be kind to us today, impart your wisdom now
> To this tortured molecule of the world. For though

They have forgotten you, still only you can stop
The mindless flock of people on the road to abyss.

(Papasian 1987, 62)

It must be the rare person who is consistently certain of his or her faith and just what it means on a daily basis. Poets such as Tekeyan express the confusion and array of attitudes felt by the less eloquent majority of people. I am including works of poetry here because they are important not only as a reflection of the general attitudes of the people but as popular and frequently heard texts that also influence the way people think and what they believe. The explicit words and thoughts give some definition to otherwise vague ruminations, for believers and nonbelievers alike.

As these poems suggest, a variety of responses vie with each other, often within the same person. Lorna Miller and Donald Miller (1986), analyzing life histories of Armenians in Los Angeles, have devised a typology of these responses: repression, rationalization, resignation, reconciliation, rage, and revenge. Within these they give examples (as I also found) of people who claimed that their faith in God gave them the strength to endure their struggle, while others found their faith destroyed.

The most common view of God, by far, in both Cyprus and London is that of a just God who punishes when angry and rewards when pleased. This is seen by Miller and Miller as part of the maintenance of a moral order (which can have a secular rather than a religious base), without which humans would flounder even more in confusion. A small number, though, as Miller and Miller also point out, are willing to allow the universe or God to operate without logic as we humans understand it. This group includes both firm Christians and equally firm atheists.[13]

The massacres remain a preoccupation, an undercurrent running through Armenian life—too much so for some, but for others in a far too superficial way. The latter prefer action of some sort—at the very extreme, revenge. Miller and Miller believe this is part of the process of healing the rupture of the moral order that the massacres inflicted on the Armenian psyche. While the first generation of survivors had to literally rebuild their lives, they and their own children have attempted to restore that moral order in community life, "bearing primary responsibility for creating and maintaining the institutions that preserve cultural and group values" (Miller and Miller 1991, 36–37).[14]

Expectations of the church's responsibility in helping people come to terms with such an event vary greatly. During and shortly after the massacres, the church often provided physical shelter and whatever practical

help could be organized. People remember the emotional and psychological help offered then as being, first, the comfort of a familiar environment
and atmosphere and, second, a place to mourn. A *hokehankist* (memorial
service) began to be held in the courtyard of the church every April 24,
both for the unknown fellow Armenians who had died and for the family
and friends of the survivors present.

The church continues the annual *hokehankist,* which today has
eclipsed the traditional religious martyrs' day, Vartanants, in popular importance. Sermons at these and other appropriate times, such as Easter,
compare the rebuilding of the Armenian people with the resurrection of
Christ, the burden of sacrifice being on the survivors of the nation. It is
significant for the church, though, that it is also possible to commemorate
these latter-day martyrs in a secular way.

The freshness and spontaneity of the sorrow has given way in recent
years to anger at the injustice of the massacres themselves and at the current denials made by modern Turkey. This anger is most effectively har-
nessed by the secular nationalists, who also organize a memorial *hantess*
on or near April 24 and who have adopted some of the main symbols of
the Christian church. Today those who died in the massacres are called
"martyrs"—not for the Christian faith or the Armenian church but for
the Armenian nation. This word is used to replace the much more debilitating and depressing "victim." The resurrection theme, used by the
priests, is also often heard at secular meetings, as is the idea of sacrifice.
Salvation for the Armenians is attainable not through oneness with God
through Jesus Christ but through sacrifice for the Armenian cause and the
restoration of dignity (and possibly the moral order) through accepting
the burden of rebuilding the diaspora and/or Hayastan.

THE CHURCH CAUGHT IN A DOUBLE BIND

Though active support is dwindling, the church is still given central symbolic importance as the institution that has survived and continued
through centuries of subjugation and dispersion. This also limits the
church, however, in its attempts to meet the needs and interests of its
members in diaspora at the end of the twentieth century.

In Cyprus today children continue to participate in church services
throughout the year, go to school beside the church, regularly meet the
priests, and learn to sing parts of the liturgy and hymns. Equally important, they are fluent in Armenian. In London, Armenian school is held on
Sunday morning, away from the church and priests, and instruction is

focused more on elementary Armenian. Thus children have infrequent direct contact with the church and priests, learn only the most basic liturgy, if any, and understand little of the language. At the same time, the physical layout of London and of Armenian homes within it, the declining usage and knowledge of Armenian, and the influence of low British church attendance all contribute toward a real decline in the activities of the London Armenian churches. This includes a seriously diminishing supply of deacons (*sargavak*), acolytes, and choir members, thus leading to further changes in the services themselves.

Changes in education also play a role, as religious concerns and expectations are affected by secular learning. As before, each generation contains considerable variation, dependent on family, educational options, and personal interests, but it can be said generally that throughout this century, in Cyprus as well as England, secular education for Armenians has become increasingly divergent from the kind of learning for and about religion and the church, in both style and content.

Whereas some are satisfied and inspired by a church of atmosphere and ritual, others ask why they are not provided with intellectual food as well. The emphasis of some priests on nationalism—via sermons on historical heroes and exhortations to be (metaphorical) soldiers for the Armenian nation—is welcomed by many, but a vocal minority prefers more emphasis on Christian doctrine and spirituality. The Western and modern emphasis on the individual also has its effect, as Armenians take an increasingly individual approach to religion, contrasted with the previous communal emphasis, which could be served only by the church. Here too the role of the priests is changing, as acceptance of their faults and frailties is not so automatic as it once was.

In the 1990s it seems that the Armenian Apostolic Church in Cyprus and in London is in a double bind. This is true throughout the Armenian world to lesser or greater degrees. On the one hand, its role as a national institution, imbued with visual, linguistic, and musical traditions, forges deep psychological links with the past. Looking at their diaspora situation, Armenians in Cyprus and London place great value on this continuing, seemingly unchanging aspect of the church. Yet at the same time the old presentation is not always understood and, worse, not even experienced, as attendance and participation dwindle with each new generation.

The final chapter explores the role of faith in religion and in nationalism, the interplay of changes in culture and religious belief, and the increasing nationalist emphasis on history as mythical charter or *raison d'être*.

Chapter 14

Faith in History

Culture is in motion. While some aspects of it may appear constant—language, history, and church, for example—ways of seeing them, treating them, and thinking about them are not. The subtler aspects of culture, values, standards, and attitudes, which are shared and passed on by family and related networks, are in continuous process, brought to bear on the changing sociopolitical and geographic environment and, in turn, affected by these things.

The dispersion of the Armenian people and the crushing loss of society as they knew it underlined the fragility of life and encouraged a deep feeling of insecurity in the early part of this century. This was brought out again by the losses in 1963 and 1974 in Cyprus and was exacerbated throughout the late 1970s and 1980s by the troubles of neighboring Armenian communities in Lebanon and Iran. The devastating earthquake in Hayastan in 1988 and continuing turmoil in the Caucasus underline the image of an endangered nation. In Cyprus, the struggle to heal the wound, or restore the moral order, has involved the rebuilding of families, of community, and of the important pieces of visible culture. The multiple changes of new places, new kinds of work, new neighboring peoples, modernization, and alignment toward the British as protectors and examples all produced a moment of extreme flux in Cyprus during the 1920s. Similar changes were repeated, with variations, around the Armenian diaspora. In these times, as with later forced physical changes, some traditions and customs proved more transportable and durable than others. Others were shored up, "restored," or invented as appropriate to the new situation and its needs (Hobsbawm and Ranger 1983; Gellner 1983).

THE CHURCH'S ROLE IN NATIONALISM

By some form of consensus, directed by poets, priests, and politicians and communicated through schools, churches, and newspapers, a message was formulated and disseminated among the Armenian people. Very roughly, this was: The homeland is lost, our people have been killed; let us work to repair and retain what we can. On a daily level, centered on family and community, Armenian life continued with myriad variations.

Having begun work in the nineteenth century, Armenian intellectuals and leaders, now spread throughout the diaspora, attempted to halt or even reverse assimilation by accenting certain identifiable, symbolic features of Armenian life. Thus while daily habits, customs, and beliefs were rapidly changing, Armenians at school and church were being taught that there was a particular way of being Armenian, and definition was given to Armenianness. Exposed to new relationships of power, and away from the homelands, Armenians' formal ideas of identity were also influenced by the increasing nationalism of the other peoples around them. The ideological construction of identity, or the reification of something called Armenian culture, was aimed at producing a cohesive collectivity out of a diverse people who did, it must be emphasized, share a sense of belonging together and of separateness from their non-Armenian neighbors.

Geertz suggests that ideologies are "most distinctively maps of problematic social reality" (Geertz 1973, 220). While certain landmarks on that map are highlighted and other features overlooked, ideologies will become part of the imagining of community only if they are indeed rooted in the shared, unconscious, everyday "social reality." As Kapferer suggests in his contrasting and linking of ontology and ideology, it is the rearrangement and particular emphasis of certain features that becomes conscious and eventually changes the way in which people unconsciously identify themselves and their group (Kapferer 1988, 80).

This formulation of conscious identity has been publicly disputed among Armenians; secular and clerical activists have disagreed over the details of the above message.[1] Some have placed the focus of community activity on the "Armenian cause" or the "Armenian question," others on the support of Hayastan. All have claimed for themselves the role of arbiter of ethnic identity. The different groups have disagreed vehemently in the past, leading many Armenians to complain that the biggest problem they face is their own divisiveness.[2] There is, however, consensus among diaspora leaders on certain ideals.

Language in particular has been emphasized, symbolizing what is special about Armenians. No one else speaks Armenian. The church, also linked to the longevity of the people, seemed relatively strong at the turn of the century and less in danger of disappearing. Indeed, it was perceived as a main instrument of maintaining both language and the people as an ethnic group or nation in exile. Religion and the church were coterminous, and both were taken for granted as part of everyday life. This, like language, was a mobile feature of culture and could be continued beyond the original homeland. Unlike language, the church was supported by a relatively powerful network. Generally the work of the church, as carried out by its hierarchy and by active lay people, was aimed at building a nation, and the church's role in that was as a teacher of language and history and as an umbrella for community government through the priests and church council. Religion was felt to be strong enough and pervasive enough to survive the church's attention being focused elsewhere. When clerical or secular leaders speak publicly about the importance of the church, it is usually in reference to its role in ensuring the survival of the Armenian people. Thus the church's spiritual message has not been expounded as clearly or emphatically as its nationalist one.

These are choices of the sort described by Susan Harding in *Remaking Ibieca* (1984), ones that appear at the time to be conservative, aimed at maintaining the status quo or rebuilding the past, but which later lead in new directions. The standard contemporary response to criticism of the church's focus on nationalism is that there was no other institution in a position to do it, but the outgrowth of this concentration is a church whose primary function many understand to be a national one, with the religious side as largely incidental. While this does not bother those who see the church as a living national museum of ritual, language, and music, even this is increasingly difficult to maintain, because fresh minds are needed for the priesthood and trained laity in order to continue the services.

The church still appears powerful, and it is very much so as a symbol; thus, in the practical sense, it can still serve as a much-needed ally to the secular nationalists. Underneath, though, the balance has shifted quite decisively, and the reins of the nationalist movement have long since passed from the church hierarchy to the political parties and their social affiliates. These continue to use the church; for example, they invite the clergy to serve as figureheads at functions. By cooperating in this relationship, the church maintains power itself in the communities while helping to sustain the secular organizations.

The basic message begun by the church and secular nationalists at the turn of the century—that of a lost homeland and a need for the survivors and their descendants to rebuild what they can—continues, but with major refinements and changes. From pride in the distant past, grief and hand-wringing about the recent past, and acceptance of the "fate of the Armenians" in the present, a more aggressive and future-oriented philosophy is emerging. This is due, at least in part, to the apparent tension between the increased confidence that comes from decades of successful rebuilding of private and public life in diaspora and the continuing physical insecurity and fears of assimilation.[3]

There are other reasons for the emergence of this outlook that are themselves developments, however unexpected, stemming from the original message. The second and third generations speak often of the images of Armenia and the Armenian people that they learned at school and at home. As the father of a large family said of his own school days in the 1940s, "We were taught we should be proud to be part of the best nation on earth! This is what we really thought." This was contrasted with the equally strong message that the Armenian people had a sad fate, that they were the victims of a horrendous crime, and that this part of the past should be held in reverence. Children were admonished to do well to make up for these personal and national losses. Like Hratch in chapter 2, some found this was not enough: "If we are so great, why do we act so pathetic?" At the same time, the general view of what was or is honorable action is the subject of debate: Should one turn the other cheek and concentrate on rebuilding, or should one rely more on better-organized self-defense (as was argued in earlier days) or political or physical revenge (as some have urged more recently)? More is known about the historical context of the time, and a different overall picture of international politics can be formed in retrospect. The actions of other minorities and displaced groups are equally influential, and aggressive rather than passive policies are admired.

Another important factor has pushed these considerations of which attitude to adopt beyond the interests of idealists, poets, and political leaders. The efforts of the Turkish government to "educate" the West on the Armenian question, funding both enormous public-relations operations and academic publishing (see chapter 3), has only fueled that idealism and aroused the attention, anger, and support of many who would otherwise not have been interested.[4] The denial by Turkey of Ottoman culpability in the deaths of so many Armenians has helped turn sorrow into righteous indignation and has stimulated the search for a response to such claims. The emotional impact of this Turkish factor has invigorated an otherwise fading concern and given definition to it.

With this last factor as a catalyst in recent years, both the pursuit and definition of "historical truth" and the political activism related to this have become an overriding concern in Armenian communities everywhere, including Cyprus and London. Nationalist rhetoric is given life and its message is made more acceptable. The injustice both of the massacres and of the denial gives a moral tone to the issue and provides a cause to preach about, believe in, and work for. History—a commitment to its continuation into the future and to the correct interpretation of the past—becomes the focus of the cause. Thus it encompasses language, church, and family, all of which become components of the historical picture. The sources of legitimacy of present-day belief and activity are attributed to the past. History becomes a *raison d'être,* a mythical charter for the nation, and what is selected as proper history in turn reflects the concerns of the present.

History has fundamental links with ethnicity, as George De Vos explains, as does a particular view of history with politicized ethnicity, or nationalism:

> Ethnicity, therefore, is in its narrowest sense a feeling of continuity with the past, a feeling that is maintained as an essential part of one's self-definition. . . . Ethnicity, therefore, includes a sense of personal survival in the historical continuity of the group. For this reason, failure to remain in the group leads to feelings of guilt. . . . Ethnicity in its deepest psychological level is a sense of survival. (De Vos 1975, 17)

FAITH IN RELIGION AND IN NATIONALISM

Benedict Anderson sees this psychological aspect of nationalism as having developed from the "religious imaginings" of the past:

> This century of the Enlightenment, of rationalist secularism, brought with it its own modern darkness. With the ebbing of religious belief, the suffering which belief in part composed did not disappear. . . . What

then was required was a secular transformation of fatality into continuity, contingency into meaning. (Anderson 1983, 19)

He suggests that the potency of nationalism should not be understood in terms of political ideologies but rather in its affinity with the psychological needs that religion had previously fulfilled.

In his book *Radical Monotheism and Western Culture,* H. Richard Niebuhr comes to a similar conclusion but is concerned more with the exploration of these needs. Where Anderson leaves religion as an "imaginative response" to suffering and desire for a sense of continuity, Niebuhr gives his attention to the problem of faith as expressed in religion and in nationalism. He sees radical monotheism, faith in God as the one beyond all the many, as being in constant conflict with polytheism and henotheism in their "modern, nonmythical guises." Monotheism is seen as the chief rival, being "that social faith which makes a finite society, whether cultural or religious, the object of trust as well as of loyalty and which tends to subvert even officially monotheistic institutions, such as churches" (Niebuhr 1943, 11). The question for Niebuhr is, Where does one derive one's sense of value or proof of worth? What is the object of one's faith? He states that

nationalism shows its character as a faith wherever national welfare or survival is regarded as the supreme end of life, whenever right and wrong are made dependent on the sovereign will of the nation, however determined, whenever religion and science, education and art are valued by the measure of their contribution to national existence. (Niebuhr 1943, 27)

For many Armenians in Cyprus and in London, faith in nationalism, in being Armenian, has upstaged religious belief. Indeed, for many it is not an issue at all. Moral fulfillment is found in working for *Hay tad* (the Armenian cause) and in other community services. For them and others the church remains important as a refuge against change and assimilation. In a chapter entitled "The Americanization of Orthodoxy," Vigen Guroian questions the meaning behind the "massive attrition" of third-generation Armenians from the church and describes trends not unlike those already developing in London and, in more subtle forms, in Cyprus as well.[5] Criticizing the Apostolic Church's evolution into a community of survivors dedicated to the preservation of their ethnic identity, Guroian notes that the secular religion of ethnicity is characterized by a lack of seriousness about worship and holiness but great seriousness about survival and success in the world. In this instance, survival and success are sought through the perpetuation of an ethnic culture such that it and those adhering to it are accepted and respected within the greater society. The Church gets defined as the instrument of this worldly activity, and the measure of the Church's value is a worldly calculus of its utility in achieving these goals. (Guroian 1987, 172–73)

As a concerned lay theologian, Guroian worries that the Apostolic Church, like many American churches and synagogues, has slipped out of the balance between worship in a culturally specific way and the worship of a particular culture.

Many anthropologists and sociologists from Durkheim onward have treated religion or divinity as society transfigured and symbolically expressed. But Gellner, writing in *Nations and Nationalism,* suggests that at the end of the twentieth century, the vehicle of religion is no longer needed to carry on the ritual confirmation of society. Rather,

a modern, streamlined, on-wheels high culture celebrates itself in song and dance, which it borrows (stylizing it in the process) from a folk culture which it fondly believes itself to be perpetuating, defending and reaffirming. (Gellner 1983, 58)

This and the shared high culture itself—that is, education, literacy, and a conscious knowledge of history and language—are outgrowths of the industrial world. Where once the folk cultures were taken for granted, they have begun to fade or even disappear in the face of ever-increasing homogeneity within each state, whether this is achieved by force or drift and assimilation.

Where does this leave religion and a national church? Does the confluence of generalized secular education and faith in nation point to an inevitable break between church and nation and beyond, to a church of "empty ritual," as the secular worship of society replaces its function? Geertz suggests that in considering religion, one should separate out its various aspects in order to understand it better (Geertz 1973). He mentions the social and the functional, two sides of the same coin, both of which have been explored to some degree in this study. There is nothing here to distinguish religion, however, from other cultural phenomena unless one looks at the third, most basic aspect: the spiritual. What is distinctly spiritual about religion is the relationship between humans and the being we in the West call God, and this leads directly to the questions of belief in the existence of such a God and to faith, which, as Niebuhr puts it, "is reliance on the source of all being for the significance of the self and all that exists" (Niebuhr 1943, 32).

Harding advises that in exploring this aspect of religion, one must ask how "the supernatural order become[s] real, known, experienced, absolutely irrefutable, in order to understand belief in God" (Harding 1987, 167). The question is essential but runs the risk of becoming sidetracked again in sociofunctional or behaviorist aspects. One must begin with the assumption that there is something to study; in other words, one must at least temporarily take the leap of faith required of religious believers of all stripes and explore the idea of "the numinous" (Otto 1923) or the wholly other being that dwells within us (Niebuhr 1943; Gadamer 1976). Niebuhr and others have written that the base of spirituality is within human nature, a raw faith ready to be touched, directed, manipulated.

For Armenians in earlier times, the reality of the supernatural order was not so much learned as imbibed or experienced in the heavily sensuous atmosphere of the church and encouraged by the interlocking network of home, community, and church. Though this is still considered the most appropriate means for Armenians to approach God, today many claim that it is not working for them. First, the constant contact and connections between everyday life and religious belief, previously mediated by the church, are made difficult by the new geography of the neighborhoods and the more separate and different lifestyles of the people. Second, secular education and the experience of living in the late twentieth century have changed the ways of thinking of later generations of Armenians. By trying to remain the same while concentrating its work on nation-building, the church has, so far, ignored its congregation's mental transition from semieducated villagers to well-educated urbanites.

The liturgy and the pageant of the Armenian Mass is clearly directed toward portraying the mystery, the awe-inspiring nature, and the otherness of God. These are aspects of religion that cannot be found in the teaching of social ethics, morality, catechism, and so on. In some ways, the prior text of having experienced the Armenian church gives many in Cyprus and older people in London an uncomfortable feeling when visiting a Protestant church because the mystery seems almost entirely lacking and everything is portrayed in intellectual terms. "There is no respect shown— it is so casual" is a complaint that is often heard. But even for these same people, the Armenian church also does not fill the other needs they feel; these needs, at least as expressed in conversations with me, almost all centered on a lack of intellectual stimulation or purpose and the frustration many feel in trying to relate the church or religion to everyday lives and ways of thinking.[6]

Instead, these "rational" questions or needs are being met by nationalism, presented as a moral cause. This has nothing to do with the numinous but everything to do with the human quest for belonging and continuity. Nationalism, while a faith, is not religion, though it can serve to replace religion in meeting some of the psychosocial needs indicated by Anderson or De Vos and by taking its form, as discussed by Kapferer. As Niebuhr points out, rationalism is also similar to religion in that it risks losing its adherents' attention to the competition of the affairs of everyday life. Not all members of the group feel the need to be part of a group equally strongly. Just as the irrational in religion is essential but not sufficient by itself, the rational in nationalism does not sustain interest and support without emotive symbols—which in the Armenian case have been in large part borrowed, or appropriated, from the church. In this vein John Armstrong adds that "the intensity of identity produced by older sacral myths—based on but not always extensive with distinctive religions—has never been exceeded by modern secular myths" (Armstrong 1982, 297).

CONCLUSIONS

The question asked in chapter 8, "How far have we come?" remains difficult to answer—but no more so than the accompanying "Where are we headed?" The complicated nature of the questions lies in the simple observation that culture at any given time is full of themes and variations. Earlier communities were not homogeneous, nor did Armenians in the homelands share a static list of identifiable cultural traits. People who called themselves Armenian also identified themselves as Adanatsi, Bolsetsi, or Zelifkiatsi, and as members of a certain family. Armenian nationalists, like others, have overlooked or disdained these local elements, viewing such diversity as the enemy of collective strength.

In Cyprus and London, Armenian daily life is diverse, private, and family-centered. Ideas, values, and behaviors are passed between generations and influenced, as always, by the wider cultural and political environment of the host culture and by the formal declarations of Armenian cultural identity. These latter appear as ideological constructions, definite, delineated, and exclusive, and though relatively few people commit themselves completely to their support, the ideas have permeated diaspora life and become part of the prior text.

Nationalism is not the only possible response to disruption or problematic social reality, of course, and should be discussed alongside parallel developments, including a less focused but equally conscious ethnic connection. Robert Murphy contends that in times of great turbulence and flux, the tendency of a given population is toward an attempted recreation of order, "to continue mundane activity as if nothing had happened." He adds further that this reaction threatens "massive personal withdrawal into private worlds, a flight from corporate illusions into personal fantasy" (Murphy 1971, 238). For Armenians in Cyprus and London, the insecurity based on memories of physical threat or fear of its recurrence, of emigration and its attendant adjustments, does often promote a conservative attitude, an attempt to re-create what is possible of that which was left behind. In the new situation, it also encourages a desire to fit into the surrounding society in order to get on with daily life or "mundane activity." This latter also means acquiescence to the host country's status quo and eventually acculturation to its values and standards. For some this becomes a complete rejection of nationalism and sometimes even of ethnicity and community. For most it is not so extreme; rather, it involves a combination of the influence of nationalist ideology, the psychological ties to one's own community and guilt feelings at failing to remain a part of it, and the personal interest in maintaining a stable everyday life.

Armenians in London as well as those in Cyprus maintain private links with other Armenians, and many more do this than are active in the political and organizational life of the community. In fact, the public, ideologically based, and more rigidly circumscribed definition of what it is to be Armenian leads to the alienation of many who do not see how they fit in. Some younger people in Cyprus and others from all but the oldest generation in London told me, "I feel Armenian until I go to one of those meetings!" The style and content of the lectures are said to be "old-fashioned"; they are too long, and the concerns expressed in them are too narrow and self-centered. More than a few have said as well that they feel uncomfortable with the "racist" slant that anti-Turkish talk often contains.

Writing about life in Ireland, Henry Glassie notes that when culture becomes politicized, certain things that previously were very much part of daily life become tainted by their association with the other side, the enemy (Glassie 1982, 642). Certainly this is also true among Armenians. Older people mention that they feel guilty when they enjoy listening to Turkish music and wonder if somehow they are less Armenian for doing so. Nasreddin Hodja stories, which were once the staple fare of repartee and storytelling, are still occasionally heard without comment in some

circles but are told with apologies in others. And yet the formal construction of ethnicity and nationalism receives its strongest energy transfusion
from the boundary-marking developed in its contrast of the good Armenian with the bad Turk (see Barth 1969). Discussing the "tension between
idealized Greek culture and the direct experience of Greek social life,"
Herzfeld points out very similar problems (Herzfeld 1987, 28). Because
Turkish or other "foreign" elements of culture are embedded in daily life,
how can one extricate a purely Armenian "culture"—or a Europeanized
version, as is often desired?

While a few young people have tried to push the Armenian cultural
and political organizations themselves to change, to be less oriented toward the status quo or more "revolutionary," to share resources and projects with other minority groups, the big majority of those who disagree
simply drop out. Some drift away. Others stay on the fringe of organized
community life, attending church occasionally (especially for weddings,
memorial services, Easter, and so on) and going to a *hantess* or lecture
when the subject is of interest or when a relative is involved. Mostly they
are caught up in their networks of family, friends, and work. The public
message and style of the politicized groups is a substantial influence for all
in the community, but people bring their own agendas as individuals and
the prior text of the culture as they live and know it. This too is part of the
dialectic that Murphy (1971) describes and the interaction between culture and ideology.

The concept of sacrifice in the Armenian world is a potent one and
resounds with pagan and traditional Christian overtones. It is embedded
in the culture, in family life, which gives it a powerful resonance it would
never have had if it had been a concept newly introduced after the massacres. Likewise, when Armenians hear ideological rhetoric about endangered peoples, it touches them because they and their families have directly experienced loss and insecurity. The ways such concepts are directed
by intellectuals and community leaders and the ways they are perceived
are constantly changing, though the major symbols representing them remain the same and thus lend them a sense of permanence and continuity.

The "witches' brew" mentioned in chapter 1, the adjustments of
western to eastern Armenians, the differences that Armenians in Cyprus
and their cousins living in London see between themselves and others in
the diaspora—all are indicative of the variety that was found within the
Armenian world in the past and which continues today. The maintenance
of ethnic identity or the promotion of nationalism is not a conscious priority of the majority of Armenians, and thus ethnicity and nationalism
take their place alongside professional, family, and other interests.

Instead, institutions—mainly the church and political parties—rightfully claim to have protected, promoted, and directed the major facets and symbols of an ideal version of Armenian culture. Individuals and their families in diaspora could not have done this in the same way. But below the surface, the institutions and symbols are also part of more mundane, everyday life—living culture—and are themselves changing. Family ties, values, and standards of behavior appear most resistant to change and also least affected by politics and institutions. Through families and their networks, a less defined, looser conception of being Armenian is nurtured and passed on. This is at least equally responsible for the continuing presence of people who call themselves Armenians in diaspora. Observing Armenian Americans, Bakalian agrees that "ultimately it is within the family that Armenianness is nourished and sustained, and it is within the family that it finds its most frequent expression" (Bakalian 1993, 441). However, when thinking consciously of being Armenian or when speaking of it, Armenians in diaspora are in dialogue, positively or negatively, with the more concrete ideas of ethnicity and nationalism spread by the church, political leaders, and teachers.

The version of nationalism that reaches Armenians in Cyprus and Cypriot Armenians in London stresses the continual history of the Armenian people, beginning on the Urartian plain some 2,500 years ago. The church and the Armenian language are both integral parts of this picture, but they are the ones that are in fact declining in terms of knowledge and participation. "History" or longevity is what appears most durable and, at the same time, encompasses the rest as symbols in nationalist terms. The rejection of fatality and the search for continuity is most comfortably served by an emphasis on the ancient roots of the people. A moral dimension is supplied by the injustices of the recent past, giving motivation and a sense of urgency to the cause. History becomes a charter or, as Glassie writes, "a prime mode of cultural construction . . . a way people organize reality to investigate truth to survive in their own terms" (Glassie 1982, 652).

"History is used in literate societies as myth is in nonliterate ones to provide a distinct but relevant realm within which to explore the validity of the current regime," adds Glassie, after Lévi-Strauss (Glassie 1982, 649). Armenians in Cyprus and Cypriot Armenians in London feel themselves very much part of a larger diaspora—connected by history, by a history of faith, by a shared past. The components of that past are not studied in detail, but the basic features have a deep resonance within Armenian life and serve as an underpinning for the mechanisms of family and community.

Armenians are conscious in their use of history as myth or social charter, and the element of faith is central. Faith in history, in a past that validates the present and spurs the future, is nurtured and encouraged. History as mythical charter does not just provide a source of pride for new immigrants in the face of more powerful, established societies but also serves as an anchor for the Armenian people, who are adrift in a sea of insecurity and caught in the unavoidable cross-currents of mobility and flexibility.

Appendix A

THE ARMENIAN POPULATION IN CYPRUS

Census year	Armenians	Total for Cyprus
1881	179	186,173
1891	280	209,286
1901	517	237,022
1911	558	274,108
1921	1,197	310,715
1931	3,375	347,959
1946	3,686	450,114
1956	4,549	—
1960	3,628	577,615
1978 (est.)	2,200	633,000
1985 (est.)	1,900	650,000
1995 (est.)	1,700	725,000

Appendix B

GLOSSARY

The following terms are frequently used throughout the text. I have chosen to use the non-English words in the original language because their translation is cumbersome, their meaning is broader than their direct English equivalent, or they are used by Armenians even when speaking English. I have used an idiosyncratic transliteration, writing these words as I hear them and as I think a speaker of American English is likely to reproduce something similar.

Note for pronunciation:

a	ah
i	ee
o	oh
gh	as in French *r*
r	is trilled slightly

AGBU: Armenian General Benevolent Union. This charitable organization, founded in Cairo, and now with its headquarters in the United States, is popularly thought to be led by people sympathetic to the Ramgavar party. Its widespread work includes the administration of a large network of schools, scholarships, cultural activities, newspapers, and magazines around the diaspora. Since the 1988 earthquake and then independence in Armenia, it has taken a very active role in reconstruction and new projects there.

aman (Turkish): "Oh!", "My goodness!", "Good grief!" and so on, depending on voice inflection and context

amot: shame, shameful

ARF: Armenian Revolutionary Federation (Dashnaktsoutiune). This political party, active in reform movements and then resistance at the end of the Ottoman Empire, governed the independent republic of Armenia between 1918 and 1920 and for many years following was popularly known as the pro-West, anti-Soviet party, although it has a socialist platform.

Catholicos: Head of the Armenian Apostolic Church. The church is presently divided between two seats. The title of Catholicos of All Armenians rests in Etchmiadzin, Armenia. The Catholicos based in Antelias is near Beirut, Lebanon. The churches in London come under the former jurisdiction and those in Cyprus under the latter.

Dashnaktsoutiune: see ARF (above)

Dashnak: member of the ARF (above)

deghatsi: native; one who is born in (and whose family is from) a certain town, region, or country

grabar: classical Armenian

hantess: event, occasion, usually large-scale and with a program; plural *hantessner*

hars: bride, daughter-in-law; also sister-in-law; woman who has married into the family

Hay, -hay: an Armenian; also used in combination. A Gibrahay is an Armenian from Cyprus; a Barskahay is an Armenian from Iran.

Hayastan: Armenia: now the Republic of Armenia, until recently Soviet Armenia; also referring to the larger territory of the ancient homelands

kahana: married parish priest

kaghtagan: refugee

khnamie: in-laws; extended family on both sides

Melkonian Educational Institute: Armenian secondary school on the outskirts of Nicosia, administered by the AGBU; historically its students were drawn from around the Near East. Currently some are also from the United States and Europe.

-ner: suffix indicating the plural

Parekordzagan: AGBU (above)

odar: a non-Armenian

pesa: husband, son-in-law; also brother-in-law; man who has married into the family

Ramgavar: political party formed from three older parties in 1921. The original Sahmanadir Ramgavar party was founded in 1908 in Cairo. The party has a Social Democratic platform and a history of support for Soviet Armenia.

Surp: saint

Srpazan: title for a bishop, equivalent to the English "Your Grace"

-tsi: suffix indicating someone who is from the country or town mentioned (i.e., Gibratsi, someone from Cyprus; Gessariatsi, someone from Gessaria)

vartabed: celibate priest

vermak: quilt, blanket, cover; also a futonlike mattress

Appendix C

All terms are Armenian unless otherwise indicated in square brackets. *-ig* is the diminutive form. Terms in parentheses were popular earlier but not today.

wife (W)	*digiin*
husband (H)	*amousiin*
bride, sister- or daughter-in-law	*hars*
groom, brother- or son-in-law	*pesa*
man and wife	*ayr yev giin*
bride and groom	*hars ou pesa*
mother (M)	*mayr, mayrig, mama; (anneh)* [Turkish]
father (F)	*hayr, hayrig, baba*
child	*zavag, yerahan; çocuk, (yavrum)* [Turkish]
daughter	*akhchig*
son	*dgha*
sister (Z)	*kuyr*
brother (B)	*yeghpayr*
grandmother	*medzmayr(ig), medzmama, mema; neneh* [Turkish]; *yaya* [Greek]
grandfather	*medzhayr(ig), medzbaba; dede* [Turkish]; *papou* [Greek]

249

grandchild	*tor(nig)*
MZ	*morakuyr, mokoor; tantig* [from French]; (*doudou*) [Turkish]
FZ	*horakuyr, hokoor; tantig* [from French]; (*doudou*) [Turkish]
MB	*moryeghpayr; dayı, dayday* [Turkish]
FB	*horyeghpayr, keri; dayı* [Turkish]
WZ	*keni*
HZ	*dal*
BW	*ner*
ZH	*kerayr*
WB	*anertsag*
HB	*dakr*
cousin	*cousin* [orig. from French, now English]; (*zarmig*)
WM	*zokanch, gesour*
HM	*gesour*
WF	*anerhayr, gesrayr*
HF	*gesrayr*
in-laws or extended family of each spouse to the other	*khnamie*
family	*undanik*
kindred, blood relations	*azkagan*
clan	*gerdastan*

Notes

PREFACE

1. Though not an ethnography, Shahgaldian 1979 provides many details about daily life in Lebanon and the context of living in the Middle East. A more recent dissertation in anthropology about Armenians in Lebanon is Aprahamian 1989.

CHAPTER 1

1. Some Turkish dialects spoken in eastern Anatolia retain this pronunciation today.

2. Loizos (1981) and Volkan (1979) write poignantly of the losses suffered by the Greek and Turkish peoples, respectively.

3. The government of Turkey insists that the deportations and massacres did not take place, saying that whatever tragedies did happen at that time were not connected with official Ottoman policy and were an accident of war and upheaval. The Turkish government also claims that at least as many Turkish people as Armenians were killed or died of disease at the time. See chapter 3 for further detail.

4. See, for example, O'Grady 1979, Phillips 1979, Talai 1989, and Bakalian 1993.

5. Armstrong uses the term "archetypal diaspora," referring to "those ethnic collectivities which have maintained persistent sacral myth" and which have

"been sustained by the highly concrete component of their myth that points to their sacral locus of origin as well as by a distinctive alphabet" (Armstrong 1982, 207). The Armenians regard Etchmiadzin, in the Republic of Armenia, as the physical site of their early fourth-century Christian roots. The alphabet used today was created by a monk in 406 C.E. Safran compares others with the Jewish "ideal diaspora," noting that Armenians also base solidarity on common religion, language, and collective memory (Safran 1991, 84).

6. Safran (1991), among others, makes this part of a general definition, with qualifications.

CHAPTER 2

1. The phrase *batmeh nayenk* is a general invitation to talk about what is new. Roughly, it means "What's up?" or sometimes, in more specific cases, "Tell us about it." Literally, it means "Tell [a story], let's see."

2. Miller and Miller (1986, 1991, 1993) have explored the effects of the massacres on the survivor generation in later years and also the variety of ways in which the younger generations absorb the anger, fear, and prolonged distress still evident in many.

3. Father Gomidas (born Soghomon Soghomonian), a priest, gathered and notated folk songs at the turn of the century.

4. By 1991 and 1992, the Surp Magar ceremony was performed by one priest and no deacons and was attended by only two or three people. The feast the following day was still shared by over two hundred.

5. After Turner 1974, 64. Dudwick (1989, 64) also discusses this in terms of the Karabagh movement in Hayastan.

6. Bakalian asked Armenian community leaders in the United States to suggest "typical" Armenian values. They listed "generosity and hospitality; hard work and industriousness; resourcefulness and ingenuity (*jarbeeg*); filial respect and loyalty; parental sacrifice and keeping the good name, honor and reputation of the family (*badeev*) by avoiding shame (*amot*)" (Bakalian 1993, 294).

7. *Hay ask* ("Armenian nation"), *Hay zhoghovourt* ("Armenian people"), or *Hayoutiune* ("Armenian people" or "Armenians"), used to refer to Armenians generally, are more forceful terms than the simple *Hayer* ("Armenians"). These words can change their meaning and emphasis, depending on the context.

8. O'Grady (1979) and Phillips (1979) focus on this aspect of Armenian life, and Phillips states, "I have described a social system within which there is a strong sense of shared culture and history juxtaposed with the reality of intraethnic conflict and political fragmentation. In this sense, Armenian identity is not derived from a particular culture or history, but an active process of symbolization" (Phillips 1979, 274).

CHAPTER 3

1. See also Maksoudian 1975 for more on the history of Armenians in Cyprus.

2. Kyrris also notes the presence of a strain of Monophysitism in Cyprus, probably connected to the Armenians there, during the sixth and seventh centuries (1985, 170).

3. More can be read about the churches of Famagusta and Nicosia, the Surp Magar monastery, and other Cyprus monuments in Mangoian and Mangoian 1947 and in Keshishian 1946.

4. An important addition to the local school system was the English school, where Greek, Turkish, and a disproportionately large number of Armenian boys went.

5. Kyrris outlines the 1931 uprising as a popular reaction to the disregard of the British administration of the "tragic financial situation of the island," combined with the instigation of an extremist group of Greek (pro-*enosis*) leaders (Kyrris 1985, 342–43). See also Loizos (1975, 35) for local reaction.

6. In Turkish, *çavuş* ("sergeant").

7. Christopher Hitchens is sympathetic to this general outline and points out that the U.S. State Department, directed by Henry Kissinger, indicated an eagerness to accept the coup. He also notes that the British government had, in 1967, anticipated and decided to accept such an eventuality (Hitchens 1984, 84, 91). He concludes that there was "collusion between unevenly matched and differently motivated forces, who for varying reasons feared or disliked an independent Cyprus" (p. 165).

8. Oberling 1982 describes the experience of Turkish villagers who fled north. Volkan 1979 analyzes psychological adjustment on the Turkish side.

9. The present alphabet contains all thirty-six of the original letters with the addition of two more in recent times. Read from left to right, Armenian script is more or less phonetic.

10. I am grateful to Deacon Hratch Tchilingirian for his help in clarifying this controversy. He adds that "the Armenian Church accepts the unity of Christ's divine and human nature as 'one nature' (Monophysite), i.e., one person composed of two natures."

11. Guroian (1995) makes a similar observation, noting that the story of Vartan Mamigonian has been transformed into a model for the Armenian struggle for survival in the diaspora. See also Tölölyan 1987.

12. See Guroian 1986.

13. Sarkis Atamian, a pro-Dashnak writer, has suggested that the existence of freedom fighters who actually fought against the Turks and Kurds has been a comfort and an aid to Dashnak supporters in adjusting in the aftermath of the massacres (Atamian 1955). Men already in diaspora, of all political persuasions,

joined the French Foreign Legion's special Armenian force, called the Gamavors, during World War I to fight against the Ottomans. Certainly today the *fedayeen,* or freedom fighters, have a most prominent place in the pantheon of heroes for roughly half the Armenians who are active in social organizations.

14. Dadrian 1986; Hovannisian 1986, 1967; Sarafian 1993–95.

15. Following the earthquake in Hayastan in December 1988, the Catholicos of Etchmiadzin and the Catholicos of Antelias announced that they were bringing forward plans for reunification and would take steps to do so immediately. They did this symbolically in a ceremony in New York, but many details have yet to be worked out below that level. Since then, Vazken Catholicos of Etchmiadzin died in 1994 and Karekin Catholicos of Antelias was elected as his successor, a move without precedent. A new man will be elected to the historic seat of Antelias, but this is seen as an exciting further step toward consolidation and the healing of old divisions.

16. Those familiar only with Armenian churches in the United States, some of which follow Etchmiadzin while the others follow Cilicia, will be surprised that churches representing "the other side" do not exist in either the United Kingdom or Cyprus. People who, for a variety of reasons, disagree with the politics of either church authority usually stop attending, at least for a time.

17. Many, if not most, of these new émigrés are families that had relatively recently settled in Hayastan.

18. Bakalian (1993, 153–54) gives many similar examples from her research among Armenian Americans. Miller and Miller (1991) analyze the family histories of several "terrorists."

CHAPTER 4

1. One *donum* is approximately one third of an acre.

2. Geddes, quoted in Zifron 1972, 33. The work and aims of the Geddes couple are described in Zifron 1972 and Mairet 1957. Briefly, small farms and interest-free loans were arranged, small craft workshops organized, and a school of sericulture set up. Some families relocated to the grounds of the Armenian monastery to reclaim farmland.

3. There are several possible reasons for this. Though the Geddes plan was far more ambitious and affected more families, the projects were short-lived. The Geddeses themselves did not stay long, and most of the families they helped moved on. Kurkjian remained in the region for many years and was very active and influential in community life. His efforts in education coincided with the concerns of the *deghatsi.*

4. A primus stove is a liquid-gas stove with a small pump that vaporizes the fuel.

5. Turkish spelling: *hoca.* In Cyprus some Armenians pronounce this *khodja.*

6. By contrast, an older woman noted that in other places there was a tradition of the man marrying into the bride's home—a "house-*pesa*." Certainly this was found in Cyprus following the arrival of the refugees.

7. Very similar stories were related by other women, all ending with the father-in-law taking pity on the young woman and sending her off to bed with her husband.

CHAPTER 5

1. Some women reported that infants' diapers were made by dipping a square of cotton cloth in wax so that it was lightly coated. Finely sieved dirt was sprinkled onto this and then a layer of gauze spread on top. The gauze layer was placed next to the baby's skin. When the dirt was soiled, it was thrown out, and the gauze and waxed cotton were washed and replaced.

2. There are formulas for greeting clergy of different ranks, but the most commonly used greeting for all is "*Astvadz oknagan*," said as the right hand is kissed.

3. Hussein Ibn Ali was driven from the Hijaz when Saudi rule expanded in the 1920s. The British brought the "King of the Arabs and Caliph of Islam" to Cyprus, where he lived in exile. The King's personal secretary was an Armenian named Simonian. When I mentioned the (to me) mysterious presence and donation of the King of Arabia to other people, one older woman, who did not know of Simonian, said, "Oh, all of those kings and such men had helpers who were Armenian, and that was how they became interested in Armenian affairs!"

4. "*Astvadz uzeneh*" or, frequently among older Armenians, "*inshallah*" (Arabic through Turkish speech). Armenians from the Arab world often use *inshallah*, which seems to reinforce or reintroduce it in Armenian Cypriot speech.

5. Another phrase often used in such contexts is "*Astvadz hokiin loosavoreh*." Young people rarely follow this custom today, except at funerals and memorial services when greeting the family of the deceased. Older people also add "*loosahokiin*" ("his or her soul is lit") after the name of the deceased as the conversation continues (for example, "Shnorig *loosahokiin*").

6. Hodja stories—so called because they are about the Hodja (Nasreddin Hodja)—are still enjoyed today, in London as well as Cyprus, but with decreasing frequency with each generation. The stories are used to illustrate a point, intimate criticism where it cannot be made directly, or just entertain. Situations often remind someone of a certain story and he or she will tell it, acknowledging that everyone else already knows it backward and forward—at times only the punchline is told. Though Armenians co-opted the Hodja into their conversation, they make no claims to his origins or "ownership" and today seem to include these stories, along with Turkish sayings that are still used, in a short list of things they admire about Turks (the list also includes hospitality and food).

CHAPTER 6

1. This was the last group to arrive during the era of colonial government. Though a break of some twenty years followed, Armenian refugees again began at least passing through Cyprus as they fled the disruptions of Beirut and the war between Iran and Iraq.

2. In speaking of the massacres, people who had been children then spoke most poignantly of their parents' (especially their mother's) pain and worries, strength and bravery. Concerning later instances of war or disruption, children again praised or worried over their parents, as parents did for their children. Very few openly expressed worry, fear, or pride for themselves, though often it could be easily deduced from what was said.

3. Similar reactions were reported by psychologists following the earthquake in Hayastan in 1988. Parents found it difficult to come to terms with their feelings of having "failed" their children. See also Erikson 1976.

4. Extract from personal communication.

5. See more on courtship and dating in chapters 9 and 10 and a very similar story (with a different ending) in chapter 7.

6. Many people worried that they might smell of garlic after eating some during a meal. It was always mentioned, by way of explanation, that the Greeks used to complain that the Armenians smelled of garlic. One woman also said she remembered a lecture at the American Academy warning the Armenian girls not to eat so much garlic at home because it was offensive; she assumed that Greek girls had been complaining.

7. Mostly boys. It seems that girls took piano lessons, for the most part. Among Mr. Vahan's students were three relatives who went on to become well-known professional violinists: his son, Haroutune Bedelian; his nephew, Manoug Parikian; and his great-nephew, Levon Chilingirian.

CHAPTER 7

1. Though Armenians lived mostly in the Turkish neighborhood in Nicosia, it is not surprising that they officially decided to join their coreligionists, the Greeks, in government. When thinking of government, the obvious contrast, influenced by the *millet* system, was between themselves as Christians and the Turks as Muslims. Older people, when asked about this decision, all said that they did not remember any debate or discussion on this at the time. It had seemed to them then (and again later, when asked about it) an obvious choice. Community leaders apparently made the decision.

2. Britain was not the only possibility. Hayastan, Australia, the United States, and various other countries also attracted Armenian Cypriots. Generally these latter went to join relatives already settled there or went for their own par-

ticular trade, business or education. Except for the university students, Armenians usually emigrated in family groups, often including grandparents or unmarried aunts and uncles.

3. This experience was widespread, and jokes developed about it (or perhaps were borrowed from other peoples). For example:

Vahram took his family to Hayastan, but his brother's and sister's families couldn't decide. Should they go? Should they stay? Vahram said, "Look, it is easy. We'll write and tell you what the situation is like."

"*Aman, janis*, but how can you write the truth if it really is very bad? They will take your letter?"

"Don't worry. We will say everything is fine, but we will include a family photo. If we are standing, everything is fine, and you must come and join us. If we are sitting, you will know it is bad. Don't come."

The next year a letter finally arrived. It said, "Everything is fine here," but in the photo everyone was lying on the ground.

4. The arithmetic does not work between official emigrants and the level of population. I think the population figures are approximately correct and the answer lies in the difference between the number of "official" emigrants and the many who left—to study, to visit family indefinitely, to stay away temporarily—if the family could afford it and had relatives abroad who could help out.

5. In 1964 the trip normally took between one and two hours, depending on blockades and diversions.

6. Françoise Zonabend, for example, who worked in a French village where violent disruption has not occurred, notes similar changes. She writes that it is unusual to see groups of people on the street: "People stay at home much more than before. They are turned in on themselves." People complain that this is related to television watching, but Zonabend notes, "In fact television has only confirmed and speeded up a trend which had already started between the two wars" (Zonabend 1984, 7).

7. Zonabend observes that houses in Minot also underwent changes in layout, encouraging more privacy and separation: "The village space seems to have become a void, and the family group, having lost its place to circulate outside, has withdrawn within its own home" (Zonabend 1984, 22).

8. Loizos, in *The Heart Grown Bitter*, quotes a survivor of the Smyrna disaster of 1922 in a similar vein, as well as an Armenian who tells the Greek refugees of 1974 that he has been a refugee five times over (Loizos 1981, 144).

CHAPTER 8

1. The Manchester Armenian community reached its peak of population and prosperity between 1875 and 1912, when approximately eighty Armenian firms were registered.

2. See Oakley 1979 for additional information on the migration of Cypriot Armenians to Britain.

3. See Attalides 1981 and Loizos 1981. Among these changes are a decrease in the number of children, an increase in emphasis on the individual and privacy (within the context of family), the increased independence of family members (including women), and an increase in secularization.

4. It was not until the Centre for Armenian Information and Advice (CAIA) began in 1986 that an Armenian center was organized specifically to meet these needs. Tala'I (1986, 254) notes that "although Armenian associations are regularly engaged in fund-raising, such funds are not then normally re-distributed in philanthropic enterprises but are used to develop and sustain the momentum of the gathering sponsored by these associations." Of course, most of these organizations were formed, or have developed from organizations that were formed, out of immediate concern for the loss of the nation itself. This continues to be their main focus but, in fact, there are Armenian philanthropic enterprises, such as Blue Cross, the Armenian Relief Fund, the Armenian Poor Board, and the Benlian and Essefian Trusts.

5. Periodically evening classes in Armenian were given, attended by non-Armenian spouses (usually wives) and young people who wanted to learn more than their basic childhood Armenian.

6. Bridgwood reports that the match of Turkish Cypriot men and Irish women is "relatively acceptable to Turkish Cypriots" and one that is not uncommon. She adds, "Both groups are migrants in London, and share a similar position as 'outsiders' in British society. . . . The Irish are also perceived as sharing some of the central values of Turkish Cypriot culture; namely control of women, an emphasis on female virginity, a belief that marriage should be permanent, and hospitality" (Bridgwood 1987, 331).

7. For example, both in Cyprus and in London, women claim that Armenians from Beirut and Iran love to dress up, wear a lot of jewelry and makeup, and generally have a much more flashy style. Those in London often find their friends and relatives in Cyprus more fashion-conscious than themselves—but this doesn't seem to be agreed on by those in Cyprus. An extremely casual style in clothes, though, is an indication of English (or American) influence.

8. Words such as *Barskahay* are used in both Armenian and English speech. In Armenian, the word is given the proper plural indicator (*Barskahayer*), but in English, the word is made plural by attaching the English *-s* (*Barskahays*).

9. Talai (1989, 47) discusses these differences, saying that each group explained to her that it was the others who didn't wish to mix.

10. But there has also been criticism of some of the elite of Soviet Armenia who spoke Russian even at home, as their first language. This has reversed dramatically following the Karabagh (Artsakh) protests of 1988. Armenians are said to be pulling their children out of Russian-language schools in Yerevan, and there is talk of a law forbidding Armenian children to attend them.

11. Talai discusses this issue as well, adding that some Iranian Armenians told her they felt their accent, being part of the eastern dialect, was more "authentic." She also notes some of the defensiveness felt at the Cypriots' better command of English (Talai 1989, 44–45).

12. This is suddenly a very different kind of question, now that the Soviet Union has disintegrated. Armenians are today rethinking their answers.

CHAPTER 9

1. Hoogasian-Villa and Matossian 1982 also gives some indication of these in the variety of responses from their informants.

2. The *Hony* Turkish dictionary shows "old Armenian woman" for this entry (*dudu*).

3. This same reason is given for the popularity of the French word *merci*, pronounced with a rolled *r*, as it is in Turkey, as a shortcut for *shnorhagal yem* (Armenian) or *tesekur ederim* (Turkish).

4. Bamberger also mentions this change, officially made in 1924, when the "steps" were reduced from seven to five (Bamberger 1986–87, 82).

5. *Amousiin,* rather than *ayr,* is used for "husband" alone. "*Amousiinis eh*" means "He is my husband."

6. Segalen questions the validity of the concept of the couple in nineteenth-century rural France and argues instead for the notion of household (Segalen 1983, chapter 2).

7. There were, of course, exceptions to this and also some times when people were uncertain what to do. Mrs. Anoush said, "In the old days you always wanted to name the child after the grandfather. But if the grandfather was still alive, it was thought to be very bad luck [for the grandfather—his death would be brought closer] to do that." This contrasts with Hoogasian-Villa and Matossian (1982, 106), who write that Armenians did not have this custom.

Sometimes the decision for a name would come through dreams. "When Louise was pregnant, some people [friends and relatives] started coming to visit and they were saying, 'We've been seeing your husband's father in our dreams. You are going to have a boy, and you must name him after him.' So she did, even though there was already another cousin with the same name."

The passing on of first names was also common among Greek Cypriots (Markides et al. 1978, 97) and Turkish Cypriots (Bridgwood 1987, 244).

8. This is also similar to figures for Greek Cypriots (Markides et al. 1978, 93) and Turkish Cypriots (Bridgwood 1987, 227). Very few mentioned world population growth as a concern, though some did.

9. Literally, "light to your eyes."

10. Mrs. Araxi continued, "We even had a superstition that the worst time

to get pregnant was right after the blood had cleared from your period. There would be something wrong with the child. We didn't realize that it was nearly impossible to get pregnant then anyway. And girls were very worried that their wedding day shouldn't fall at just that time."

11. People said that this was because the Catholic Church would not recognize marriages performed in the Apostolic church and that one must convert to Catholicism to marry in the Catholic Church.

12. Hirschon quotes a Greek proverb: "Shoes from your homeland, even if they are mended" (Hirschon 1989, 111).

13. Turkish, "my child"; literally, the young of an animal or bird.

CHAPTER 10

1. Nasreddin Hodja stories are traditional Turkish tales. See chapter 5.

2. Loizos 1981, 169–70.

3. Crawford (1985, 28) describes a similar custom among Greeks in Kalavassos.

4. In Cyprus the church grants divorce, as it is the institution that legalizes marriage. A couple must appear (together or alone) before a special council of clergy and lay people and present their case. The lay members should be married and over forty years old. A lawyer can be used for advice, but is not necessary. I asked one lawyer what grounds for divorce were allowed. She consulted her books and found nine possibilities, which she gave in condensed form: (1) tough, hurtful, or intolerable behavior; (2) immoral behavior; (3) diseases or epidemics; (4) sterility (for either); (5) atheism; (6) mutual hatred; (7) homosexuality or bestiality; (8) physically hurtful behavior; (9) desertion (after seven years). The parish priest in Cyprus later said that the most common grounds he had observed was the first—interpreted liberally as incompatibility.

5. As in other cultures, it is Armenian men and not women who grill meat. Kebabs are especially popular.

6. Bridgwood discusses similar child-rearing methods for Turkish Cypriots and suggests that "socializing children, then, is not so much a matter of moulding them, as of curbing their worst excesses until they reach an age when they know better" (Bridgwood 1987, 255). She adds that this attitude is now changing, especially in London. This is true among Armenians both in Cyprus and in London.

7. Boyarin quotes an Armenian tailor in Georgia, speaking to his Jewish friend. "You made a mistake sending your son off to the university, Moshe. I'm having my three sons trained as artisans; they'll come and have a drink with me at the end of the day. But your son—what will he have to say to you?" (Boyarin 1991, 169)

CHAPTER 11

1. Peter Trudgill defines it as "first language learnt" (Trudgill 1974, 125).

2. By contrast, a teacher who had worked many years in Cyprus asked me what my mother tongue was. Before I could answer, he asked further, "What language do you use for counting? *That* is your mother tongue!" He does, however, agree that ideally, Armenian is the mother tongue of Armenians.

3. Comparisons can be made with the rapid learning of Hebrew in Palestine and Israel, but in Cyprus (and other communities around the Near East) the return to an ancestral tongue took place outside the homeland. Armenians in diaspora did not have a language comparable to Yiddish, which would have provided sentimental or nostalgic competition. Village or town dialects were neither widely shared nor highly regarded. The existence and continuation (however faltering) of Yiddish literature is a further contrast with the former dialects of western Armenia, where intellectuals wrote primarily in classical Armenian or in the Istanbul vernacular dialect (cf. Boyarin 1991).

4. *Bakkal* means "grocery store." Although *patate* and *tomate* are French words, they are often thought of as Turkish.

5. This was a common practice in certain regions of the Ottoman Empire. Bibles, hymnbooks (for Protestants), and newspapers (see chapter 4) were printed in this way.

6. Trudgill suggests the following explanation for similar observations in other societies: "Men and women's speech . . . is not only different: women's speech is also (socially) 'better' than men's speech. This is a reflection of the fact that, generally speaking, more 'correct' social behavior is expected of women" (Trudgill 1974, 94). He also notes "that working-class speech, like certain other aspects of working-class culture in our society, has connotations of or associations with masculinity, which may lead men to be more favourably disposed to non-standard linguistic forms than women" (Trudgill 1974, 93).

7. In Turkish *siktir* is an extremely insulting obscenity, never used as a joke. Greeks and Romanians use it often, again in milder, joking terms. "*Ah, siktir*" can mean "Oh, go on," "Get out of here" (Ruth Mandel, personal communication).

8. With the increase in knowledge of English, the repertoire of puns includes some that cross three languages. In the case of *hivant yeghnig,* Armenian words meaning "sick deer," Armenian speakers of Turkish recognize the English words as sounding like *siktir*. Again, this moves toward joking rather than insulting relations.

9. At this time it seems the administration of the Melkonian Institute itself discouraged many Cypriot students from attending, as it wished to remain a boarding school, separate from the community. Though it was no longer an orphanage, it still aimed at providing an education for needy students from around the Near East. Students in Cyprus were thought to be better-off financially.

10. There were stories of Greek or Turkish apprentices who learned Armenian while learning a trade from an Armenian and a few maids who learned while working in an Armenian household.

11. By Taniel Varoujan, translated by John Papasian. From *Sojourn at Ararat: Poems of Armenia,* compiled and edited by Gerald Papasian (1987, 35).

12. Several people mentioned they had heard or read that Margaret Mead suggested that Armenian be used as a world language at the United Nations, for international business, and so on because, people said, "it is so rich" and it is "phonetic and the alphabet contains every sound" (it doesn't). Mead saw it as a possibility because it is not associated with any of the world's dominant powers but has a long history of written and oral use (Mead 1969, 409–12).

13. Like the telling of stories and jokes in Turkish mentioned earlier, Hodja stories are almost always enjoyed in intimate situations, that is, with close friends and/or family. They are not part of the public, formal self-image of Armenians (cf. Herzfeld 1987).

CHAPTER 12

1. This is very likely brought over from French through Turkish, where it is also used frequently. The Turkish expression for "thank you" (*teşekkür ederim*) is as long as that in Armenian.

2. *Tamam* and *maşallah* are Arabic words that have entered Armenian speech through Turkish.

CHAPTER 13

1. Interestingly, Hirschon reports that the Greek refugees of Asia Minor criticized their old neighbors, the Armenians, for emphasizing the Epiphany rather than Easter as the major religious festival (Hirschon 1989, 29). Both in London and in Cyprus, Armenians make exactly the same distinction between themselves and "the English" (or Americans), as the latter appear to give Christmas more importance. The misunderstanding of the Greeks may stem from two sources: (1) the Armenian celebration of the Nativity and Epiphany on January 6 comes at a quiet time for the Greeks and thus appears to lend it special emphasis; (2) their own grander, more outward celebration of Easter, especially the carrying of the *epitaferon* through the streets, somewhat dwarfs the relatively private Armenian celebration.

2. In Armenian, the verb "to eat" (*oudel*) has many uses beyond describing the consumption of food and is often used in a play on words such as this. Just as someone can embezzle money by "eating" it, the priest can do away with parts of the service by "eating" them.

3. For example, one service that was mentioned in this vein was *dassuh*

gousank, based on the parable of the ten virgins and their lamps, a service in which the girls used to participate. An older woman said that she remembered it well, though she hadn't taken part. Girls would wear the *shabig* and hold candles during the service. Five would stay lit, and five were extinguished. "And every time, some of those girls would come out crying—because theirs had to go out!"

4. Some whom I asked later claimed they never did this. Others agreed with Araxi's interpretation. One woman said that her family took the flower home and pressed it between the pages of the family Bible. A young woman told me that the custom was also to bring flowers to lay on the *keresman* before the service. She did this, but most did not. A few people mentioned that before 1963, in the old church, the *keresman* was a rectangular carved box that could be decorated and then lifted up and carried around the courtyard of the church in a procession, the small boys leading. One would hold a cross, and they and the priests sang special hymns. "Like the Greeks," someone said, "only their *epitaferon* is much grander!" Another person said that the *keresman* is still carried around churches in Lebanon.

5. Greek for "my dear"; literally, "my mother." This is used between men, between women, or between men and women. It is a term of affection used very often among the younger Armenians when speaking Armenian or English as well as Greek.

6. Traditionally, eggs are boiled (often with onion skins, to give a rich reddish brown color) and a contest is held to see whose egg can withstand being knocked against another. Each person holds an egg with only the tip showing (whichever end is judged the strongest) and uses that to hit the tip of his or her partner's egg. The egg that cracks is the loser. The winner continues with other people's eggs until that also cracks.

7. Interestingly, God is not thought of as an Armenian God, nor is the church (its doctrine or ritual) thought to be the one true church, except for Armenians. Proselytizing is not done, though *odar* spouses who marry into the church are welcomed. The Armenian church is of and for Armenians only, and it appears that Armenians, at least in Cyprus and London, have a similar view of Christianity, that is, it is for Christians. The idea of conversion is somehow suspect and certainly not something to promote.

8. "*Astvadz uzeneh*" (Armenian) or often "*inshallah*" (Arabic or Turkish).

9. "*Astvadz hoki loosavoreh,*" literally "May God light his/her soul." Traditionally this precedes the name of a dead person when introduced in conversation. Young people rarely follow this custom, except at funerals and memorial services when greeting the family of the deceased.

10. I assume that below the surface level described above, there must have been considerable variety in earlier years as well, as evidenced in literature and poetry.

11. This was again strongly expressed following the 1988 earthquake in Hayastan.

12. Pre-Christian Armenian gods.

13. Miller and Miller would perhaps classify these under rationalization or reconciliation—or both—as they affirm that most people span several categories, depending on the day and situation (Miller and Miller 1986, 190).

14. Though I found the articles by Miller and Miller very helpful and sensitively written, they make some points that I find do not coincide with my own research. This could easily be due to the very different places in which our research was done (theirs was in Los Angeles). Whatever the reason, the contrasts are worth mentioning for the sake of future studies. In "An Oral History Perspective" the Millers note that "there is little question that the *degree of suffering* experienced by survivors, and/or witnessed by survivors, plays a key role in their response. Those who were not deported, or did not suffer extreme deprivation during the deportation, tend to be more reconciled to the massacre and less resentful toward the Turks" (Miller and Miller 1986, 189). While the *deghatsi* in Cyprus *are* remembered today for their relative disinterest and lack of understanding at the time, I found no such correlation among the refugees. Among the most bitter were some people who had lost material wealth but who had traveled in wagons or trains to simple but relatively comfortable new homes, whose families stayed intact for the duration. This is said not to deny the sadness and the shock of losing one's home and community but only in response to the point made above about varying reactions. I found women to be as outspoken as men (see Miller and Miller 1986, 190) in their own ways, in their anger and sorrow. Men could be outspoken, but often in terms of a formula, one I heard variations of at many community meetings.

CHAPTER 14

1. This struggle over image and meaning continues today as divisions remain between secular and clerical factions, between political parties, and between different regions of the diaspora and Hayastan. Cf. Bakalian 1993; Suny 1993; Talai 1989.

2. Talai (1989) discusses the intraethnic political behavior of Armenians in London, concluding that the conflict that surrounds it is, in the end, a constructive way to establish and reaffirm ethnic identity in a dispersed and diverse community. Though she notes that only a small percentage of Armenians are active in the organizational life of the community, Talai does not really acknowledge the negative aspect noted by Fischer (1986), where conscious teaching and sermonizing about being Armenian can have the effect of turning people off rather than on and driving people away from the organizations themselves.

3. The answer to the twin fears of assimilation and insecurity, many Armenians say, is a land of one's own. This has been the ideal virtue of Hayastan for many, but up until the country's recent independence, it had not been considered a real option for emigration from Cyprus (or London) for some time. As men-

tioned earlier, this attitude has changed greatly over the course of the century among different groups of Armenians. It is changing again today as more people visit Armenia and as they consider the implications of the 1988 earthquake and interethnic troubles in the former Soviet Union.

4. A partial explanation for this long and expensive campaign of disinformation is that successive Turkish governments have had a great fear of information or "evidence" that in any way feeds or confirms what is perceived as the long-held and deep-seated European prejudice against the "barbaric Turks." Unfortunately, Armenians have often presented their claims in exactly this language, seeking acknowledgment and sympathy from the United States and Europe in terms of "we the civilized Christian West against the barbaric Muslim East." Cf. Mandel 1988 on mutual fears of Germans and Turks in Berlin. See also Herzfeld 1987, 28; Suny 1993.

5. Bakalian's research in the United States demonstrates this point more dramatically, as tables show that each progressive generation has substantially less contact with the church (Bakalian 1993).

6. The other major complaint was about the clergy, sometimes connected to these same problems.

References Cited

Alishan, Leonardo
   1985   Crucifixion Without the Cross: The Impact of the Genocide
               on Armenian Literature. *Armenian Review* 38(1):27–50.

Anderson, Benedict
   1983   *Imagined Communities: Reflections on the Origin and
               Spread of Nationalism.* London: Verso.

Aprahamian, Sima
   1989   The Inhabitants of Haouch Moussa: From Stratified Society
               Through Classlessness to the Reappearance of Social
               Classes. Ph.D. dissertation, McGill University.

Apte, Mahadev L.
   1985   *Humor and Laughter: An Anthropological Approach.* Ith-
               aca: Cornell University Press.

Armstrong, John
   1982   *Nations Before Nationalism.* Chapel Hill: University of
               North Carolina Press.

Atamian, Sarkis
   1955   *The Armenian Community.* New York: Philosophical
               Library.

Attalides, Michael
   1981   *Social Change and Urbanization in Cyprus: A Study of Nic-
               osia.* Nicosia: Zavallis.

Bakalian, Anny P.
1993   *Armenian-Americans: From Being to Feeling Armenian.*
                New Brunswick, N.J.: Transaction.

Bamberger, Joan
1986–87   Family and Kinship in an Armenian-American Community.
                Journal of Armenian Studies 3(1–2):76–86.

Barth, Fredrik
1969   Introduction. In Fredrik Barth, ed., *Ethnic Groups and
                Boundaries: The Social Organization of Culture Difference.*
                Boston: Little, Brown.

Bhachu, Parminder
1985   *Twice Migrants: East African Sikh Settlers in Britain.* Lon-
                don: Tavistock.

Birand, Mehmet Ali
1975   *Thirty Hot Days in Cyprus.* Ankara: Milleyet.

Bowman, Glenn
1993   Tales of the Lost Land: Palestinian Identity and the Forma-
                tion of Nationalist Consciousness. In Erica Carter, James
                Donald, and Judith Squires, eds., *Space and Place: Theories
                of Identity and Location.* London: Lawrence and Wishart.

Boyarin, Jonathan
1991   *Polish Jews in Paris: The Ethnography of Memory.* Bloo-
                mington: Indiana University Press.

Bridgwood, Ann
1987   Marriage, Honour, and Property: Turkish Cypriots in North
                London. Ph.D. dissertation, London School of Economics.

Christian, William A.
1972   *Person and God in a Spanish Valley.* New York: Seminar.

Clifford, James
1982   *Person and Myth: Maurice Leenhardt in the Melanesian
                World.* Berkeley: University of California Press.

Crawford, Sheena Enid
1985   Person and Place in Kalavassos: Perspectives on Social
                Change in a Greek-Cypriot Village. Ph.D. dissertation, Cam-
                bridge University.

Dadrian, Vahakn
1986   The Naim-Andonian Documents on World War I: Destruc-
                tion of Ottoman Armenians: The Anatomy of a Genocide.
                International Journal of Middle East Studies 18(3):311–60.

Deutsch, Karl W.
1963   *Nation-Building*. New York: Atherton.
1979   *Tides Among Nations*. New York: Free Press.

De Vos, George
1975   Ethnic Pluralism: Conflict and Accommodation. In George
            De Vos and Lola Romanucci-Ross, eds., *Ethnic Identity:
            Cultural Communities and Change*. Chicago: University of
            Chicago Press.

Dubisch, Jill
1991   Gender, Kinship, and Religion. In Peter Loizos and Evthy-
            mios Papataxiarchis, eds., *Contested Identities*. Princeton:
            Princeton University Press.

Dudwick, Nora
1989   The Karabagh Movement: An Old Scenario Gets Rewritten.
            Armenian Review 42(3):63–70.

Edwards, John
1985   *Language, Society, and Identity*. Oxford: Basil Blackwell.

Erikson, Kai T.
1976   *Everything in Its Path: Destruction of Community in the
            Buffalo Creek Flood*. New York: Simon and Schuster.

Fischer, Michael M. J.
1986   Ethnicity and the Post-Modern Arts of Memory. In James
            Clifford and George E. Marcus, eds., *Writing Culture: The
            Poetics and Politics of Ethnography*. Berkeley: University of
            California Press.

Gadamer, Hans-Georg
1976   *Philosophical Hermeneutics*. Berkeley: University of Califor-
            nia Press.

Geertz, Clifford
1973   *The Interpretation of Cultures*. New York: Basic Books.

Gellner, Ernest
1983   *Nations and Nationalism*. Oxford: Basil Blackwell.

Gilsenan, Michael
1982   *Recognizing Islam: Religion and Society in the Modern Arab
            World*. New York: Pantheon.

Glassie, Henry
1892   *Passing the Time in Ballymenone*. Philadelphia: University of
            Pennsylvania Press.

Grosjean, François
    1982   *Life with Two Languages: An Introduction to Bilingualism.*
                Cambridge: Harvard University Press.

Gulesserian, Babgen
    1936   *Hay Gibros* [Armenian Cyprus]. Antelias, Lebanon: Semi-
                nary Press.

Gumperz, John
    1972   The Speech Community. In Pier Paolo Giglioli, ed., *Lan-
                guage and Social Context.* London: Penguin.

Guroian, Vigen
    1986   Collective Responsibility and Excuse Making: The Case of
                the Turkish Genocide of the Armenians. In Richard G. Hov-
                annisian, ed., *The Armenian Genocide in Perspective.* New
                Brunswick, N.J.: Transaction.
    1987   *Incarnate Love: Essays in Orthodox Ethics.* Notre Dame,
                Indiana: University of Notre Dame Press.
    1995   Towards a Diaspora Theology. In *Faith, Church, Mission:
                Essays for Renewal in the Armenian Church.* New York: Ar-
                menian Prelacy.

Halbwachs, Maurice
    1992   *On Collective Memory.* Edited by Lewis A. Coser. Chicago:
                University of Chicago Press.

Harding, Susan F.
    1984   *Remaking Ibieca: Rural Life in Aragon Under Franco.* Cha-
                pel Hill: University of North Carolina Press.
    1987   Convicted by the Holy Spirit: The Rhetoric of Fundamental
                Baptist Conversion. *American Ethnologist* 14(1):176–81.

Herzfeld, Michael
    1985   *The Poetics of Manhood: Contest and Identity in a Cretan
                Mountain Village.* Princeton: Princeton University Press.
    1987   *Anthropology Through the Looking Glass.* Cambridge:
                Cambridge University Press.
    1991   *A Place in History: Social and Monumental Time in a Cre-
                tan Town.* Princeton: Princeton University Press.

Hirschon, Renee
    1989   *Heirs of the Greek Catastrophe: The Social Life of Asia Mi-
                nor Refugees in Piraeus.* Oxford: Clarendon.

Hitchens, Christopher
    1984   *Cyprus.* London: Quartet.

Hobsbawm, Eric, and Terence Ranger, eds.
    1983   *The Invention of Tradition.* Cambridge: Cambridge University Press.

Hoogasian-Villa, Susie, and Mary Kilbourne Matossian
    1982   *Armenian Village Life Before 1914.* Detroit: Wayne State University Press.

Hovanessian, Martine
    1992   Le lien communautaire: Trois générations d'Arméniens. Paris: Armand Colin.

Hovannisian, Richard
    1967   *Armenia on the Road to Independence.* Berkeley: University of California Press.

Hovannisian, Richard, ed.
    1986   *The Armenian Genocide in Perspective.* New Brunswick, New Jersey: Transaction, 1986.

Kapferer, Bruce
    1988   *Legends of People, Myths of State.* Washington, D.C.: Smithsonian Institution Press.

Keshishian, Kevork
    1946   *Romantic Cyprus.* Nicosia: Printco.

Kherdian, David
    1981   *I Remember Root River.* Woodstock, N.Y.: Overlook Press.

Kugelmass, Jack
    1988   Introduction. In Jack Kugelmass, ed., *Between Two Worlds: Ethnographic Essays on American Jewry.* Ithaca: Cornell University Press.

Kurkjian, Vahan
    1901   *National Educational Orphanage in Cyprus: Report of the Fourth Year.* Translated by V. Kerovpyan and A. Kerovpyan. Vienna: Mekhitarian.
    1903   *Gibros Gughzi* [The Island of Cyprus]. Cyprus: National Orphanage Press.

Kyrris, Costas
    1985   *History of Cyprus.* Nicosia: Nicocles.

Ladbury, Sarah, and R. King
    1982   The Cultural Reconstruction of Political Reality: Greek and Turkish Cyprus Since 1974. *Anthropological Quarterly 55*: 1–16.

Loizos, Peter
1974   The Progress of Greek Nationalism in Cyprus, 1878–1970.
               In John Davis, ed., *Choice and Change: Essays in Honour of
               Lucy Mair*. London School of Economics and Political Sci-
               ence, monograph no. 5. London: Athlone.
1975   *The Greek Gift: Politics in a Cypriot Village*. Oxford: Basil
               Blackwell.
1981   *The Heart Grown Bitter*. Cambridge: Cambridge University
               Press.

Loizos, Peter, and Evthymios Papataxiarchis, eds.
1991   *Contested Identities: Gender and Kinship in Modern Greece*.
               Princeton: Princeton University Press.

Magnarella, Paul J.
1974   *Tradition and Change in a Turkish Town*. New York: John
               Wiley and Sons.

Mairet, Philip
1957   *Pioneer of Sociology: The Life and Letters of Patrick
               Geddes*. London: Lund Humphries.

Maksoudian, Noubar
1975   A Brief History of the Armenians in Cyprus. *Armenian Re-
               view* 27(4):378–416.

Mandel, Ruth
1988   We Called for Manpower, but People Came Instead: The
               Foreigner Problem and Turkish Guestworkers in West Ger-
               many. Ph.D. dissertation, University of Chicago.

Mangoian, L., and H. A. Mangoian, eds. and comps.
1947   *The Island of Cyprus*. Nicosia: Mangoian Bros.

Markides, Kyriacos C., Eleni S. Nikita, and Elengo N. Rangou
1978   *Lysi: Social Change in a Cypriot Village*. Nicosia: Social Re-
               search Centre.

Markowitz, Francine S.
1993   *A Community in Spite of Itself: Soviet Jewish Emigrés in
               New York*. Washington, D.C.: Smithsonian Institution Press.

Mead, Margaret
1969   Language in Diaspora. In Jack Antreassian, ed., *Ararat: A
               Decade of Armenian-American Writing*. New York: Arme-
               nian General Benevolent Union.

Miller, Donald E., and Lorna Touryan Miller
1986   An Oral History Perspective on Responses to the Armenian
               Genocide. In Richard G. Hovannisian, ed., *The Armenian
               Genocide in Perspective*. New Brunswick: Transaction.
1991   Memory and Identity Across the Generations: A Case Study
               of Armenian Survivors and Their Progeny. *Qualitative Soci-
               ology* 14(1):13–38.
1993   *Survivors: An Oral History of the Armenian Genocide*.
               Berkeley: University of California Press.

Murphy, Robert
1971   *The Dialectics of Social Life: Alarms and Excursions in An-
               thropological Theory*. New York: Columbia University
               Press.

Nassibian, Akaby
1984   *Britain and the Armenian Question, 1915–1923*. London:
               Croom Helm.

Niebuhr, H. Richard
1943   *Radical Monotheism and Western Culture*. London: Faber
               and Faber.

Oakley, Robin
1979   Family, Kinship, and Patronage: The Cypriot Migration to
               Britain. In Verity Saifullah Khan, ed., *Minority Families in
               Britain: Support and Stress*. London: Macmillan.

Oberling, Pierre
1982   *The Road to Bellapais: The Turkish Cypriot Exodus to
               Northern Cyprus*. New York: Columbia University Press.

O'Grady, Ingrid
1979   Ararat, Etchmiadzin, and Haig (Nation, Church, and Kin):
               A Study of the Symbol System of American Armenians.
               Ph.D. dissertation, Catholic University.

Ortner, Sherry B.
1989   *High Religion: A Cultural and Political History of Sherpa
               Buddhism*. Princeton: Princeton University Press.

Otto, Rudolph
1923   *The Idea of the Holy*. London: Oxford University Press.

Papasian, Gerald, ed. and comp.
1987   *Sojourn at Ararat: Poems of Armenia*. Mars, Penn.: Publish-
               ers Choice.

Phillips, Jenny King
    1979   Symbol, Myth, and Rhetoric: The Politics of Culture in an Armenian-American Population. Ph.D. dissertation, Boston University.

Safran, William
    1991   Diasporas in Modern Societies: Myths of Homeland and Return. *Diaspora* 1(1):83–99.

Said, Edward
    1985   *After the Last Sky.* New York: Pantheon.

Sapir, Edward
    1970   *Culture, Language, and Personality: Selected Essays.* Berkeley: University of California Press.

Sarafian, Ara
    1993–95   *United States Documents on the Armenian Genocide.* 3 vols. Watertown, Mass.: Armenian Review.

Segalen, Martine
    1983   *Power and Love in the Peasant Family.* Oxford: Basil Blackwell.

Shahgaldian, Nikola
    1979   Political Integration of an Immigrant Community into a Composite Society: The Armenians in Lebanon, 1920–1974. Ph.D. dissertation, Columbia University.

Smith, Anthony D.
    1986   *The Ethnic Origins of Nations.* Oxford: Basil Blackwell.

Stirling, Paul
    1965   *Turkish Village.* New York: John Wiley and Sons.

Suny, Ronald G.
    1983   *Armenia in the Twentieth Century.* Chico, Calif.: Scholars Press.
    1993   *Looking Toward Ararat: Armenia in Modern History.* Bloomington: Indiana University Press.

Tala'I, Vered Amit
    1986   Social Boundaries Within and Between Ethnic Groups: Armenians in London. *Man* (n.s.) 21(2):251–70.

Talai, Vered Amit
    1989   *Armenians in London: The Management of Social Boundaries.* Manchester: Manchester University Press.

Tölölyan, Khatchig
    1987   Martyrdom as Legitimacy: Terrorism, Religion, and Sym-
                  bolic Appropriation in the Armenian Diaspora. In Paul Wil-
                  kinson and Alasdair M. Stewart, eds., *Contemporary Re-*
                  search on Terrorism. Aberdeen: Aberdeen University Press
    1988   The Role of the Armenian Apostolic Church in the Dias-
                  pora. *Armenian Review* 41(1):55–68.

Trudgill, Peter
    1974   *Sociolinguistics: An Introduction.* Middlesex: Penguin.

Turner, Victor
    1974   *Dramas, Fields, and Metaphors.* Ithaca: Cornell University
                  Press.

Volkan, Vamik
    1979   *Cyprus: War and Adaptation: A Psychoanalytic History of
                  Two Ethnic Groups in Conflict.* Charlottesville: University
                  of Virginia Press.

Walker, Christopher
    1980   *Armenia: Survival of a Nation.* Beckenham, Kent, U.K.:
                  Croom Helm.

Wolf, Eric R.
    1982   *Europe and the People Without History.* Berkeley: Univer-
                  sity of California Press.

Zifron, Abbie
    1972   Part One: Biography. In Marshall Stalley, ed., *Patrick Ged-
                  des, Spokesman for Man and the Environment.* New Bruns-
                  wick, N.J.: Rutgers University Press.

Zonabend, Françoise
    1984   *The Enduring Memory: Time and History in a French Vil-
                  lage.* Translated by Anthony Forster. Manchester: Manches-
                  ter University Press.

Index